Population Growth and Family Change in Africa

Population Growth and Family Change in Africa

The New Urban Elite in Ghana

John C. Caldwell

AUSTRALIAN NATIONAL UNIVERSITY PRESS
CANBERRA

LONDON: C. Hurst & Co.
NEW YORK: Humanities Press

First published 1968

Library of Congress Catalog Card No. 68-18427
National Library of Australia Reg. No. AUS. 67–1337

Foreword

The world is in the sweep of a 'population explosion'. In the industrialised countries this has been contained by the voluntary choice of millions of parents to restrict their family size, so that in all of these countries birth rates and rates of population growth are now modest. Not so in the developing countries. Great advances have been made in saving lives and postponing death. Death rates are falling rapidly. But in most of the underdeveloped world the birth rates remain very high, rates of population growth have been accelerating, and the burden of supporting a rapidly increasing population is a major handicap in achieving the economic and social development to which all aspire. Population growth is greatest in those areas least able to afford it.

In Asia and in North Africa these dangers have been recognised; some twenty countries in these regions have adopted national family planning programs. Thus far awareness and concern about these problems have been less in tropical Africa; only one African country, Kenya, may be said to have a national policy and program promoting family planning. The reasons for this lower interest in tropical Africa are understandable: there is less overt manifestation of overpopulation than in Asia; there is more land, more natural resources in relation to population; death rates have been reduced only very recently and are still among the highest in the world; every African country is confronted with immediate overwhelming problems of maintaining political stability and of establishing a viable state. It has also been argued that African culture is not conducive either to the idea or to the practice of restricting family size.

During his residence at the University of Ghana in the years 1962-4 Dr Caldwell set out to determine the attitudes and practices of Ghanaians concerning fertility and family size by field investigation. The results of his study of rural regions have been published elsewhere. But, reasoned Dr Caldwell, if harbingers of future reduction of the birth rate exist in Ghana they surely are to be sought in the most modernised section of the population, the urban elite.

Before undertaking this and his other field surveys Dr Caldwell was warned that such studies were difficult and perhaps politically awkward; that African respondents would not give valid information, if any, on such topics; and that African interviewers could not be expected to carry out successfully the rigid instructions concerning sampling and interviewing necessary to assure scientifically valid results. Happily the Cassandras were proved wrong on all counts. Especially gratifying were the African interviewers' dedication to, interest in and understanding of the scientific objectives of the study. Many of Dr Caldwell's students served in this capacity.

Dr Caldwell's study is noteworthy on several counts: (1) its demonstration that a study on such a sensitive topic could be carried out successfully in a tropical African country; (2) the reliability of the results

v

—especially impressive is the remarkable correspondence between the responses of men and women despite the fact that these were completely separate samples separately interviewed (i.e. *not* husbands and wives married to each other); (3) the regularity of the patterns that emerge— seldom in social investigation is it possible to have so logical an unfolding of the results. The organisation of the book reflects both the regularity of the findings and systematic and logical presentation by the author.

The book is an important contribution to the study of the demographic transition in developing countries. Dr Caldwell is the pioneer for such studies in tropical Africa.

The value of the book is enhanced by an appendix, which analyses some of the relevant results of the Ghanaian Census of 1960, the first taken by an independent tropical African country.

DUDLEY KIRK

The Population Council (New York)

Stanford
September 1967

Acknowledgments

In a work of this sort, where the planning, execution, and writing spans several continents, the writer necessarily incurs many obligations of gratitude.

The first is to the Population Council, which established and supported the demography post at the University of Ghana which the writer occupied, and financed all survey work in Ghana. In addition, Dudley Kirk, the Council's Demographic Director, assisted personally in many ways, particularly as a consultant in the type of population work in which he has had much experience.

The University of Ghana provided a happy home for the work, and members of many disciplines, particularly Ghanaians, were able to throw light on aspects of the country's society, or to suggest changes in questions so as to make them attune more to the ways of the society. The members of the Sociology Department, under two successive heads, K. E. de Graft-Johnson and N. Elias, assisted in many ways.

In a field survey one's most heartfelt thanks must inevitably go to the survey workers with whom one undertook the practical tasks and who shared the day-to-day problems. In this case the thanks are strengthened because the survey workers were mostly drawn from the writer's demography students, who had served as a critical and constructive audience since the beginning of the project.

Most of the analysis and all the writing up of the survey has been carried out at the Australian National University. Thanks for the use of facilities, for co-operation, and for a congenial intellectual climate must go to the University's Department of Demography and to its head, W. D. Borrie.

J.C.C.

Canberra
January 1967

Contents

Tables

Appendix

Figures

Introduction

When this study was planned and executed in 1962 and 1963 there was no certainty that the population attitudes or reproductive behaviour of the urban elite in Ghana differed in any way from those of the majority of the population. One could but surmise from experience elsewhere and from knowledge of what was necessarily a limited range of Ghanaian friends.

No evidence on the point could be adduced from available censuses or other official material. The 1960 Census had already been taken but during the survey planning stage little was known about its findings except that the enumerated population was so much larger than that counted in 1948 that the growth rate was probably very high. In the latter stages of the project two complete volumes and an advance volume of the census became available. These appeared to confirm that fertility levels were lower in the towns than elsewhere and that the explanation must lie in the nature of the urban society. Not until very recently, with the publication of the *1960 Population Census of Ghana, Special Report 'A': Statistics of Towns,* have data been available on subsections of urban population. These have now been analysed in the Appendix to this book. A prior glance at this Appendix might well provide the reader with a better perspective; indeed, one considerably better than that possessed by the writer during the survey itself. It can no longer be doubted that, in Ghana's four major towns, there is a true fertility differential between the suburbs where educational, occupational, and income levels are higher and those where they are not. In the former, family size is somewhat smaller than in the latter. The major reason is delayed female marriage, but very probably some of the reduction in fertility amongst the elite can be ascribed to the attempts to prevent pregnancy examined at some length in this book.

At the outset a study of family change and of shifts in social values which might affect birth rates was planned. It was a case of searching for evidence of future trends, and as such there was a clear realisation that measurable change would probably be confined at present to a minority. Specifically it was suspected that such change might be in evidence amongst the economically 'better-off' residents of the 'better-off' suburbs of the largest towns, for necessarily these persons had already been forced to make many adjustments to the way of life inherited from the culture of agrarian villages.

The study was a specialised one, and, at least in West Africa, of a new type. Thus in the following chapters the reader will rarely discover comparison of the findings with those of earlier studies. Nevertheless, the

1

orientation of the study did owe much to the work of those in allied disciplines who had systematically examined aspects of West African, and particularly Ghanaian, society.

There is, for instance, a growing body of studies of tropical African cities, of Accra, Lagos, Freetown, Kampala, and Dar es Salaam, to name just a few in ex-British colonies. Leslie's study of Dar es Salaam is suggestive (Leslie, 1963), but it describes a pre-independence city unlike anything that Accra, for example, has been for many years. Marris's work on Lagos (Marris, 1961) and Banton's on Freetown (Banton, 1957) are studies of much poorer sections of African society. As background material for any investigation of Ghana's larger towns Ioné Acquah's *Accra Survey* (Acquah, 1958) is valuable, but it hardly touches on the main matters concerned here.

Perhaps the most important study of social change in urban areas was Busia's of Sekondi-Takoradi (Busia, 1950), carried out fifteen years before our survey and a decade before independence. Nevertheless, some of his remarks find reflections in the observations of respondents quoted in this book. He draws attention to the different treatment received by school-children (pp. 38–9) and to the greater amount of money spent on schoolgirls (p. 39). He discusses the problems of the town and of sexual *mores*, and even then the most quoted problems were those connected with schoolgirls.

> Criticism of laxity in sexual morality among schoolgirls appeared to be well-founded, for it was not difficult to obtain evidence of this in the course of the Survey. There were instances of pre-marital sexual relations between school girls and working men, as well as between school girls and school boys. Authentic cases of conceptions and even abortions were reported. Though pre-marital sexual relations prevail, its extent appears to be much exaggerated by popular reports (p. 60). Parents blame teachers, and teachers the parents for the "misbehaviour" of school girls, though sometimes "misbehaviour" just means non-conformity to the ways traditionally approved by the community (p. 38).

Amongst writing not specifically on Ghana, a thought-provoking article had been published in 1959 by Tanya Baker and Mary Bird on 'Urbanisation and the Position of Women' (Baker and Bird, 1959). They argued that, 'The process called urbanisation spreads through a whole society affecting even those who do not live in towns. Nevertheless, it is in the large new towns of Africa that it has gone furthest. These new towns act as catalysts. They are the core of the modern changes' (p. 100). Summarising, they wrote,

> We have also tried to show how the process of urbanisation isolates from the extended family of the compound the small family, which may comprise man, wife and children, or even mother and children. We have indicated that the social and economic position of the woman in such a unit is radically different from her position in an extended family. In fact, when a woman leaves the support and succour of the compound, whether as an individual or as a wife, she increases her personal liability and her dependence on herself (p. 118).

They emphasised that the small family was becoming increasingly common in urbanised Africa (p. 113), and that at the same time there was growing pressure on women in elite groups to work both before and after marriage (pp. 113–14). They stressed the social implications of the fact that earnings were secured individually and not merely as a member of a kinship group (p. 101).

Just available at the time of planning was Kimble's *Tropical Africa,* which contained little on family change but a great deal on Westernisation in the towns (Kimble, 1960). And in the final stages of the survey Gamble's study of the Temne family in a modern Sierra Leonean town appeared (Gamble, 1963). It emphasised the plight of the clerical workers, teachers, and civil servants, whose pay was too low for the standards they hoped to achieve and whose prestige was often connected to a surprising degree with their children's education (pp. 219–21). It also contained some interesting comments on well-to-do, non-'white-collar' urban groups, especially on the payment for their children's education (pp. 214–16). Subsequently, Little's 'West African Urbanization as a Social Process' became available (Little, 1964). In it the author pointed out that migration to the town removes one or both spouses from constant contact with relatives, and argued that the problem of jointly earning a living in the town tends to produce companionate marriage (p. 141).

A great deal of writing has dealt with general problems of social change in West Africa but much of it has not been greatly concerned with family change or population movements. Apter's *Ghana in Transition* was basically concerned with political transition (Apter, 1955). In the *Social Implications of Industrialization and Urbanization South of the Sahara,* Fortes, Steel, and Ady (1956) were concerned, when describing 'The Ashanti Survey', with rural life, while Forde's (1956) 'Introductory Survey' touched only passingly on the problems examined in this book. Similarly, the *Contemporary Africa Trends and Issues* number of the *Annals of the American Academy of Political and Social Science,* issued almost a decade before the survey, had very little to say on family, marriage, or population (Brown, 1955). Of more value, although it became available only in the final part of the survey, was Paulme's *Women of Tropical Africa,* but the major study of West Africa, Falade's 'Women of Dakar and the Surrounding Urban Areas', was concerned with groups very unlike the Ghanaian urban elite, groups where 'the life of a woman today does not appear to be very different from what her mother's or her grandmother's must have been' (Paulme, 1963, p. 217).

A growing, and surprisingly large, literature does exist on the African elite. As early as 1956 Busia was writing searchingly, and necessarily introspectively, of the Ghanaian (Gold Coast) elite. In the *International Social Science Bulletin* of that year he wrote,

> It is against the historical background of five centuries of trading contacts with Europe, two centuries of Christianity and European education, and a century of British rule that the present situation of elites in the Gold Coast should be studied . . . . The introduction of schooling into a non-literate society creates a new elite. Africans who become literate are able to share the white man's civilization. They learn to speak his language, and they copy not only his manners and his dress, but also aspire to his occupations and manner of living in every way. Literacy enables them to share the power and enjoy the

prestige which literacy gives to one in a predominantly illiterate society, and the literate looks away from the traditional culture to distant Europe for their goals. They [the professional elite] set standards for society in all walks of life. These standards show a large degree of approximation to those set by the European group . . . . It is permissible in the Gold Coast situation to regard all who are literate as an elite, because their patterns of aspiration are 'Western': that is, European orientated (Busia, 1956a, pp. 425-9).

Subsequently he remarks, 'A popular song already refers to "been-tos, car-ful, frig-ful", those who have been educated overseas, and own cars and refrigerators, as being the most desirable husbands'. Two years later he was writing of the strains of assimilating a new culture in West Africa, and emphasising that it was urban housing which made family structure different in the towns (Busia, 1961, pp. 177–8).

Other work on the Gold Coast elite had been done by Jahoda. In 1954 and 1955 he published two articles on 'The Social Background of a West African Student Population', emphasising in the earlier the self-reinforcement of elite groups and the fact that the male elite take to a considerable degree elite wives (Jahoda, 1954, pp. 360–1, 364; 1955).

Other writers have written of elites in general terms or in circumstances approximating to those of Ghana. In 1955 Little wrote of the great social and economic changes which have occurred this century in West Africa and of the new way of life, very different from the traditional, led by the elite (Little, 1955). In the mid-1950s Frazier (1956) and Leith Ross (1956c) were emphasising at conferences the importance of Western education and literacy in creating the elite. McCall, in 1961, was defining elites in very similar terms to those found in this survey, and claiming that it was the difficulties of town conditions which made the urban family approximate to the nuclear family (McCall, 1961, pp. 193–4). During the late 1950s Hugh and Mabel Smythe were studying the Nigerian elite (Smythe, 1958; Smythe and Smythe, 1960). They also pointed out that 'education is a minimum requirement for elite status', but defined 'eliteness' more strictly than in this study, so that by their broadest definition only 20,000 to 40,000 or at the most one-tenth of 1 per cent of Nigerians were included. Their main interest was in political change and little attention was devoted to population, the family, or the children of the elite.

Other material which became available too late to affect the work was Peil's study of Ghanaian university students, which confirmed that those entering the elite by means of university education contain a wholly disproportionate number from urban, 'white-collar' backgrounds (Peil, 1965), and Lloyd's *New Elites of Tropical Africa* (Lloyd, 1966). The latter contained an introduction by Lloyd and two papers which in general supported many of the findings of this study. They were de Graft-Johnson's 'The Evolution of the Elites in Ghana' (de Graft-Johnson, 1966), which included a valuable historical account of Ghana's elite, and Little's study of 'Attitudes towards Marriage and the Family amongst Educated Young Sierra Leoneans' (Little, 1966).

A growing literature exists on aspects of marriage and family life amongst urban Africans and especially amongst the elite groups. The best overall survey probably remains Little's 'Some Urban Patterns of Marriage and Domesticity in West Africa' (Little, 1959). In it he claimed that most urban households in British West Africa took the form of nuclear families (p. 68). He also wrote, referring perhaps chiefly to the Yoruba, 'Monogamy occurs more frequently as educational standards improve and it is practically incumbent upon professional men, politicians, senior civil servants, Christian teachers and ministers', and quoted Crabtree's findings (Crabtree, 1950) that, in a sample of 113 persons in Accra, 94 per cent of the educated were monogamously married compared with 64 per cent of their fathers (pp. 72–3). Leith-Ross published in 1960 a discussion of the coming into being in Nigeria of wives suited to companionate marriage and described them as the product of secondary or higher schooling (UNESCO, 1956).

A considerable amount of the writing is on Ghana. As early as 1949 Acquah had written an unpublished thesis on 'Marriage and Family Life Among the Educated Africans in the Urban Areas of the Gold Coast' (Acquah, 1949). Jahoda carried out research in 1955 which appeared in subsequent years. In his 'Aspects of Westernization: A Study of Adult Class Students in Ghana: I' (Jahoda, 1961) he discussed the increasing proportion of nuclear families and claimed that very few of his adult students regretted the passing of traditional ways and customs. He also found amongst the males a significant fertility differential by education, the more educated having fewer children, apparently because of delayed marriage. In his 'Boys' Images of Marriage Partners and Girls' Self-images in Ghana' (Jahoda, 1958) he revealed among schoolboys much discussion on the relative advantages of literate and illiterate wives and amongst schoolgirls a tendency to identify themselves with Western roles. In 'Love, Marriage and Social Change: Letters to the Advice Column of a West African Newspaper' (Jahoda, 1959) he examined the letters of a group similar in social characteristics to the sample in this study. The letters placed much emphasis on the selection of marriage partners and on adherence to and changes from traditions which were obviously as much mission-induced traditions as the more indigenous forms. The major problems involved in marriage to an illiterate girl were apparently the self-consciousness caused when bringing friends to the house and the danger of the children being ill-bred.

Omari studied 'Changing Attitudes of Students in West African Society Towards Marriage and Family Relationships' (Omari, 1960), taking in 1957 a sample of final year students, aged 17 to 31, in Ghanaian secondary schools and teachers' colleges. He found that the group had participated in rapid social change, especially with regard to attitudes towards marriage, and that the women particularly desired more change. He found a strong desire for companionate marriage, and concluded that, 'The traditional family can be said to have become completely Westernized when monogamy becomes the completely accepted highly valued norm'. Hunter, summarising some of these studies, wrote, 'In Ghana the influence of Christian teaching and modern manners has been so strong that until recently no educated person would have liked to argue the case for polygamy. It was assumed to be part of the old unregenerate attitudes' (Hunter, 1962).

Busia had earlier commented on some of these aspects of urban marriage, finding that almost a third of all marriages in Sekondi-Takoradi were inter-tribal (Busia, 1950, p. 29). He commented about that town in 1947-48,

> The educated woman married under the Ordinance . . . expects a companionship and equality which the illiterate woman does not expect . . . . The effect of monogamy as enforced by the Ordinance and by Christian teaching is to strengthen the bond between husband and wife at the expense of the strong sibling bond in the old matrilineal society (pp. 43–4).

On the more strictly demographic side there was little work closely allied to the present study, the most important being that found in Lorimer's *Culture and Human Fertility* (Lorimer, 1954). In it Busia reported on 'Some Aspects of the Relation of Social Conditions to Human Fertility in the Gold Coast', analysing data from a 1952 survey. He adopted the view held in this study, that 'changes in attitudes may precede marked changes in actual behaviour' (p. 343). His data indicated completed fertility (including miscarriages and stillbirths) as 7·3 per woman beyond the reproductive years, the possibility of a slight rural-urban fertility differential and lower fertility amongst women with secondary or tertiary education (pp. 344–6). Busia related the latter differential to a later age at marriage. He also drew attention to the determination of parents to secure more schooling for their children (p. 349). The description of the Ashanti survey by Fortes in the same book provides valuable information on the rural backgrounds of some of the kinds of people examined in this study but does not of course examine urban society.

Elsewhere, Dorjan had undertaken some specific work on the demography of polygyny in Sierra Leone (Dorjan, 1958; 1959). Light was thrown on African demography by Lorimer and Karp, *Population in Africa: Report of a Seminar held in Boston University* (Lorimer and Karp, 1960) and Lorimer's *Demographic Information on Tropical Africa* (Lorimer, 1961). These have been added to recently by Lorimer, Brass, and van de Walle, 'Demography', in Lystad's *The African World: A Survey of Social Research* (Lystad, 1965), the Economic Commission for Africa's 'Recent Demographic Levels and Trends in Africa' in the *Economic Bulletin for Africa* (E.C.A., 1965) and by Coale's 'Estimates of Fertility and Mortality in Tropical Africa' in *Population Index* (Coale, 1966). All provide background material but none broach the questions raised in this study. However, two current research projects may do so, although without specific reference to the elite. They are two studies of fertility which were reported to the African Population Conference, held in Ibadan in January 1966, one by Pool in Ghana (Pool, 1966) and one by Ohadike in Lagos (Ohadike, 1966).

In addition much general background information for the study has recently become available in the two-volume economic and social work, *A Study of Contemporary Ghana* (Birmingham, Neustadt, and Omaboe, 1966 and 1967).

To a large degree the impetus for this work came from outside Africa, and was provided by a series of studies of population change and by a body of theory known as *demographic transition theory* which has been created to explain the observed changes.

Much of this work was undertaken on European populations and much centred on the fact that initial fertility declines in the nineteenth century were amongst the urban population of higher socio-economic class. Innes found that in England and Wales,

> ... fertility rates started downward in every class but miners by 1861–71, and amongst miners by 1871–81. This ... was qualified only by the existence of some inverse association between fertility and status even for marriages contracted in 1851–61, which may have signified a somewhat earlier decline among the higher ranks (Innes, 1938, pp. 65–6).

Glass and Grebenik, reporting on *The Trend and Pattern of Fertility in Great Britain* for the Family Census of 1946, found a decline in completed fertility consistent with the year of marriage from at least 1862, confirmed the early socio-economic fertility differentials, and pointed to the marked lowering of fertility caused by delayed marriage (Glass and Grebenik, 1954, pp. 131–5). Sydenstricker and Notestein had found early fertility differentials, with fertility inversely related to social class, in the United States (Sydenstricker and Notestein, 1930), and Borrie showed that urban-rural and occupational differentials in Australia stretched back to 1880 and probably earlier (Borrie, 1948).

Such findings had produced generalised statements about the process of demographic transition and of initial fertility decline, noted as early as 1929 in an article by Thompson (Thompson, 1929), but later with continuing research and experience spelt out more fully by Notestein in 'Population—the Long View' (Notestein, 1945) and Davis in 'The World Demographic Transition' (Davis, 1945).

The most extensive examination of a group akin in many ways to the Ghanaian elite is Banks's *Prosperity and Parenthood: A Study of Family Planning among the Victorian Middle Classes* (Banks, 1954), and accordingly a few lengthy quotes are justified. Their relevance will be seen repeatedly in the rest of the book.

> As opposed to an average size in family of 5·5 to 6 live children born to couples married in the mid-Victorian years, among the couples married in 1925-29 the figure has been estimated at 2·2. The families of five, six, and seven children which were formerly the most common had been replaced by one- and two-child families while those of more than six had virtually disappeared (pp. 3–4).
> The salient factor in the decline of population growth over the past eighty years or so has been a radical change in the attitude towards parenthood. People no longer wish to have the large families which were customary in the days of their grandparents (p. 4).
> ... the retreat from parenthood has not proceeded uniformly throughout the community ... it is no distortion of the truth to say that the earliest signs of the change in reproductive habits took place amongst the families of military and naval officers, clergymen, lawyers, doctors, authors, journalists and architects. Not far behind them came civil service officers and clerks, law clerks, dentists, schoolmasters, teachers, professors and lecturers, people employed in scientific pursuits and accountants .... In general, the decline in family size commenced as

an upper- and middle-class phenomenon at some time in the 1860's
and 1870's. It was not until some time later that the new reproductive
habits began to spread amongst the less privileged social groups
(pp. 4–5).

The importance of education, already accepted by many in the prosperous years of the 1850's and 1860's might well have been enhanced
during the lean years of the 1870's and 1880's, and the greater demand
for specialized training through the mechanism of a rise in the prices
charged for tuition, increased the expensiveness of placing a child in
a chosen career and hence may have become a factor in the fall in family
size (p. 201).

The study which follows has been written so that readers do not have
to spend much of their time referring to the Appendix. Hence, the
questions asked of respondents are, with the exception of the formal
collection of data on personal characteristics, placed in the body of the
book in the form of table headings. The complete questionnaire can be
reconstructed by reading the successive tables of this type. In addition
the tables themselves have been formally constructed on a fixed pattern
so as to avoid the repetition of such tables in the Appendix and so as
to allow direct comparison between tables. This means that the presentation
of tables may sometimes appear either repetitious or stilted, but the writer
believes that in this form they do make the study more scientifically
meaningful.

Reference to some of the findings has already been made in the
writer's contribution to *A Study of Contemporary Ghana,* Vol. II
(Caldwell, 1967a), in a paper presented to the International Conference
on Family Planning Programs, Geneva, August 1965, which has been
reproduced in *Family Planning and Population Programs* (Berelson *et al.,*
1966) and in a paper in *Population Studies* (Caldwell, 1967d, pp. 5–21).
Any discrepancies between the data presented are insignificant and have
been caused by recoding together with some redefinition.

One of the difficulties met in describing a single research project, which
nevertheless formed but a segment of an integrated research program,
is the necessity for referring frequently to the location of findings published
elsewhere. In order to minimise references to the author's writings specific
note has usually been made only when important quantitative results need
to be quoted in order to buttress the argument found here. However, when
text without references concerns population trends or characteristics, the
argument can usually be found in the author's contribution to *A Study
of Contemporary Ghana,* while the major reports on work on university
students and on the survival of descendants appear in *Population Studies*
(Caldwell, 1965; 1966a) and that on rural population in *Economic
Development and Cultural Change* (Caldwell, 1967b). These and other
locations of the research program's findings can be identified by consulting
the bibliography. Most of the results of the examination of rural-urban
migration, referred to here in passing, have not yet appeared.

1

The Population Problem and the Urban Elite

Few parts of the world have ever experienced such sudden social and economic change as that which has convulsed tropical Africa within the last three-quarters of a century. Much emphasis has been placed by writers on the low levels of literacy and of schooling, the limited extension of the cash economy, the shortcomings of the communications network, and the low proportion of urban population. What is less frequently observed is that few if any of these things existed a hundred years ago except in a few small coastal enclaves. Modern industrial society came late to tropical Africa, so late that many old men still living spent their childhood in societies which were in all essentials very similar to those existing in the region centuries before. This is no longer the case. Much change has occurred and much more is expected. 'Perhaps nowhere in the non-Western world is there as passionate an attraction to the Idea of Progress as amongst Africans affected by modernity . . . . The literature of modern Africa is saturated with such words as "upliftment", "development", "trusteeship", "progress reports", etc. In general, this has meant a strong orientation towards futurism in popular attitudes and values . . . .' (Coleman, 1960, p. 285).

Demographic phenomena have been important in this revolution. Population growth in Ghana has been rapid, even by the standards of most contemporary developing countries. Figure 1 shows that the apparent growth between the first census after the country had attained its present borders and the most recent census amounted to almost a trebling of the country's population in thirty-nine years. There may well have been considerable underenumeration at the earlier census, but the fact remains that enormous population growth has occurred. It has been great, not only in comparison with such economically developed countries as modern Britain, but also in comparison with Australia, a developed country which has quite a high birth rate and which has encouraged immigration and praised its industrial economy for being able to absorb the substantial additions to its people's numbers. There is no real comparison with Britain of an earlier period, as is shown by the line on the graph depicting population growth in England immediately before the birth rate there began to fall.

Modern Ghana has become conscious of its high rate of population growth, for it is now known that the two post-World War II censuses claimed an increase in the country's inhabitants of almost two-thirds in the twelve-year period from 1948 to 1960. This would mean an average

9

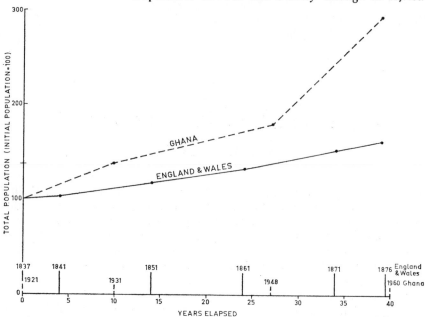

Fig. 1:1　*Population growth in Ghana, 1921-60 and in England and Wales, 1837-76 (initial population = 100)*

Note: 1876 has been chosen as the date when the number of births per 1,000 females, 15-44, was at a level which it did not subsequently attain again.
Source: 1960 Population Census of Ghana; B. R. Mitchell with Phyllis Deane, *Abstract of British Historical Statistics,* Cambridge, 1962, pp. 8-9, 28-9.

annual growth rate of 4·2 per cent or double that in India during the same period. In reality the rate of population increase was probably some-what lower, as there appear to have been defects in the 1948 population count. Nevertheless, it probably amounted to over 3½ per cent per year (Caldwell, 1967a, pp. 78–83).

This rate of population growth would appear to many to be astonishing for it has occurred in a continent where death rates are the world's highest and where, until comparatively recently, demographers were claiming that there was little change in population numbers. Part of the explanation in Ghana has been immigration. The 1960 Census claimed that an eighth of the population of the country was of foreign origin and a twelfth of foreign birth. The true figures were probably even higher, and the contribution made to population growth by immigrants and their children born in Ghana was almost certainly a quarter or more of the total 1948–60 increase (Caldwell, 1967a).

Nevertheless, almost three-quarters of the population growth must be explained in terms of the natural increase of the population already living within Ghana in 1948. Even after adjustments are made to the 1948 Census population, the average annual rate of natural increase between that Census and the 1960 one can hardly have been less than 2·9 per cent. By the latter year it had almost certainly passed the 3 per cent mark and by the time of writing is probably around 3¼ per cent.

The truth would seem to be that there has been very considerable natural growth throughout this century. Mortality rates have been very high and are still high, but they are probably lower than those found elsewhere in West Africa. The reason lies in Ghana's wealth: cocoa, gold, industrial diamonds, tropical hardwoods, manganese, bauxite, and other produce have made the populace on average the wealthiest in tropical Africa. By 1960 the gross national income per capita was £63,* reaching £176 in the Accra Capital District (Szereszewski, 1966, p. 92). The cash economy was dominant in the southern part of the country and was even penetrating the north. Hospitals and medical services continued to spread, a process which had been going on for at least two generations. Thus, a great many people, especially in the south, where four-fifths of the population lives, had access to modern health services. By 1960 the expectation of life at birth may well have been about 45 years and the crude death rate somewhere around 21 per thousand (Caldwell, 1967a, p. 93). These figures, if correct, show a level of mortality which is low by tropical African standards.

However, expectations of life are still less than those found in North Africa and in other continents. Even India is slightly ahead. The reason why the high level of mortality has not checked population growth has been the very high level of fertility. Birth rates in West Africa are the world's highest, and are possibly above 50 per thousand in almost every country in the region. In contrast, birth rates in North Africa, Asia, and Latin America range on the whole between 40 and 50, while most of those of Europe, North America, and Australasia lie between 15 and 25. Thus, even high death rates in West Africa do not forbid considerable natural increase. With the extension of modern health services, the region has the potential for the world's most rapid rate of population growth. In theory, there is nothing to forbid the attainment of annual rates of natural increase around 4 per cent.

In Ghana one estimate places the crude birth rate at about 52 per thousand and the average size of the completed family around 7·3 children (Caldwell, 1967a, p. 93). Many more of these children are now surviving to adulthood, as is evidenced by a net reproduction rate which was possibly about 2·2 in 1960. It is likely that infant and child mortality rates have decreased more rapidly than have adult mortality rates, so that, even in a society where orphans are distributed between relatives, parents are actually rearing more children. A comparison of the 1948 and 1960 censuses suggests that child dependency increased very significantly during the intervening period. The ratio of the number of persons under 15 years to the number above that age rose by 14 per cent, implying that the child-dependency burden upon the work-force and the household had risen by about one-seventh in twelve years. There is in fact a surge of population moving from infancy up through the age groups, now demanding more educational facilities and soon to require employment.

Rapid population growth changes many facets of a society. No country can treble its population within less than two generations, as has Ghana, and absorb the increase into the various parts of its society in exactly the same proportions as had previously obtained. Some social and economic institutions have greater absorptive power than others. Necessarily the

* Ghanaian pounds, at par with sterling.

pattern of residence and of occupation changes. This has certainly been the case in Ghana.

There has been a tendency for the population increment to spill out of the countryside into the towns and to forswear farming for urban occupations. Thus, although the towns (as defined in censuses) housed only an eighth of the population in 1948, they absorbed two-fifths of the population increase between the censuses, so that by 1960 almost a quarter of all Ghanaians lived within them. At the same time population was becoming increasingly concentrated in the more economically advanced south. The most densely settled part of the south constituted less than a quarter of the country's area, but it contained in 1948 almost six-tenths of the population and absorbed seven-tenths of the 1948–60 population increase. A major explanation was rural-urban migration. Between 1948 and 1960 over a quarter of the increase in rural population had moved to the towns. It was especially the young who were moving. Thus, the 1960 Census showed that while five-sixths of males, 60–64 years old, lived in rural areas, only two-thirds of males 20–24 years old did so, and while three-quarters of the former were farmers or fishermen only half of the latter were.

The growth of town population is one of the clearest examples of the magnitude of the changes which have affected Ghana. It is itself a product of some social and economic changes and the cause of others. Between 1921 and 1960, the rural population multiplied less than two-and-a-half times, but the urban population increased over eight-and-a-half times. It was the growth of town life that allowed modern nationalist movements to develop. Thus, Accra contained no more than 19,000 people immediately before World War I, and the number of its inhabitants had grown to only a little over 60,000 by 1931; in 1960 it had reached a more suitable size for a national capital with over a third of a million people in the main town and almost 400,000 in the municipal area.

Between 1948 and 1960 the population of Ghana's towns grew astonishingly rapidly, from just over half a million people to well over one-and-a-half millions. Where did the extra million come from? Analysis shows that the natural increase of the urban population accounts for about a quarter of the growth and immigration from other countries for approximately one-fifth, but well over half must be explained by movement from Ghana's own countryside.

This movement from village to town is not a case of the transfer of the surplus poor and illiterates of the rural areas. It is highly selective in terms of age and education and somewhat selective in terms of sex. On the whole it is the young adults who are moving to the towns and more of the migrants are males than females. Education is also important, for since the arrival of the missions, schooling has usually transformed farmers' children into young people who could obtain what in more temperate lands would be called 'white-collar jobs'. Furthermore, most of these jobs were to be found in the towns and very largely in the few big towns. A survey in the demographic program carried out in rural areas in 1963 showed that, while over three-quarters of children without education were likely to remain in the countryside, only one-third of those with secondary

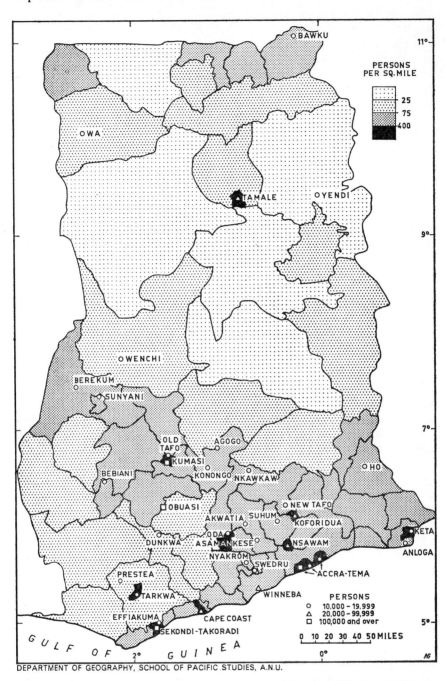

Fig. 1:2   Major towns and patterns of settlement, Ghana, 1960
Source: 1960 Population Census of Ghana.

education would do so. Three-quarters of illiterate people stay, but only a quarter of the literate do.

Thus the growth of urban population has been the result of economic and social revolution. Economic change has created ever more town jobs and social change has brought into being people capable of filling the positions and has given them the desire to undertake the new way of life found in urban areas.

In the process urban population has become differentiated from rural population in many ways. An obvious example is provided by occupation, but education is another. Not only were towns first to be provided with schools, as well as continuing to be better provided with them, but the migrants from the countryside have on average better educations than those who remain on the farms.

Not all centres that qualify for the census definition of urban exhibit a distinctive town life. Some are little more than bloated villages; but this is not true of the larger centres. The four biggest, Accra-Tema, Kumasi, Sekondi-Takoradi and Cape Coast, all had more than 20,000 inhabitants by the end of World War II and more than 40,000 by the 1960 Census. In 1960 their combined populations exceeded three-quarters of a million. Each has been associated with the history of modernisation, although Kumasi has also deeply entrenched traditional associations, as have to perhaps a lesser degree each of the others except Takoradi and Tema. Cape Coast and Accra have both been the seat of government. All are regional headquarters and so are centres for a considerable amount of governmental and semi-governmental employment. Takoradi and Tema are creations of the modern economy, both being artificial harbours associated with modern industries. Accra is the home of the government of independent Ghana, and of its ministries. Table 1:1 demonstrates some of the ways in which these towns are distinctive and have concentrated within them a special cross-section of Ghanaian society.

Though these four towns contain less than an eighth of the population of Ghana, over half of those who have been to secondary school and seven-tenths of those who have been to university are found there. Similarly, they house the majority of those employed in government services and three-quarters of the more highly paid group found in central administration and defence. On the other hand, employment in agriculture is rare. The lure of highly paid town jobs has repercussions. The four towns contain over a quarter of the unemployed, most of them being young adults with a disproportionate representation of rural-urban migrants. The attraction of the large towns is felt far beyond the borders of Ghana, drawing foreign immigrants who give Ghana's main towns a rather cosmopolitan atmosphere.

Immigration affects the structure of the towns' populations. Towns attract a large number of young adults, more males than females. Migrants think the inhabitants of the towns to be richer than those of the countryside, and in terms of average income per head they are right. The average income per head is £176 in the Accra Capital District compared for instance with £53 in the adjoining Eastern Region and £30 in the far north (Szereszewski, 1966, p. 92). But the contrasts in the towns are

TABLE 1:1   Contrasts between the Four Towns* and Ghana as a whole, 1960

(a) Concentration: Percentages of the total number of various types of person in Ghana found in the Four Towns

All persons	12
Those with some university education	69
Those with some secondary education†	52
Those over 6 years of age with no schooling	8
Those employed in all government services	52
Those employed in central government, administration, or defence services	74
Those employed in agriculture	2
Those over 15 years of age unemployed	27
Those of foreign origin	35
Those of foreign birth	33

(b) Differences in structure (as percentages of total population except where stated)

	Four Towns	All Ghana
Persons, 0–4 years	17	19
Persons, 15–44 years	51	43
Persons, 65 years and over	2	3
Males, all ages (as percentage of persons, all ages)	53	51
Males, 15–44 (as percentage of persons, 15–44)	58	49
Persons, 6–14, attending school (as percentage of all persons 6–14)	62	40
Persons born in the locality	45	58

* Accra-Tema (= Accra Municipality and Tema Development Corporation), Kumasi Municipality, Sekondi-Takoradi Municipality, and Cape Coast Municipality.
† All persons who had undertaken secondary, commercial, technical, or university education or teacher training).
Source: 1960 Population Census of Ghana, Vol. II, Advance Report, and Special Report 'A'.

great: the migrant may be attracted to Accra by the vision of how the senior public servant lives in the Ridge area, but he may well find himself settling in the congested squatter area of Nima on the northern outskirts. Furthermore, town life can be relatively very expensive in that nearly all food and housing must be paid for in cash. There are pressures also for other types of expenditure. There are more schools and fewer jobs which can be obtained without schooling, so inevitably parents feel stronger obligations to educate their children.

Modernisation, Westernisation, the extension of schooling, and the growth of towns have all been interrelated. The spread of education in rural areas has certainly speeded up the rate of urbanisation. Town life has of itself wrought further change. The following picture of the general position in tropical Africa certainly applies to Ghana:

Urban life is a new experience for most Africans. The new cities accelerated the intensification of the division of labour. As urban Africans became increasingly dependent upon their occupational specialities or salaried jobs they lost the economic security of the lineage and the self-sufficient rural community. The impersonality, heterogeneity, and competitiveness of urban life accentuated their personal insecurity as well as their individualism which became more pronounced as they sought status and prestige within the urban social structure. The cities were also centres for intensive acculturation, for it was there that Africans came into daily and intimate contact with all aspects of modernity (Coleman, 1960, pp. 270–2).

The leading sector of this headlong rush to modernity has been the group described in this study, for want of a better term, as the 'urban elite'.* Obviously no moral judgment is implied, nor would those politically in command of modern Ghana tolerate a social judgment. All that is meant here by the term is those Ghanaians who have enjoyed superior education, earn superior wages, occupationally hold more prestigeful positions, and live in the suburbs of Ghana's main towns with more expensive housing. In modern Ghana most of these characteristics are closely related. Most of the superior jobs are now controlled by the government and the great majority are secured by high educational attainments. The society has assumed since far back in colonial times that an individual's earning power should be related to the educational investment in him.

Perhaps the most remarkable feature of Ghana's recent history has been the growth of this elite. In 1948 only one Ghanaian over 12 years of age in every forty had received education beyond the sixth grade of the primary school, but by 1960 the proportion had risen to more than one in seven. At the same time the development of the economy and the Ghanaianisation of public service and other higher positions with the approach and achievement of independence meant that many more high-income jobs were available for the educated. This was even more the case because of the increased governmental expenditure which became possible with buoyant revenues resulting largely from high cocoa export prices triggered off

* After the completion of the author's work in Ghana, the International African Institute held a seminar in July 1964 at the University of Ibadan on the 'New Elites of Tropical Africa'. As mentioned in the Introduction to this book, the record of the conference, *The New Elites of Tropical Africa* (Lloyd, 1966), became available only after the writing of the present study was finished. Nevertheless, the book has provided a valuable, and reassuring, source of comparative material. Lloyd shares the view that 'elite' is a more suitable term than 'middle class' or 'upper class' in contemporary Africa, and a contributor on Ghana agrees that 'it is more meaningful to speak of elites rather than social classes in Ghana' (de Graft-Johnson, 1966, p. 105). Lloyd's reasons for preferring the description 'elite' is the present fluidity of the upper strata of society, the lack of class awareness, and the fact that their position is guaranteed largely by the possession of power, which in turn often rests on their acquisition of a Western education. De Graft-Johnson points to the somewhat peculiar nature of the Ghanaian elite, formed in a country where there had long been a native intelligentsia and administrative group, but where a successful political party had more recently swept a whole 'new class' into positions of power and affluence (p. 109). Most contributors agree that the elite do enjoy what Lloyd describes as a 'style of life'; This is usually expressed in residential terms, which offer a better chance for the success of survey techniques than do the other attributes of the elite.

by the Korean War. Other positions were created by the expansion of the army and of the political machine and parapolitical organisations like the Trade Union Congress and the press. The small Ghanaian middle class of a generation earlier, many of them with some European ancestry, had swollen by 1963 into something very much larger and also more purely African. The new African elite moved into the suburbs which had once been mainly the preserve of the colonial rulers. By 1960 less than an eighth of the residents of Accra's blue ribbon Cantonments area were non-African, and even in Kumasi's Ridge area more than five-sixths of the population had been born in Africa. The rate and direction of social change in Ghana will be immensely affected by the urban elite, not merely because they control so many decision-making positions, but also because they form the main channel through which external influences act upon the society.

The urban elite must necessarily be concerned with population questions. On the macroscopic scale, their literacy and education make it possible for them to understand the problems of economic development. Indeed much of the published discussion of development plans is meant for their consumption. Many of them are actually concerned in either the planning or in the development or enforcing of policies which have some relevance to economic change. The *Seven-Year Development Plan* stated the country's basic objectives as 'the development ... of a consistent strategy ... to yield the most rapid rate of economic development possible within the limits of Ghana's generous endowment in human and material resources' (*Seven-Year Development Plan*, p. 1). The planners were not very perturbed by the rate of population growth, perhaps because they almost certainly underestimated it, but they did point out that, 'The success that we have had in bringing down the death rate in one generation will not be matched by a similar rapid success in bringing down the birth rate. Until the birth rate is reduced the population will continue to grow and the numbers of the dependent young will remain proportionately large' (*Seven-Year Development Plan*, pp. 7–8). It is certain that many of the urban elite, either in their official capacity or as part of a kind of Ghanaian 'establishment', will have to develop viewpoints during the coming years on the effects of both immigration and high birth rates upon the Ghanaian economy and society.

However, they may find more pressing needs to formulate viewpoints on high fertility at their own family level. It would seem likely that urban living, opportunities of occupational mobility, changing attitudes towards the upbringing of children, the spread of schooling and especially advanced schooling, and other social changes would bring upon them, to an increasing degree, pressures essentially similar in kind to those which have led, since the late nineteenth century, to a restriction in the size of the European family. A study of the population of rural Ghana (Caldwell, 1967b) had already shown that large families were creating economic problems for parents even in farming and to an increasing degree even in the far north. Large families had not been a problem in the fully subsistence agrarian economy which had once prevailed, but these times had either passed or were passing everywhere in Ghana. The spread of the cash economy, the increasing desire to purchase a wide range of goods, and the wide extension of schooling facilities had radically changed the situation. By 1963 two-thirds of rural households in central and southern Ghana felt that parents were made relatively poorer by having large numbers of children, and in the southern coastal areas, where traditional society has been subject to the most change, a quarter of all rural families approved of attempts to restrict family size.

Partly on the grounds that pressures to reduce family size are probably felt up to now more by the urban elite than by most other sections of the society, and partly on the grounds that any action taken by the elite to limit the size of their families is likely ultimately to influence the whole society, the writer, while directing a program of demographic research, felt that it would be profitable to study in some depth the population attitudes of this group. Such a study, it was argued, might well be of more than demographic significance, for no previous attempt had been made in tropical Africa to identify quantitatively the members of the urban elite and to determine their characteristics and attitudes toward any aspect of life.

The initial aim of this survey was to identify the families living in the wealthier suburbs of Ghana's four major towns. This object has recently been assisted by the publication of the 1960 Census findings for urban tracts, findings which are analysed in the Appendix to show amongst other things the differences between rich and poor suburbs in such matters as occupation and education. Ultimately the research was designed to discover if this group felt pressure to restrict the size of their families, what that pressure was, and whether such restriction was taking place for this or other reasons. Some of the examination was carried out so that one could at least surmise whether family planning ideas or practices were likely to spread and whether any effect was likely to be had upon the national rate of population growth.

Surveying the Urban Elite

It was suggested above that the urban elite might be defined in some way by education, income, occupation, or residence, or perhaps by a combination of these characteristics. In fact it is impossible to obtain complete, graded lists of persons by education, income, or occupation. When, in early 1963, it was finally decided to go ahead with an investigation of population attitudes, preliminary investigation soon revealed that the definition would have to be made according to residential area and residence. This posed no very great problems, as a cursory inspection of Ghana's towns is enough to distinguish between the wealthier and poorer suburbs and this division approximates to lines of educational and occupational cleavage.

However, such subjective estimates were not relied upon, and a series of small sample surveys were conducted to determine by inspection a position on a socio-economic scale for each of the suburbs of the four towns, based mainly on the quality of the residences and the occupations and education of the householders. Some parts of certain suburbs and some houses considered sub-standard for the general area were omitted, while in some suburbs, such as Jamestown, Accra, a traditional Ga area, some houses of old Ga families had to be included because they were above the general standard of the suburb. In the Appendix some of these problems are illuminated. Later, the publication by the Census Office of its special report on the statistics of towns (*Special Report 'A'*) broadly confirmed the choice of residential areas. For instance, taking residents who had been to university as an index of the socio-economic position of suburbs, the census enumeration areas containing the surveyed suburbs of the four towns housed in 1960 a little over a third of the total population but almost four-fifths of those who had been to university. In these census enumeration areas ten persons per thousand had been to university while in the other enumeration areas of the towns only one per thousand had. The selected suburbs or parts of suburbs did not make up all the census enumeration areas enclosing them, and even within the suburbs some areas had been excluded. In fact the total surveyed area had contained at the time of the 1960 Census only about 185,000 persons, forming a little less than a quarter of the population of the four towns or about 2¾ per cent of that of the whole country.

The preliminary sample surveys had indicated that the residential structure of the suburbs was not such as to permit a sampling of all households within the selected area. Within each area large numbers of poorer persons lived, some as relatives of the wealthier and others as servants. Many houses contained subtenants whose socio-economic position was well below that of the house owner or chief tenant. Finally, it was decided that the problem could be overcome only by taking houses as sampling units and interviewing within each house only the householder (i.e. the owner, lessee, or renter) or his wife. Where the householders were an older couple, so that the wife did not meet the survey age requirements but lived with a married child and spouse who were eligible for interview, one of the latter couple was included in the sample.

The survey was confined to wives between 18 and 44 years of age and to husbands whose wives were of this age. In accordance with Ghanaian law, no stricter definition of marriage was demanded than that the couples considered themselves in this state. Only persons of African descent were included in the survey. In the case of polygynous marriages where both wives lived under the same roof, it had been found necessary when interviewing females in previous survey work to question the first wife to present herself, for otherwise ill-feeling was aroused. This practice was followed also in this survey in the very few cases where it was needed, for, although some polygyny is found amongst the elite, it is rare for the wives to be housed together. When interviewing males in such marriages, a husband was questioned only when the age of the wife with whom he usually resided, or the senior wife where there was more than one wife in the house, fell within the selected range. In preliminary discussions some attention was paid to the fact that the whole four towns were situated amongst cultures where husband and wives had traditionally lived apart, either with the families of their own lineage or in housing provided separately for the sexes. However, pre-testing and the main survey showed that, amongst the urban elite, even in the comparatively few cases where spouses were living apart, the position was stated to be temporary, usually for occupational reasons.

The actual interviewing occurred only after prolonged planning and training. First it was necessary to find interviewers and to determine what questions should and could be asked. From a series of seminars attended by interested students and staff we built up a preliminary set of generalisations and hypotheses about the social change that was occurring amongst the urban elite. This proved to be a subject of absorbing interest to the Ghanaians because many of the students and all of the staff belonged to this group. Discussions centred on the characteristics of the elite, their awareness of population questions, change in family structure and behaviour, attitudes towards family size, and measures taken to avoid pregnancy.

A set of questions was then constructed on these matters and a group of undergraduate sociology students specialising in demography were trained as interviewers so that they could be tested in the suburbs which had already been selected as housing residents of relatively high position in the socio-economic scale. In fact most testing was done in Accra because its nearness to the University of Ghana allowed work there to be undertaken in term time.

As a result of these preliminary tests some of the questions were modified and some were omitted, while a few new lines of inquiry were suggested. It was discovered that less suspicion and impatience was engendered by asking for a list of personal data at the conclusion of the interview rather than at the outset. More importantly, it was established that nearly all interviews could be held in English and that detailed translations would not be needed. In the whole demographic survey program this was to be the case on only one other occasion, a study of university students. It was found that a few wives would have to be interviewed in African languages, and for this reason student interviewers were later allocated to towns in areas from which they originally came. This did not solve every linguistic problem during the main survey because of the heterogeneous nature of urban population, but the residue of respondents who each had subsequently to be interviewed by a student re-allocated because he spoke the respondent's language was very small indeed.

The most important point established during the preliminary testing was that our original idea of including matching couples made up of pairs of husbands and wives presented greater problems than had been anticipated. Such an arrangement would obviously have yielded some information, especially on spouses' understanding of each other's attitudes, not otherwise obtainable. However, this gain did not seem to outweigh the other disadvantages. We required truthful answers on many intimate questions and had accordingly planned to have wives interviewed by female students and husbands by male students. The arranging of two separate interviews was awkward and consumed a great deal of time. More seriously, it aroused the justifiable suspicion that we were comparing the answers of husband and wife and so reduced the amount of co-operation received from respondents. Furthermore, the actual pairing of spouses was sometimes rendered difficult by the existence within the society of such institutions as polygyny and unstable marriage. Ultimately, it was decided to hold two entirely separate surveys, one of wives and the other of husbands, in the same suburbs and using very similar schedules. Accordingly, it was also decided that two unrelated samples would have to be used.

One feature common to these surveys and to most others in the demographic survey program was the extensive use of open-ended questions. The director of the program came from another type of society and the Ghanaians with whom he worked originated from either another stratum of the society being examined (although this was not the case in the survey described here) or lacked sufficient experience in thinking analytically about their own society and producing hypotheses upon which a satisfactory range of possible question answers could be constructed. Experience had shown that a large preliminary survey would be necessary to design an exhaustive series of answers, and it seemed to be more economical in terms of time and money to leave the answers open and to have Ghanaians subsequently codify the responses in committees chaired by the director. The codification was in continuous review during the preliminary processing.

During the original sampling of the towns to determine which suburbs were to be included in the survey and the subsequent building up and testing of the questionnaire, a body had been formed of students who were familiar with most aspects of the project. To achieve the full complement of male interviewers a few more sociology students were recruited. Amongst females, however, the search for suitable interviewers had to be widened to other university departments, because of the scarcity of female students, who made up only one-tenth of all students. The interviewers attended lectures on the project and undertook first mock interviews and then trial interviews in the field. A few who were not suited for the task were weeded out, but, on the whole, the students made excellent interviewers. They belonged to a society which rather strongly favours the discussion of problems and in which it is usual to show a considerable interest in personal affairs. They regarded the subject as important; so did the respondents, and in many interviews the completion of the schedule formed only a part of a much more extensive discussion.

Once the suburbs in which the urban elite lived were defined, no sampling of areas was required as all areas were surveyed. It was estimated that the selected suburbs contained between nine and ten thousand houses, and hence that a sampling ratio of one house in thirty would probably yield somewhat more than three hundred interviews in each survey. In the absence of a complete house list, a systematic sample was organised along selected interviewing routes which gave each house the same chance of selection.

The surveying was carried out in the latter part of 1963. Hence, when its findings are compared with those of the 1960 Census it must be remembered that the two investigations were separated by a period of about three-and-a-half years.

Very few problems were encountered during the actual survey, many fewer in fact than the preliminary tests had led us to anticipate. Substitution of the next house on the route, or, failing it, the previous house, had only to be employed by most interviewers in cases where the householders originally selected were not eligible for interview, usually because of racial origin or the wife's age. It was very rare for an interview to be refused outright, although some households may have intended to achieve this by asking the student to call back later. However, as the interviewers were under firm instructions to call a second, third, or even fourth time, if necessary, practically all intended interviews were ultimately carried out. Sometimes the whole schedule was completed only by one or two subsequent visits, but even the deferring of the whole or part of interviews was rare. Amongst males it was most common in the wealthiest of suburbs, where the husbands, who usually held very important jobs, were either a little apprehensive about being interviewed, or lived such busy lives that they were frequently called away to genuine engagements. Amongst wives the most common reason for deferment was that their husbands were at home and they would prefer to make an appointment for a subsequent time when he would be absent.

The interviewers reported a great deal of interest and co-operation and an earnestness about arriving at exactly defined answers. The interviewers for their part reported that they remained scrupulously neutral and did not ask any questions emotively, especially those on population growth, so as to influence the answers.

The holding of separate female and male surveys was not all loss. They did provide a check on each other, a check which was on the whole most reassuring, and which has given us very considerable confidence in the validity of the findings which are presented in the balance of this book. The major discrepancy was in the number of interviews. This arose partly from certain problems of route plotting, but partly also from one misinterpretation and one difficulty about the limits of the survey area, one in each survey and both acting to increase the difference between the number of interviews in each survey. The difficulty was that army officers queried our right to interview husbands in the officers' section of the military camp at Accra, while no obstacles were put in the way when interviewing their wives. Thus in the end the female survey consisted of 331 interviews and the male survey of 296. This discrepancy is tolerable if it is kept in mind that there were in fact two surveys, and not two divisions of a single survey. The universe varied slightly, but the extra included and excluded areas in the female and male surveys respectively were not atypical and could hardly affect the general characteristics of the population surveyed. This is substantiated by the fact that there are no significant differences between the data collected in the two surveys, except where one might reasonably expect to find them because of the different experiences or social positions of the two sexes.

The surveys were initially processed by students of the University of Ghana in order to codify answers and so that any defects in the data could be detected and remedied on the spot by subsequent re-interviews or whatever else was needed. However, the final coding and programming, analysis, and writing was undertaken at the Australian National University in Canberra.

2

The Characteristics of the Urban Elite

The Ghanaian Elite

The new education systems have been of paramount importance in bringing into existence the socio-economic class studied here. One authority on sub-Saharan Africa has written,

> Western education has created the new African elite . . . . In general, the new classes emerging from the Western impact (doctors, lawyers, teachers, businessmen, artisans, traders, clerks, cash crop farmers, etc.) have not only moved into the upper strata in territorial stratification systems; they have also displaced the upper strata in traditional societies . . . . It is doubtful whether in the modern world such rapid vertical mobility has been equalled (Coleman, 1960, pp. 278, 283, 279).

At the time of the survey the numbers of the elite had been swollen by those who had achieved occupational success by belonging to the politically successful group who took over power during the transition to independence. Such people worked not only in the public service but in the higher ranks of political or quasi-political organisations, such as the party machine, the press, the Trade Union Congress or various bureaus. Most, but not all, of the elite lived in the suburbs studied in the survey.

The 1960 Census yielded some information on the size of the country's elite. For instance it showed that of the population over 25 years old (and it seems reasonable to suppose that Ghanaian men at least would not achieve great occupational success nor on the whole get married until after this age) 3,800 males and 800 females, forming 0·3 per cent and 0·1 per cent respectively of the whole, had attended university at some time. Those with at least some secondary education made up 2·6 per cent of males and 0·6 per cent of females. However, the new elite contains a considerable number with only middle school education, and therefore it might be noted that 14·7 per cent of males and 2·9 per cent of females had experienced some middle school or higher education. Using occupational measures, it was found that 47,200 males and 6,800 females, forming 3·5 per cent and 0·5 per cent respectively of the two groups, did professional, technical, administrative, executive, or managerial work, while a further 28,100 and 1,200 respectively were clerical workers.

However, these measures are not entirely satisfactory. A considerable number of the most highly qualified persons would not have been Africans. Furthermore, the occupational categories are rather too comprehensive to separate the modern, urban elite. Even if we subtracted those identifiable as midwives, native physicians, herbalists, jujumen, fortune tellers, fetish priests, chiefs, cashiers, stenographers, typists, letter writers, and postal agents, many others do not appear even in the detailed census tables as separate categories.

It is much more satisfactory to adopt the approach of this survey. Who are the chief tenants of the modern houses of the richer suburbs in Ghana's four largest towns? What are their qualifications and what their occupations? What form does their family life take and to what extent has it parted with that traditionally Ghanaian?

Before describing the surveys' answers to these questions, it is necessary to consider just whom the surveys do cover. The methods adopted to identify the urban elite avoided the pitfalls into which the census must necessarily fall even when dealing with the wealthiest suburbs on a strictly areal basis, but at the same time they raise considerable difficulties in accurately defining the universe of the study.

Because of the use of a sampling ratio of one house in thirty, the 331 female respondents surveyed can be taken to be typical of a universe of about 10,000 women, while the 296 males represent about 9,000 men. Various tests can be employed to compare this group with the population enumerated in the 1960 Census. Educational characteristics prove to be more satisfactory for such a comparison than do occupational data, for, in spite of detailed statements in the Census volumes, there were found to be many problems in matching occupational data and in determining precisely what criteria were employed by the census when allocating occupational classifications. When using educational data, it is much more satisfactory to use the most advanced educational classifications, for, although not all who have attended universities will have secured places in the elite, let alone the urban elite, the loss rate will undoubtedly have been lower than amongst those with lesser education.

Even if the examination is confined to those who have been to university, there are still problems. Many university graduates have come from outside Africa. On the other hand the numbers of Africans with university education had risen greatly between 1960 and 1963. It may be that these two factors tend to cancel each other out. Numbers of graduates, such as schoolteachers and agricultural officers, would have been forced to leave the major urban areas precisely because of their qualifications, which earned them employment which could mean service in any part of the country. Many males with university training would still be unmarried because of the relatively late age of male marriage, which adds to the complexity because such a high proportion of the university trained are still young adults. For this reason, it may be that the use of female figures for comparison is more meaningful, in spite of the stronger link between residence in superior areas and the husbands' occupations.

It might be noted that the survey sample implies that the survey universe contained only one-half as many females who had been to university as the 1960 Census had enumerated in the four towns and not much more than a quarter of the number in the whole country. The balance within the towns probably lived in poorer suburbs or as subtenants in the surveyed ones. It should be understood that the great majority of females surveyed had not had university training. This qualification is being used here merely as an index of the distribution of the elite. The fact that the country as a whole contained four times as many university-trained women as the survey universe does not indicate that four times as many women necessarily think in much the same way as the respondents described in the succeeding pages of this book. For necessarily many of the female graduates elsewhere, whether teaching in rural areas or living in small towns or the poorer suburbs of the large towns or as poorer subtenants in the wealthier suburbs, are not surrounded by nearly as many women who have attitudes which resemble those of the urban elite. The total number of women in the whole country who do view life along similar lines and experience a similar family life is undoubtedly greater than the 10,000 of the survey universe but their numbers may not exceed 20,000.

A similar analysis is rendered more difficult still amongst males, because this study is concerned only with husbands, and as discussed later the average age of first marriage amongst the male urban elite is 26 years. Thus a comparison of those who have attended university might best be made with the population shown by the 1960 Census as over 25 years of age. Unfortunately, this data is available only for the whole country and not for the separate towns. This comparison indicates that the male survey universe contained only a fifth of those with university attendance in the country. The main reason for the discrepancy between this proportion and that found for females may be that there are disproportionately more male expatriate graduates in the country. There may also be relatively more males serving outside the large towns. Probably somewhat more than 20,000 males think as do those in the survey.

The female survey universe represents about three-quarters of 1 per cent of females, 18–44, in the country, and about 1 per cent currently married and living with their spouses (Caldwell, 1966, p. 599). Thus, it is likely that in Ghana at least one couple in every fifty in which the wife is between 18–44 years of age lives a life something like that pictured in the following pages and shares similar views on population growth, family relationships, and family size and limitation.

The Characteristics of the Surveyed Group

Averages are not always very meaningful, and in this study an attempt will usually be made to describe the distribution of respondents in any particular. However, only averages can provide a succinct glimpse of what might be regarded as typical specimens. Table 2:1 shows all family data that can easily be expressed as single figures.

The picture of the average elite couple is clear enough, even if, for the moment, there appear to be small anomalies between the two surveys. The wife is around 30 years of age and the husband is some seven years her senior, almost certainly a smaller margin than has traditionally existed in rural Ghana. The age gap at first marriage appears at first sight to be irreconcilable with that presently existing, for the men were little more than four years older than the women at the time of that event. The explanation lies in the 28 per cent of males and 12 per cent of females not experiencing their first marriage, for, in subsequent marriages, the men, growing older, tend to choose wives ever younger than themselves. Nevertheless, most marriages have been astonishingly stable compared

TABLE 2:1   Average characteristics of the urban elite

	Female survey	Male survey
Age of wife (in years)*	31·4	29·1
Age of husband (in years)	38·8	36·0
Age difference between spouses (in years)	7·4	6·9
Age at first marriage (in years)	21·6	25·8
Percentage of respondents enjoying first marriage	87·0	72·0
Percentage of cases where husband currently has no other wife	83·0	91·0
Number of children ever born to respondent†	3·4	4·4
Number of children still alive	3·2	3·9
Number of children by present spouse	3·0	3·4
Number of children recommended to a friend	4·4	4·6
Number of children hoped a daughter will have	4·3	4·7
Average number of other persons living with the family‡	1·4	1·5

* In the case of polygynous marriages in the male survey, this referred to the wife currently being lived with for most of the time; in the relatively rare cases of polygynous households it referred to the oldest wife.
† I.e. of whom the respondent was the biological parent.
‡ I.e. other than spouses and their children, but excluding other households in the same building, even if composed of relatives, and servants.

with the traditional pattern, for in about three-quarters of all cases respondents have participated in only a single, monogamous marriage. This does not necessarily mean that there have been no other liaisons, or that further liaisons or marriages will not be formed as the respondents, who are on the whole still relatively young, grow older. However, other investigations have confirmed that polygynous and unstable marriage patterns, as distinct from temporary liaisons and the possession of mistresses, are in contemporary Ghana very much more a feature of village life than of urban residence (Caldwell, 1967a, pp. 67–74; Tetteh, 1966, pp. 209–10). The nature of town dwellings and of 'white-collar' occupations enjoyed by the urban elite may stabilise marriage, at least partly because increased social and economic pressures are exerted to prevent the casual dissolution of existing unions.

By the time the wife is thirty, she has had three to four children, in the majority of cases all of them by her present spouse; what is more startling in terms of African social history is that in four cases out of five all have survived. Each of the four major urban centres has good medical facilities, and the respondents have usually had the influence and money to make full use of them. There may have been some omissions in replies about the deaths of children, but the general picture, one in which children have almost as much chance of survival as those in the West, is almost certainly a reasonably accurate one of the well-off urban family. It might be noted that mortality has been higher amongst children recorded in the male survey. One reason is that the children of women other than the present wife or wives, averaging one per respondent, are very likely raised elsewhere, in material conditions and perhaps propinquity to medical services inferior to those enjoyed by the families being surveyed. Families recommend on average about one more child than they themselves have by the time the wife is thirty. However, unless social change in this matter is proceeding much more rapidly than appears to be the case, they will overshoot this target by a considerable margin. Those urban elite women who have already completed their reproductive span or are drawing near to its close have on average borne about six children, not appreciably fewer than is typical of Ghanaian society as a whole.

Finally, in what ways are the figures in Table 2:1 worrying? It should be remembered that they apply to the results of two separate surveys, not the wives and husbands of the same couples, and, as such, the correspondence of many of the replies is reassuring. Nevertheless, there are some anomalies. More females reported that their husbands currently had other wives than did males when describing their own marital condition. This was in fact in keeping with the reports of some of the interviewers, who believed that wives were more likely to list their husbands' wives in the home villages or describe another town liaison as marriage than were the husbands themselves. Most other differences can either be related to the fact that husbands are on average older than their wives, and are less likely to be experiencing their first marriages or more likely to have had children outside that marriage, or to chance variations between two fairly small samples.

A more comprehensive picture of the elite can be obtained only by describing the distribution amongst them, not only of the characteristics glanced at above, but of such key matters as occupation and education, as well as religion, birthplace, child-bearing history, and marriage history.

In any study of a socio-economic elite it is meaningful to begin with an examination of occupation, for this is usually the major source of both the prestige and spending power which give rise to the description 'elite'. Especially is this the case with regard to husbands' occupations. In each of the surveys, just under a tenth of the husbands were in professional or highly skilled technical positions and a similar fraction were administrators or executives. Over a tenth were teachers and considerably over a third occupied clerical or other similar 'white-collar' posts. Thus, as can be seen in Table 2:2, two-thirds of the male household heads were employed in such categories, the great majority by governmental or semi-governmental authorities. A few of the husbands worked for large private firms but, as most of these were foreign-owned, the employment conditions were not dissimilar to those found in the public service. Only one in forty described himself, or was described by his wife, as owing his position to being a successful businessman. Thus the elite of Ghana's cities are essentially an administrative elite; they are not counterbalanced by an equally large, indigenous, commercial bourgeoisie. This situation arose partly from the policies of the Nkrumah Government, but the same position holds true to a very considerable extent in all the new African states. They have inherited from the colonial régimes a situation in which lucrative

TABLE 2:2   Male occupations as revealed by survey and census
(percentage distribution)

Occupational classification	Female survey (husbands)	Male survey (respondents)	All employed persons Four Towns	Ghana
Urban, upper*	66	66	19	6
Urban, lower†	27	29	74	31
Farming, etc.‡	2	3	7	63
No response, no occupation	5	2	—	—
Total	100	100	100	100

* Professional, higher technical, administrative, executive, managerial, clerical, teaching.
† All other urban (including nursing).
‡ Farming, fishing, etc.
Source: Surveys and *1960 Population Census of Ghana, Advance Report.*

business is to a marked degree in foreign hands and where high salaries are paid to indigenous population in return for executive and professional skills, often attested by educational qualifications. Even in Lagos, the greatest commercial mart of West Africa, the indigenous, city bourgeoisie does not contain nearly the same proportion of businessmen as does London, let alone New York.

Table 2:2 shows that the elite embody in an intensified manner the contrast between urban and rural life. These Ghanaian cities are not 'agrotowns'. Although none of them is far from the main tree-crop, cash-farming areas, they contain few farmers living away from their holdings, and fewer still of the elite described themselves as primarily farmers.

Finally, the elite found in the 'urban, lower' occupations category are found in its upper echelons. None of them was described as 'unskilled' or 'semi-skilled'; a third were skilled workers, a fifth connected with commerce or marketing, and a fifth with services and entertainment.

Although, in the recent flux of change in African society, it would be quite reasonable to picture an urban elite maintained by the husbands' positions, with wives undertaking jobs more akin to the general female employment position in the country, this is not in fact the case. Table 2:3 shows much more employment amongst survey wives in 'urban, upper' occupations than is found throughout the four towns or country. However, 'urban, lower' occupations not only form between a third and half the occupations, but there is a discrepancy between the two surveys. Half this group earn income in marketing, and re-interviewing revealed that there was disagreement, especially between husbands and wives, about whether some involvement in marketing constituted a form of employment. Husbands were more likely to assert that it did and to record its existence. In fact, the two surveys were in agreement in a subsequent question, that 28 per cent of wives contributed nothing towards their own or their children's support. Usually, the type of marketing involved was on a

TABLE 2:3   Female occupations as revealed by survey and census
(percentage distribution)

Occupational classification	Female survey (respondents)	Male survey (wives)	All employed persons Four Towns	Ghana
Urban, upper*	27	22	4	1
Urban, lower†	33	49	52	24
Farming, etc.‡	1	1	4	34
Homemakers§	34	26	40	41
No response	5	2	—	—
Total	100	100	100	100

* Professional, higher technical, administrative, executive, managerial, clerical, teaching.
† All other urban (including nursing).
‡ Farming, fishing, etc.
§ Includes 'no occupation'.
Source: Surveys and *1960 Population Census of Ghana, Advance Report.*

considerable scale; wives used the substantial amount of capital available in the household to buy on a large scale and then to sell, often to lesser traders.

Hardly any wives held professional or executive positions, and comparatively few were clerks. In fact, two thirds of those in 'urban, upper' positions were teachers, who make up almost a sixth of the wives of the elite. Of the 'urban, lower' occupations, those not marketing usually were employed in skilled work, frequently nursing and dressmaking.

It is noteworthy that more wives amongst the elite are employed than amongst all women of the four towns. The explanation may be that such qualifications as teacher-training or the availability of some finance for marketing make jobs both easier to get and more tempting. Comparison with all women in the country would be less valid, as many of the women returned as 'homemakers' in rural areas certainly do a substantial amount of work connected with farming.

In addition, occupational data over two generations and before and after the marriage of wives provide valuable information about how the urban elite is formed. The value of the data in Table 2:4 is reduced by the large number of female respondents giving no answer or claiming not to be certain about their fathers' occupations. Almost a third fell into this category. At first it was believed that the interviewers were at fault, but further examination showed that, because of the unstable marriage pattern, many of these respondents had lost contact with their fathers, at least to a sufficient degree to be uncertain about their employment in younger life or before death. It might be noted that the great majority of respondents came from matrilineal societies. In addition, many of the fathers were long since dead, as men in traditional Ghanaian families were often very much older than their wives and hence were separated by a large age gap

TABLE 2:4 Comparison of occupations of respondents' fathers, respondents before and after marriage and female respondents' husbands (percentage distribution)

Occupational classification	Female survey				Male survey	
	Respondents' fathers	*Respondents before marriage*	*Respondents after marriage*	*Respondents' husbands*	*Respondents' fathers*	*Respondents*
Urban, upper*	24	44	27	66	20	66
Urban, lower†	16	40	33	27	29	29
Farming‡	22	1	1	2	42	3
Homemakers	0	13	34	0	0	0
No response, no occupation, unclassified	38	2	5	5	9	2
Total	100	100	100	100	100	100

* Professional, higher technical, administrative, executive, managerial, clerical, teaching.
† All other urban (including nursing).
‡ Farming, fishing, etc.

from their children. Fathers seemed to have taken relatively more care to keep in touch with their sons than with their daughters. A similar pattern of response to a question of this type was subsequently reported from Lagos, Nigeria (Ohadike, personal communication). Nevertheless, our impression was that most of the fathers of unknown occupation had been farmers or fishermen, a feeling which received support from the fact that a very large proportion of the respondents concerned were of rural origin.

Even with these qualifications, the table clearly establishes two points. The first is that the 'urban, upper' classes are not a closed group. They could hardly be so, as the type of occupational position they hold, and indeed the total urban population, has been increasing so rapidly that self-recruitment alone would not suffice. Only about a quarter of the socio-economic elite seemed to have been recruited from similar parental stock. Nevertheless, in view of the very small size of the elite a generation ago, such a proportion provides very significant evidence of the tenacity with which the children of the urban elite cling to their way of life. They are, of course, greatly assisted by their usually superior educational opportunities in a society where occupational advance to the higher urban positions is dependent very much on educational qualifications. It is striking that, although only about a tenth of the population lived in urban areas a generation ago (i.e. in centres with more than 5,000 inhabitants in 1931), probably about half the urban elite have been recruited from the towns. Even the urban families of lesser occupational status have contributed far more than their proportional share to the urban elite of the next generation.

Table 2:4 also shows that marriage was by no means the only way whereby females achieved town residence and higher living standards.

Nearly all those born in rural districts had moved to urban areas prior to marriage. In fact it was often the securing of posts as teachers or clerks which led to their 'successful' marriages.

The key to occupational success in such new African nations as Ghana is education. Nor is this resented. The society is very conscious of educational success and assumes that such success should be rewarded. A common type of complaint is that some person holds a responsible position although his education was not particularly extensive.

The surveys bore evidence on this point. At the outside, only 1·3 per cent of the male respondents (assuming that no response indicated no formal education) had achieved their socio-economic success, as judged by their residence, without education, in a country where five-sixths of the adult population in 1960 had never been to school. Half the male respondents had education beyond the middle school level, a stage which still marks the completion of schooling for the great majority of the country's children. While the relationship does not hold so clearly for wives, a sixth of whom may not have been to school at all, it is abundantly clear that one can place little faith in the view, expressed frequently in Ghana, that educated men seek uneducated women as wives. There is a high correlation between the education of spouses. Furthermore, the lower educational qualifications of the wives is merely a reflection of relatively low educational opportunities for females; the survey females stand out more markedly from the general community levels than do the survey males.

Care should be taken when interpreting Tables 2:5 and 2:6. 'Technical training' as used in the survey referred to any specialised training subsequent to middle schooling or higher education, and thus included, for instance, training in nursing or teaching where no secondary or university

TABLE 2:5   Highest level of education attained
(percentage distribution)

Highest level of education reached	Female survey	Male survey
University	2	8
Secondary school	9	22
Technical training	25	22
Middle school	44	34
Primary school	3	13
Other: mass education	0*	0*
Arabic school	0	0
None	12	0*
No response	5	1
Total	100	100

* One case.

qualifications were demanded as prerequisites. The figures in this category for the four towns or the whole country are merely the aggregate of those shown in the census as having been to teacher-training institutions, or commercial or technical schools. The census figures are proportions, not of the married, but of all persons over 6 years of age not currently at school. The large numbers now at school, especially in the four towns,

TABLE 2:6   Persons reaching a certain standard of education or higher
(cumulative percentage distribution)

Standard	Female survey	Females Four Towns*	Ghana*	Male survey	Males Four Towns*	Ghana*
University	2	0	0	8	1	0
Secondary school	11	2	0	30	7	1
Technical training†	36	3	0	52	8	2
Middle school	80	15	4	86	41	15
Primary school	83	21	8	99	47	21
Other‡	83	21	8	99	49	22
None or no response§	100	100	100	100	100	100

* Percentages of all persons over 6 years of age and not currently at school.
† For census figures includes only teacher-training, commercial and technical schools.
‡ For survey includes mass education; for census includes Arabic schools.
§ No 'no response' figures are found in the census.
Source: Surveys and *1960 Population Census of Ghana*, Vol. III and *Special Report 'A'*.

render this treatment less dangerous for comparative purposes than it would otherwise be.

The category, 'other', includes Arabic schools and adult mass education courses, the latter in the surveys alone and only so far as literacy results. This raises another important point. In the Four Towns, 2·4 per cent of males have been to Arabic schools but no member of the elite had been trained in them. Entrance to the elite is almost exclusively through Western-type schools, which provide the qualifications recognised by the public service, universities, and even private firms.

Religion is related to education. The first Western-type schools were mission schools, and the acquisition of a modern education went hand in hand with at least nominal conversion to Christianity. Some of the residential secondary schools, which have played such an important role in producing the elite, still have church connections. Even later government schools often assumed that their non-religious role meant that their influence should be non-sectarian Christian, and sometimes non-sectarian Protestant. Thus, the urban, socio-economic elite is overwhelmingly Christian, and very largely Protestant. One could almost talk of a 'Protestant ethic' amongst the successful.

Furthermore, there is a statistically significant avoidance of mixed Protestant-Catholic marriages. Of the 277 marriages in the female survey and 240 marriages in the male survey where both spouses were listed as either Protestant or Catholic, in well over 90 per cent of all marriages both spouses were of the same persuasion.

TABLE 2:7 Religion as revealed by survey and census
(percentage distribution)

Religion	Female survey (respondents)	Male survey (respondents)	Four Towns*	Ghana*
Protestant	79	76⎱	66	43
Catholic	12	12⎰		
Moslem	0†	1	15	12
Traditional	0†	0	11	38
Other‡	6	8	—	—
No religion	1	2	8	7
No response	2	1	—	—
Total	100	100	100	100

* Persons over 15 years of age.
† One case.
‡ Usually Christian unspecified but in a minority of cases 'no religion' would be the better description.
Source: Surveys and *1960 Population Census of Ghana,* Atlas.

The towns are more Christian and less traditional, but not less Moslem, in religion than the countryside. The urban elite is Christian to the almost complete exclusion, not only of traditional religions, but also of Islam.

A possible factor in determining social change amongst Ghana's elite is not merely whether its members are at present subjected to urban influences but whether they were during their formative years. In addition to the towns surveyed Tamale, Koforidua, and Tarkwa all had more than 50,000 people within them or their immediate environs (i.e. within the urban council area) at the time of the survey, and, with the exception of the last, had numbered over 10,000 inhabitants for at least a generation.

By this criterion of 'urban', Table 2:8 reveals a statistically significant (1 per cent level) difference between the origins of the female and male

TABLE 2:8 Birthplace of respondents
(percentage distribution)

Origin	Female survey (respondents)	Male survey (respondents)
Urban (large towns)*	56	45
Small towns and villages	43	54
No response	1	1
Total	100	100

* Born in Accra, Kumasi, Sekondi-Takoradi, Cape Coast, Tamale, Koforidua, Tarkwa.

respondents. In the past it has almost certainly been relatively much harder for a girl in rural Ghana to obtain the necessary education to give her a chance of reaching the urban elite than it has been for a boy. In the large towns the odds against her were not so great. Even by 1960 the urban-rural differential in the education of the sexes was still considerable; for every 100 girls at school there were 133 boys there in Accra, 152 boys in all urban areas, 227 boys in rural areas, and 359 boys in the rural part of the remoter Northern Region. If the urban elite want educated wives they may have to seek them predominantly from the town-born.

In fact the urban elite has been recruited in disproportionate numbers from the towns with regard to both sexes. Even amongst male respondents almost half came from these seven towns, which contained only one Ghanaian in ten in 1960 and one in fifteen a generation earlier. The explanation does not lie merely in the immobility of the population, for, even between 1948 and 1960, natural increase accounted for much less than half of urban growth. Admittedly, the 1960 Census found that four-ninths of the people in the four towns had been born there, but a very large part of this group were undoubtedly children. If the examination is confined to what may be described as Ghana's 'cities', Accra and Kumasi, the only centres which have housed more than 50,000 people for a generation, and the only ones with more than 100,000 inhabitants at the time of the survey, we find that a third of all respondents were born in them, although a generation ago they would have contained no more than a twenty-fifth of the country's population.

The age distribution of respondents was determined largely by the definition of the survey, the relatively late age of marriage of the group, and the predominance of the young in such a rapidly growing population, and contained no real surprises. The numbers of female respondents in each age group was 18–19 years, 2 per cent; 20–24 years, 16 per cent; 25–29 years, 27 per cent; 30–34 years, 24 per cent; 35–39 years, 16 per cent; 40–44 years, 13 per cent, while 2 per cent were subsequently found to have disregarded the initial instruction and to have been over 45 years. Thus half the respondents were aged between 25 and 34 years, and two-thirds between 20 and 34 years. Most had been children until after World War II and had married and faced decisions about family formation and child-rearing in the exciting years of social and political change which followed, to select one turning point, the 1948 riots in Accra. The husbands were on average five to six years older and more of them had experienced their formative years in the 1930s. Nevertheless, most had likewise not faced questions of marriage and the upbringing of children until after World War II, when Ghana's towns were growing fast, its economy booming, and the indigenous, urban elite expanding as never before.

The urban elite probably marry later on average than other residents of the towns, while the marriage age pattern in the towns certainly indicates the delay of female marriage compared with traditional society. An important reason is the spread of education, coupled with the fact that average age is higher for each school grade than is common in the West. A ninth of the female respondents had had at least some university or secondary education and four-ninths had been trained beyond the middle school level. Because the education system is still in the process of con-struction, because many children are delayed in the early stages by a switch in the language of tuition, because most must go to middle school prior to secondary school, and because some have had to miss periods of school while money for fees was found or earned, students are often relatively old at the end of training. At the time of the 1960 Census, females in the last year of middle school (bypassed by many on the way to secondary school) were most frequently 16 years of age, in the last year of commercial schools 18 or 19 years, and in the last year of secondary school 19 or 20 years. More than half the female students in the second year of teacher-training were over 20 years and very few even began university before 20 years of age. These are no longer the social conditions which favour universal female marriage at puberty.

TABLE 2:9   Age at first marriage of respondents
(percentage distribution)

Age (in years)	Female survey	Male survey
Under 20	21	1
20–24	62	36
25–29	12	49
30 and over	2	13
No response	3	1

As can be seen in Table 2:9, only a fifth of female respondents married for the first time before 20 years of age. An examination by single years of age showed that only one in twenty married before 18 years; thereafter the incidence increased until 20 years, an age at which a fifth of all respondents married, and then decreased as down a sloping plateau, which fell away sharply only after 24 years. This does not mean that sexual experience or the risk of pregnancy has been postponed for this group by five or more years. Indeed, a high proportion of discussions in Ghana on familiarity with contraceptives or the need for abortions centres on the problems of girls still being educated. Admittedly, few of the respondents may have become pregnant during their education, as such an event may well terminate education and greatly reduce the chance of entering the urban elite.

Half the male respondents married for the first time between 25 and 29 years of age. Marriage amongst the males does not become really common until about 23 years of age, and thereafter the frequency plateau ascends until 25 years, an age at which about a sixth marry, and then descends, steeply after 28 years of age.

An investigation into the factors influencing delayed female marriage showed a statistically significant relation (at 1 per cent) with education beyond middle school. Such a relation could not be shown in the case of the male respondents, who normally married at a later age even than the completion of the most extended education. Background seems also to play a role, although the link may be partly through the greater likelihood of having been given an extended education by well-off, urban parents. In the case of both female and male respondents marriage was significantly (at 5 per cent level) later in the case of children of fathers with 'urban, upper' occupations than of children of farmers or those with 'urban, lower' jobs. No other relationships could be established.

There is quite a marked age gap between spouses, although it is almost certainly less than that found in the traditional society. Nevertheless, in each survey only one husband was found who was younger than his wife and only one more of the same age. In each survey four-fifths of all spouses were separated by a gap of two to ten years and two-fifths by four to seven years. The average and median gaps were between five and six years.

It would seem to be a reasonable surmise that the age gap between spouses would narrow with social change as marriage became more of a partnership. If this is so, the surveys failed to find the evidence. The age gap between monogamously married younger couples experiencing their first marriage was not significantly less than that between older couples in the same condition. Nor did modernisation appear to play a role. The level of education of the spouses could not be shown to have influenced the position. Nor could the town of residence, although in this case, the geographical mobility of the elite might militate against distinguishing any regional cultural traditions.

Any analysis of marriage in tropical Africa is rendered complex by the great numbers of persons who marry more than once, either successively, concurrently, or both. However, the survey showed that a surprising number of the urban elite had been married only once. Table 2:10 shows this to have been the case for 87 per cent of female respondents and 72 per cent of male respondents. The discrepancy between the sexes is to be explained partly by polygynous marriages and partly by the fact that successive or unstable marriage is somewhat commoner amongst males, a

TABLE 2:10   Number of times respondents have been married
(percentage distribution)

Number of marriages	Female survey	Male survey
1	87	72
2	8	20
3 or more	2	7
No response	3	1
Total	100	100

position which can exist because of the age gap between spouses and the high rate of population growth (Caldwell, 1963a). Nevertheless, such figures show a surprisingly stable marriage pattern compared with that described in the traditional society. A similar position has recently been found in the wealthier suburbs of Lagos, Nigeria (Ohadike, personal communication). The explanation is that an unstable marriage pattern is not easily adjusted to the living conditions of the urban elite—to the greater interest in the upbringing and education of the children, the arrangement of superannuation schemes connected with 'white-collar' employment, to the acceptance of the provision of a house by the government and so on. Questions of respectability also arise; so does the difficulty a husband finds in divorcing his wife, which might well be an expensive affair by the time all costs and recompenses have been paid. Furthermore, the wife is likely to have an influential family who are capable of exerting considerable pressure. They may even have insisted on a 'marriage under the ordinance' in the first place, which means that divorce must be secured through a law court on grounds similar to those obtaining in Britain. This does not, of course, mean that the husband might not have mistresses or keep other households or children, although such practices can prove expensive in an urban environment, but it does mean that the socially recognised marriage is comparatively stable.

The two surveys produced answers about the number of wives previously possessed by husbands which were not significantly different. This, as mentioned before, was not the case when inquiring about whether the husband currently had more than a single wife. Rechecking suggested to interviewers that husbands were less likely than were their wives to suggest that another woman kept elsewhere was in fact a common-law wife. Thus 8 per cent of male respondents described themselves as polygynously married at the time of the survey while 13 per cent of female respondents claimed that their husbands were.

Female respondents were asked how many years they had been married, either for one continuous period or for a total of several discontinuous periods. Presumably this period roughly approximates for most with the main period during which they have been at risk of pregnancy. The answers accord with what has already been stated about age, marriage patterns by age, and incidence of stable marriage. Table 2:12 shows that over half the female respondents had been married for less than ten years.

TABLE 2:11   Number of wives currently possessed by husbands
(percentage distribution)

Number of wives	Female survey	Male survey
1	83	91
2	10	7
3 or more	3	1
No response	4	1
Total	100	100

Data was collected on the number of live births to which parentage was biologically attributable to the respondents. Rates for males were higher than those for females even when standardised by the age of

TABLE 2:12   Female respondents, number of years married
(percentage distribution)

Years	Female survey
0–9	53
10–19	32
20–29	12
No response	3
Total	100

the oldest wife, averaging between a quarter and a third higher. The difference is attributable to polygynous and unstable marriage patterns. Detailed analysis of the male rates is made difficult and not very meaningful by the different age patterns of wives in polygynous or successive marriages.

This is not the case with regard to the female respondents, although the numbers in certain age groups are so small as to produce random fluctuations in the fertility pattern. In Table 2:13 the average number of live births for respondents in each age group has been compared with three other sets of survey results from Ghana. The survey of the elite, unlike the other surveys, was confined to married women and so these rates must be regarded as marital rates only, but, because of near universal marriage and remarriage, the difference can be regarded as unimportant for the 25–29 years of age group. The numbers of urban elite survey respondents in the last two age groups are too few to make comparison meaningful; but certain conclusions can reasonably be drawn. Firstly, these surveys showed, as did the 1960 Census, that there is an urban-rural fertility differential in Ghana. Completed fertility (i.e. the average number of children borne by women by the end of their child-bearing span) in the urban areas of the country is apparently about 8 per cent below the national average or 10 per cent below that obtaining in rural areas. In southern Ghana large towns appeared to exhibit fertility levels about one-eighth below those of the surrounding regions (see Appendix). The survey of the urban elite produced rates generally in line with the two other urban surveys, and thus gave no indication of a differential within urban areas by socio-economic class, except possibly amongst younger parents. However, the Appendix does establish that a small socio-economic differential exists. In the surveys it may be masked by a greater ability or willingness among the elite to recall dead children, and by the fact that the elite survey measures marital fertility. Secondly, the surveys showed that family size in Ghana, even amongst the urban elite, is still so large as to be equal to the national figures recorded in the world's highest fertility countries. There is, then, little evidence from this source of any particularly effective use of methods for limiting family size, even amongst the small, select group being investigated. One female respondent in eight had borne no children, but many were still young and recently married. Only 5½ per cent of respondents over 30 years of age had not had any children, a figure which probably closely approaches natural infecundity. On the other hand, a third of the women over 30 had borne six or more children and two over ten children.

A statistical investigation was made of all influences likely to affect fertility amongst the urban elite. A significant (5 per cent level) fertility differential by education was found amongst both female and male respondents. The fertility of female respondents who had been educated beyond the middle school level was in each age group no more than nine-tenths of that of the respondents with lesser education. A similar, but necessarily more complex, pattern was found amongst male respondents. No other significant differentials, not even one between Protestants and Catholics, could be established.

About 93 per cent of their children are said by the elite mothers to be still alive. There may be some failure or refusal here to recall infant deaths, a phenomenon found by other surveys in the society in general. If the figure is correct, and if at this level of mortality the Ghanaian pattern is similar to that found outside Africa, then the expectation of life at birth of these children is above 65 years and only a little behind that of the advanced countries of Western Europe. This is certainly not impossible or even improbable, as this select group can command similar medical facilities. The failure of the proportion surviving to drop much with increase in the age of the mothers and hence the number of older children suggests that the great majority of mortality is restricted to infancy, as

TABLE 2:13   Average numbers of live births per female by age

Age (years)	Female survey No. of respondents	Average live births	Accra survey*	Urban survey*	Rural survey*
15–19	5	0·4	0·3	0·5	0·6
20–24	47	1·2	1·3	1·3	1·7
25–29	89	2·2	2·4	2·5	3·0
30–34	80	3·8	3·2	3·6	4·1
35–39	53	4·7	4·2	4·6	5·0
40–44	43	6·3	5·1	5·5	6·1
45+ (completed)	—	—	5·6	6·2	7·4
No response	14†				
Total number of respondents	331				

* Accra and Conjugal Biography Surveys, data taken from J. C. Caldwell, 'The Forces of Change', in Walter Birmingham, I. Neustadt, and E. N. Omaboe (eds.), *A Study of Contemporary Ghana*, Vol. II, *The Social Structure of Ghana*, London, 1966, p. 102.
† Respondents failing to state age, number of live births, or both.

would be expected from experience elsewhere of such low child mortality. Such a high level of survival does mean that the elite are likely to be rearing more children than are poorer parents, for typically in many rural areas only about two-thirds of the children born are found by investigators to be still alive.

Over four-fifths of the female respondents' children were living with them, although almost a third of their husbands' children were elsewhere, frequently, presumably, with their mothers. These fractions are in fact larger than the proportion of children by spouses other than current ones. Nine-tenths of the children borne by female respondents had been by their present husbands and over three-quarters of the children fathered by male respondents were those of women to whom they were currently married.

Summary

The above description of the urban elite does not illustrate the purpose for which the survey was organised. Indeed, to collect accurate information upon such matters would require a much larger sample than two surveys of approximately 300 persons each. This is especially so with regard to the kind of demographic information about mortality of children and fertility by age of mother just described. For this reason no great weight has been put on the findings.

The purpose of the surveys was to gather the kind of information about changing family structure and attitudes, together with some views on wider population matters, of the kind which is described in the rest of this book. To draw a picture of this sort, 600 interviews, investigating perhaps a fifteenth of the households of the required kind in the interview areas and perhaps a thirtieth of all such households in the country, is quite adequate. Indeed, to administer properly a complex series of interviews of this type, each containing well over a hundred questions, many of which involved lengthy consideration and answers, and often revisits, would not have been possible without a much larger and more complex organisation.

The present chapter has not aimed at accurately describing in statistical terms the characteristics of the urban elite. Its function has been to delineate the kind of people making up that elite to further understanding of the 'new class' in countries like Ghana and to permit an understanding of the kind of people who answered and argued in the way described in the balance of this book.

The general picture emerges quite clearly. The upper socio-economic stratum of Ghana's major towns is composed largely of families with male household heads employed in administrative and professional occupations which they have been able to secure because of their educational quali- fications. Many of their wives have made their own way into such employ- ment, which has led to their marriage, rather than the other way round. More than half the males and over a third of the females have been educated beyond the middle school level.

Access to the elite has, over the last twenty years, not been particularly difficult, although urban and especially urban elite background has helped very substantially. It is, therefore, likely that the children of the elite will for the most part manage to remain within this group. A large proportion of the wives still do some work outside the home, often assisted by the fact that one or more relatives live with the family. Practically all are Christian and a very large majority Protestant.

The females are likely to have married first between 20 and 24 years of age, which is late by traditional standards, and in fact no earlier than American women. The males, perhaps five or six years older than their wives, are most likely to have married between 25 and 29 years of age. Probably four-fifths of the wives are married for the first time, and perhaps two-thirds of all the households involve first and monogamous marriages. The most educated have slightly fewer children than the others but, unless family patterns change, five living children is a likely number for the completed family. In the great majority of cases husbands and wives will be living in the same house and usually all the children of the existing marriage will be living with them.

This pattern differs in many ways from the traditional Ghanaian pattern and could be said to be more Western. Thus, the respondents are not likely to answer the survey questions in a way completely typical of their society. Probably about one household in fifty in the whole country is of the type described here, but such a fraction does not represent their importance or militate against the significance of the study. For the urban elite are significant in two ways: firstly, their numbers are likely to increase and ultimately their way of life might become fairly general; secondly, and in the shorter perspective, they serve to channel new patterns of living into the country and aspects of their way of life will, in perhaps diluted form, have a much wider influence in the society than the mere spread of their numbers would indicate. Even more important is likely to be their effect on the formation of governmental policy.

3

The Awareness of Population Questions

Taking up first the final point of the last chapter, it is pertinent to ask what influence on population policy is likely to be exerted by the urban elite. After all, by definition they comprise all the higher public servants and most of the politicians and publicists. Do they in fact share any awareness of or views on population matters?

The survey included four questions, each subdivided into two parts, on this subject. Beginning with a general inquiry about future population size, the questions subsequently became more specific as they tested reactions to current growth rates, immigration, and the relation between population growth and economic development.

Future Population

The survey was carried out during the period when the results of the much publicised 1960 Census were being released. Amongst the elite it was widely known that the Census had enumerated six and three-quarter million people compared with little more than two, three, and four million in 1921, 1931, and 1948 respectively. It was also known that it had established that the rates of both natural increase and net immigration had been very high indeed during the 1950s. Perhaps less widely appreciated were the facts that the 1948 and 1960 enumerations had implied an average annual intercensal growth rate of 5 per cent, staggeringly high in terms of most precedent elsewhere, and that the Census Office had suggested that the apparent rate had been raised by defective census-taking in 1948 so that the real rate, even including immigration, might not be above 3 per cent (see Caldwell, 1967a, for the author's views).

Nevertheless, an awareness of rapid population growth did exist. This was by no means universally associated with apprehension. Indeed, it is surprising that any apprehension was felt. The Nkrumah Government expressed confidence that its policies could cope with, and even benefit from, population increase of any size, especially the natural increase of the Ghanaians themselves. For a man in a responsible position to express any other view could easily be taken as a sign of lack of confidence in the régime. Certainly the mass communications media, all in the hands of the government or party, rarely exhibited lack of confidence on this point. Some apprehension was to be expressed in the *Seven-Year Development Plan*, but its release occurred after the completion of the survey.

The strong expression of the official viewpoint may have led some members of the elite to rationalise their own viewpoints. It may even have denied them sufficient data to judge the problem correctly. However, it was rarely felt by interviewers that it led to the expression of untruthful

42

answers during the survey. University surveys had prestige and university students were trusted. Furthermore, there is a distinction between the expression of views on political occurrences and on demographic and economic policy matters, and there was no great apprehension about the private expression of views in the latter field.

Question 1 (a) of the survey asked, 'Do you hope that in future the number of people living in Ghana will be (i) less than now, (ii) the same as now, (iii) more than now, or (iv) much more than now?' Question 1 (b) sought reasons for the answers given. It was the latter part of the question which revealed that answers to the former part should be treated with great caution. In spite of checks and counterchecks on question interpretation and on translation—for even when the questionnaire was administered in English, conversation between the interviewer and interviewee often changed to Ghanaian languages—unexpected semantic difficulties occurred here. In fact difficulties of this order were not encountered with any other question in the whole series of surveys. 'Hope' was often confused with 'expect' or 'anticipate', and in most Ghanaian languages any distinction can be made only with difficulty. Thus, most respondents discussed the question in terms of probable demographic trends. However, no information was completely lost as Question 2 served as an adequate check and supplement to Question 1.

Replies to Question 1 (a) are shown in Table 3:1. The differences between the replies of female and male respondents may largely arise from the greater involvement of the latter in administration and their consequent awareness that population will inevitably increase. In replies to question 1 (b), five-sixths of the respondents in each survey appeared to reveal some confusion between 'hope' and 'expect'. Of those who

TABLE 3:1   Responses to question, 'Do you hope that in future the number of people living in Ghana will be, (i) less than now, (ii) the same as now, (iii) more than now, or (iv) much more than now?'

Response	Female survey (n = 331)		Male survey (n = 296)	
	No.	Per cent	No.	Per cent
Less than now	33	10	20	7
Same as now	33	10	7	3
More than now	129	39	187	63
Much more than now	129	39	79	26
No response	7	2	3	1
Total	331	100	296	100

desired no further population increase, the difficulties of individual families and national economic problems were cited as reasons to about the same extent.

Some of the individual comments were interesting. Amongst those mentioning sexual morality, there was general agreement about increasing laxity especially amongst girls in towns. Some went on to argue that this must lead to more conceptions, while others insisted that 'good-time girls' were so averse to pregnancies interfering with their way of life that they were taking ever more care to see that this did not happen. Improved health facilities were mentioned frequently as the cause of a marked decline in infant and child mortality and occasionally as producing a rise in fertility. One young male school-teacher said that population growth would inevitably accelerate because 'our illiterate masses will not control births'.

Present Population Increase

Question 2 approached the question of rapid population growth in a way which did not give rise to confusion and which did not lead to the awkward dichotomy between what one hopes and what one feels to be inevitable. As shown in Table 3:2, respondents were told that Ghana's population was increasing exceptionally rapidly and were then asked if they regarded this as being good, bad, or immaterial.

Amongst every ten respondents, seven viewed such rapid increase as being 'good', an attitude in line with both traditional beliefs and what the government claimed to be the most modern economic and political concepts. Thus, it is of very considerable interest that one out of every ten did not consider the phenomenon to be intrinsically good, while two

TABLE 3:2   Responses to question, 'At present Ghana's population is increasing much faster than is the case in most parts of the world. Do you think this is (i) a good thing, (ii) a bad thing, or (iii) does not matter?'

Response	Female survey (n = 331)		Male survey (n = 296)	
	No.	Per cent	No.	Per cent
A good thing	227	68	214	72
A bad thing	65	20	51	17
Does not matter	34	10	29	10
No response	5	2	2	1
Total	331	100	296	100

regarded it as a bad thing. It is the emergence of this latter view which will be considered in further detail below.

Who are the fifth of the elite who maintained against the apparently accepted official view in the society that such a rate of population increase in the country was a bad thing? It should be noted that statistically there is no significant difference in response by sex.

The examination then turned to other characteristics of the households and respondents. In much of the examination that follows, the age group of the spouses is determined by whether the wife, or at least the wife currently living in the household or the senior wife where there is more than one, is under or over 30 years. Similarly, the major educational grouping of respondents has been determined by whether they have been formally educated beyond the middle school level or not.

Using these major divisions, age did not appear to affect the replies of female respondents but, in the case of males, it was significant (5 per cent level). Over a fifth of younger respondents thought such rapid increase to be bad, compared with fewer than an eighth of those who were older. Rather surprisingly, education showed no differentials significant at even the 5 per cent level, although it might be noted that 20 per cent of male respondents with more than middle school education described the increase as bad, compared with 15 per cent of those with lesser education. Neither religion nor the number of marriages experienced could be related to the replies at all.

However, there is a connection, amongst the Ghanaian elite, as there presumably is elsewhere in the world, between personal practices and views on national phenomena. When a person decides to limit the size of his family for its own good, he is quite likely to adopt the same views about the condition of the nation. Thus respondents who were using family planning methods or had done so in the past were much more likely to be apprehensive about rapid population increase. Such growth was described as bad by 27 per cent and 32 per cent of female and male respondents respectively who had ever used methods to restrict family size, but by only 17 per cent and 12 per cent of those who had not. There was a less clear-cut connection with merely favouring the establishment of family planning clinics or expression of desire to use them, the relations being statistically significant (1 per cent level) only in the case of male respondents.

Amongst those who favoured rapid population increase, over two-thirds believed it would benefit economic development. About an eighth of respondents mentioned national status and another eighth military manpower, while a tenth talked of filling the country. Repeatedly reference was made to the government's plans for industrialisation and the consequent need of additional workers. In one sense, replies were markedly different from those obtained when interviewing the rural population, for amongst the elite only one in twenty spoke of 'God's will', 'nature' or some equivalent concept. Admittedly, the framing of the question may well have appeared to call for an answer more in terms of the country than in terms of the domestic situation of individual families.

The case against rapid increase was framed to an even greater extent in economic terms. Every respondent in this group made at least one reference to either the threat of unemployment, particularly in the towns, or the possibility of food shortage. Some discussed housing shortages in the towns. A fifth referred to family costs, especially the increasing need for seeing that all children were well educated. Some took it as a sign of social slipshodness. One female teacher, herself a mother of ten and married to a chief accountant, described rapid increase as bad and complained that 'Many people bring forth just for the sake of it, while they leave the children to wander about'.

Immigration

In Ghana one cannot speak of population increase, or approve or disapprove of its rate, without clearly distinguishing its two components. Directly or indirectly immigrants were probably responsible for over a fifth of population increase between 1948 and 1960 (Caldwell, 1967a, pp. 78–83). By the latter date persons of foreign birth made up at least a twelfth of the population and, with their children, constituted an eighth. To a resident of one of the surveyed towns the impression of massive population increase arising from immigration is probably even stronger than these figures convey. The 1960 Census showed that a sixth of the population of the four towns is of foreign birth and a quarter of foreign origin. In Accra and Kumasi, the only centres for which the necessary data have been published, a third of the male population, 20–44 years of age, was of foreign origin.

TABLE 3:3   Responses to the question, 'A large number of people now live and work in Ghana although they were born in other African countries, especially Togo, Nigeria and Upper Volta. Do you think it would be best if there were (i) fewer immigrants in the country, (ii) about the number there are now, or (iii) more immigrants?'

Response	Female survey (n = 331)		Male survey (n = 296)	
	No.	Per cent	No.	Per cent
Fewer immigrants	127	38	131	44
About the existing number	65	20	54	18
More immigrants	134	40	106	36
No response	5	2	5	2
Total	331	100	296	100

As shown in Table 3:3, this position was briefly described to the respondents and then their reactions were sought. The answers did not differ significantly by sex. Approximately two-fifths of those interviewed preferred fewer immigrants, one-fifth the existing number, and two-fifths more. Thus hardly more than half of those favouring rapid population increase wish to see it achieved with the help of immigration. Nevertheless, there is no evidence here of the marked antipathy to immigrants found in many immigrant societies. That this is so is confirmed by the immigrants, most of whom claim to feel no great hostility, although they do relate hearing about themselves the usual kinds of petty prejudices and stock tales (Caldwell, 1967a, pp. 118–19).

Of those opposed to continuing immigration, almost half expressed fears about competition with Ghanaians for employment, especially in the towns. This was disputed by some on the grounds that large numbers of immigrants performed necessary but menial tasks scorned by Ghanaians. Others conceded this to be partly true, but nevertheless urged a brake on immigration, claiming that there were already sufficient foreigners to meet all these needs and in addition that Ghanaian prejudices against lowly jobs were declining. Almost a fifth of respondents in this group expressed in some way the view that the migrants had contributed to the country's economic welfare in the past but that the same need of them no longer existed. Worries about urban employment were often interwoven with fears of overcrowding and of accommodation shortages in the towns accompanied by inflating rents. A quarter of those favouring fewer immigrants spoke of the very real financial problems which can result from the unrestricted remittance of earnings. One in eight, a smaller number than expected from a survey of the general populace, spoke of undesirable personal characteristics, referring to theft, dirtiness, and a propensity for living in overcrowded conditions. Others talked of lack of loyalty. Respondents favouring the existing number of immigrants gave similar answers but included a larger number who thought that a halt would have to be called because of the climbing rate of natural increase.

Of the respondents desiring more immigration, half claimed that it was necessary to sustain the highest rate of economic growth, many citing the willingness of the migrants to engage in unpopular forms of work. A quarter spoke of African brotherhood. An officer of the party youth movement said that the continued right to enter the country freely was 'in consonance with the Constitution—the ultimate aim of African unity'. A surprising number of respondents spoke of the exchange of ideas.

Population Growth and Economic Development

Ultimately Ghanaians are likely to favour certain population policies and oppose others according to the effect of such policies, or at least what they believe to be the effect, on their standards of living. Therefore respondents were questioned on their beliefs about population growth, care being taken to equate this with individual economic well-being. Necessarily, the question was subdivided into growth arising from natural increase and that resulting from immigration.

The responses are shown in Table 3:4 and they record a phenomenon which persisted right through the surveys. Table 3:2 has shown that there was little difference between the attitudes of male and female respondents

TABLE 3:4   Responses to the questions 'Plans are being made to increase the economic development of the country and to raise the standard of living (i.e. to make people richer). (a) Do you think that this would be helped if parents had (i) more children, (ii) the same amount of children, (iii) fewer children?'

Response	Female survey (n = 331)		Male survey (n = 296)	
	No.	Per cent	No.	Per cent
More children	79	24	154	52
The same amount of children	57	17	55	19
Fewer children	187	57	83	28
No response	8	2	4	1
Total	331	100	296	100

'(b) Do you think that this would be helped if there were (i) more immigrants, (ii) the same amount of immigrants, (iii) fewer immigrants?'

More immigrants	74	22	81	27
The same amount of immigrants	53	16	66	22
Fewer immigrants	194	59	145	50
No response	10	3	4	1
Total	331	100	296	100

to population growth in general, and Table 4:1 will reveal that men and women are not widely divided in their appreciation of the advantages and disadvantages of large families, at least once they are formed. Similarly the migration section of Table 3:4 demonstrates no very striking difference between male and female views on population increase arising from immigration.

The major difference occurs when population growth is related to the bearing of children. Women have different and often stronger views on this point, partly we gathered because they are well aware of the problems of bearing large numbers of children, and partly because they often shoulder more of the day-to-day responsibility for seeing that the monthly housekeeping money goes the full distance or earning the extra money needed if children are to stay at school. Thus men's reaction to the question of population growth is frequently that, if it must occur, then the extra might as well be made up by Ghanaians. Twice as many in fact believe that greater numbers of children would raise living standards than credit increased immigration with being able to achieve this. On the other hand, the female respondents, faced with the suggestion that the number of children borne by Ghanaian women, already averaging six or seven, should be raised further, reacted on the whole against the idea and against the view that such an effect could do something to accelerate the improvement of living standards.

Thus, over half of all female respondents and more than a quarter of the males believe that living standards could be raised by restricting family size. Even in the male survey this represents a substantial break with both traditional *mores* and what was the official viewpoint of the time. The male survey showed less doubt about the cutting of immigrant numbers, although the important role of migrants in the growth of the economy during the last few decades might well provide evidence for their continued value. However, many respondents felt that migrant policies should not be decided merely on economic grounds. Thus Table 3:4 shows a significant number of respondents as feeling that maximum rates of economic growth could be achieved by restricting immigration, but in Table 3:3 they are shown as not favouring such a course. Many feel quite strongly that West Africans should be free to move from country to country.

The most radically changed ideas attested by Table 3:4 are held by those respondents who answered 'fewer children', and a determined effort was made to identify them. Town of residence did not affect the pattern of replies; in the male survey, but not the female one, age did. There was a significant difference (at 5 per cent) between the replies of husbands with wives under 30 years old and those of husbands with older wives. Amongst the former 34 per cent replied 'fewer children' compared with only 21 per cent in the latter group. Education also appeared to affect replies, although it achieved statistical significance (at 1 per cent) only in the female survey. Amongst women, 50 per cent with middle school or lesser education said 'fewer children' compared with 67 per cent of those with more extended education. The respective proportions amongst males were 25 per cent and 31 per cent. Religion did not affect male replies at all, but did exhibit a significant association (at 1 per cent) in the female survey for, while three-fifths of Protestant respondents said 'fewer children', only one-fifth of Catholic women did so. Thus there has apparently been a shift in viewpoint amongst Protestant women without an equivalent movement amongst Protestant men. The views of women did not appear to be affected at all by the religion of their husbands, but the relatively small number of Protestant-Catholic marriages made the analysis difficult.

Where strong associations were found was in the relation of this general question of national matters to private behaviour and views on family size and restriction. Thus statistically significant associations (nearly all at 1 per cent) could be shown in both surveys between the reply 'fewer children' and the awareness that more children were now surviving to adulthood, the belief that the government would some day have to appeal to citizens to cut family size, the view that friends or grown-up children should limit their completed family size to less than five children, the holding of discussions between spouses on how many children they should have, the current or past use of contraception, and the desire to restrict family size. This relation between private and public 'population' policies is likely to prove of increasing significance in Ghana, and probably elsewhere in the developing world. In Table 3:5 the interrelation between

TABLE 3:5 Relation between belief that bearing fewer children would assist economic development and replies to certain other questions on family size

Other question	Responses to other question	Percentage of respondents in category of responses to other question believing fewer children would assist economic development	
		Female survey	Male survey
Do you think that women have to give birth to fewer children now if they want to make sure that some grow up?	Yes	67	32
	No	50	20
Do you think it possible that some day the government will have to ask people to try not to have so many children?	Yes	68	43
	No	58	20
If a friend were about to get married, and asked you the best number of children to have, what would you answer?	Up to 4	64	37
	5 or more	50	25
How many children do you hope your daughter will have?	Up to 4	64	38
	5 or more	51	20
Have you ever discussed with your husband/wife how many children he/she thinks is the best number to have?	Yes	60	38
	No	50	20

the belief that having fewer children would assist economic growth and
the replies to certain other questions dealt with in Chapters 4 and 5 is
examined.

Finally, it should be noted that the government's attitude towards
population growth had produced some conflict in many respondents. In
almost identical words, a 34-year-old woman, who was married to a
businessman and had borne him seven children, and one of the wives of
a building contractor, herself the mother of three and previously married,
said, 'People should have less children but the government is encouraging
more'.

Summary

In Ghana the 1960 Census has produced amongst the literate and
sophisticated group surveyed an increased awareness of the high rate of
population growth and of the role that both large family size and massive
immigration have played in attaining that rate. Some of the most significant
reactions to these facts are shown in Table 3:6.

TABLE 3:6 Summary of certain responses to questions on population
attitudes

	Female survey (n = 331) Per cent	Male survey (n = 296) Per cent
Economic development would be helped if there were fewer immigrants	59	50
Economic development would be helped if parents had fewer children	57	28
It would be better if there were fewer immigrants	38	44
The present rate of population increase is a bad thing	20	17

The salient point is that most respondents regard population growth
as a matter on which they might be expected to have views. Furthermore,
not all these views, in spite of what appeared from the press to be a
populationist and pro-natalist official attitude of an almost mercantilist
nature, were either populationist or pro-natalist. Those that were not are
of particular interest as denoting a change in attitude which may spread
and are accordingly the ones selected for the table.

Half or more of respondents feel either that immigrants have never
assisted economic development, at least in the sense of speeding up the
rate at which Ghanaians improve their individual economic well-being, or
have done their job and have less to offer in the future. A majority of
females, but only about half as many males, have similar feelings about
the large family. However, of the respondents aware that children have
an increasingly greater chance of survival to adulthood, two-thirds of
the females and one-third of the males had strong doubts about the large
family. Social as well as economic arguments count. Only two-fifths of

respondents think that the country would be better with fewer immigrants. Similarly, only one-fifth regard the present high rate of population growth as a bad thing, although it might be noted that another tenth are not prepared to say that it is a good thing.

Doubts about high rates of population growth and very large families will presumably increase. Such doubts are felt to a greater extent by the young and the better educated, and it can be assumed that education will extend and that many of those now young will retain their present views as they grow older. Doubts about the large family are stronger amongst wives, who may, as Chapter 4 suggests, come to have an increasing say in family matters.

Perhaps the most important findings, obvious once noted but possibly far-reaching in their consequences, are the relations between attitudes and practices within the family and views on national welfare. Husbands and wives who talk about the number of children they should have, or who hope that their children will have small families, or who practice contraception or hope to do so, are much more likely to view high rates of national population growth with disquiet. The process may well also work the other way; in fact it is probably circular. Persons beginning to wonder whether high population growth rates are one cause of difficulties with economic development plans may begin to look askance at the size of their own families. Presumably the Malthusian debate of the nineteenth century had some influence in hastening the restriction of individual family size in the West. More likely still, some rather complex form of interaction occurs.

4

The Changing Family

The way of life of the new Ghanaian elite is very different from the traditional way of all Ghanaians and even very different from that experienced by most of the country's people today. It is inevitable that changes should have effects upon the structure of the family and upon the relations of its members. The world of such families is an urban one, where most fathers work in offices and where the children aspire to do so; it is also one where they may well only achieve such goals with the help of both the family and the state education system over a prolonged period. It is an existence lived out in adequate housing, very different from most village shelter and often provided by the government. It is a life where such activities as shopping and even owning a car are important. It is a kind of life much less distinctly Ghanaian and more cosmopolitan in its details than village life has been. It may well be that such families are subject to many of the same forces that have produced the contemporary Western family and that the similarity between these two types of family is increasing. It has been agreed elsewhere that social change is militating against polygyny and the extended family and perhaps against unstable marriage (Goode, 1963, 1964; Caldwell, 1963a, pp. 23–4). Certainly, such institutions have evolved in rural and subsistence conditions and are usually somewhat difficult to adjust fully to town life. In the analysis that follows evidence will be sought of changes within the family and of attitudinal shifts which may be the precursors of such change.

The Large Family

The most striking difference between families in developed and developing countries is their size. In the former, women in the reproductive years usually average less than three live births compared with more than five in the latter (Berelson, 1966, p. 658). West African families have been very large indeed; in Ghana completed families (i.e. the children born to a woman in the course of her reproductive years) have averaged well over six and perhaps over seven (Friedlander, 1966; Gaisie, 1966; Caldwell, 1967a, pp. 84–9). As seen in Chapter 2, the oldest women in the survey had averaged over six births, and there is no certain evidence that their fertility was lower than their poorer and less educated urban sisters, although both were probably somewhat less fertile than village women. The Appendix shows that this position is probably changing with regard to current birth levels.

If change is to occur, it will presumably be anticipated by some shifts in attitudes towards family size. Accordingly, respondents were questioned about the things to be said both for and against large families. One striking difference between the replies to the two sub-questions shown in Table 4:1 is that, whilst considerable numbers of respondents insisted

TABLE 4:1   Responses to the question, 'Most parents in Ghana have always had quite a large number of children. (a) What are the good things about having a large number of children?'

Response	Female survey (n = 331)		Male survey (n = 296)	
	No.*	Per cent	No.*	Per cent
Parents helped in sickness, old age, and need	97	29	82	28
Children help in the house (and on the farm)	90	27	68	23
Gain in prestige or assurance of continuation of family	68	21	54	18
Source of happiness either for parents or each other	40	12	28	10
National good	25	8	15	5
Nothing good	44	13	63	21
No response	22	7	15	5

'(b) What are the bad things about having a large number of children?'

Parents unable to afford sufficient training	212	64	194	66
General problems of supporting large number	103	31	46	16
Behaviour problems, quarrelling, sibling jealousy	77	23	51	17
Nothing bad	14	4	1	0
No response	11	3	13	4

* Some respondents gave more than one answer, and hence columns do not total to numbers of respondents or 100 per cent.

on volunteering the view that there was 'nothing good' to be said about the large family, there was not an equal sized group asserting that there was 'nothing bad'.

The pattern of response is clear enough and does not vary unexpectedly between the two surveys. In urban conditions expenses do increase with family size while income does not. Neither point may hold in a fully subsistence rural economy (Caldwell, 1967b, p. 2), but it is abundantly clear that both do in the town. Furthermore, in a society where most of the jobs which could secure for the children in later life the kind of socio-economic conditions in which they have been raised are attained through qualifications earned by examination, the difficulties met in educating a large family were very much in the respondents' thoughts. A nurse married to a lawyer, said, 'Children in large families do not have the same opportunities because of financial difficulties'. A 44-year-old woman teacher, who had raised five children, claimed that, 'Sometimes parents become poorer in that proper education is not given to all the children'. It is not surprising that mothers bear more of the brunt of children's quarrels, nor that they mentioned domestic expenditure more frequently, for many women support the children partially, or even wholly, while most receive from their husbands fixed housekeeping allowances which do not seem to rise in proportion to family size.

The case for the large family is the one which is made throughout most of Ghanaian society, help in old age, help in the house, and family prestige. Their value as a kind of consumption good, increasing family happiness, was more rarely expressed, perhaps only because it seemed obvious, and national welfare was mentioned more rarely still. A civil servant observed that, 'The parents become dignified and earn the praises of all the people, and may be well cared for when they grow old and infirm'. A 30-year-old domestic science teacher, mother of three children and married to an engineer, told the interviewer, 'It is prestigeful to have as many children as possible and to educate them to the best of your ability'.

Polygyny

Polygyny is much more common in rural areas than in towns. There are real problems in supporting more than one urban household on a salary. In the town, food and housing must all be paid for in cash, while young dependants, especially with the ever greater pressures to keep them at school, cannot be expected to contribute any considerable earnings to the household. Nevertheless, perhaps an eighth of husbands in the surveyed group were currently polygynous. Probably a somewhat larger proportion were contributing to the support of more than one woman and perhaps children as well. Almost always these women live in different places.

Respondents were asked whether they approved of the institution. The question has several interesting aspects. Firstly, it may involve reactions best described as African cultural nationalism. Many monogamously married persons will forcefully defend polygyny because they regard the assault on it by the Christian missions to have been motivated more by a desire to promote European values than Christian ones. Protestant churches in West Africa have frequently split on the issue. Secondly, males, even when monogamously married, may feel that their rights or prestige demand that they defend the institution. However, Table 4:2 shows that three-quarters of the female respondents and two-thirds of the males stated that polygyny was not a good thing.

The most persistent argument against polygyny, one voiced by over half of all female respondents, was that it gives rise to intractable emotional problems. The existence of such problems, at least on the scale which is attested, may itself be a sign of social transition. It seems hard to believe that they would be found, or at least realised and described with such forcefulness, in a rural society which had long practised polygyny and taken its existence for granted. The strains are usually those occurring between wives but impinging, according to many male respondents, upon the husband as well as the wives. However, the support of more than one household by fathers was also said to reduce the care they could devote to the rearing of their children. The wife of a timber contractor said of

TABLE 4:2   Responses to the question, '(a) Do you think that it is a good
thing for a man to have more than one wife at the same time
if he wants to?'

Response	Female survey (n = 331)		Male survey (n = 296)	
	No.	Per cent	No.	Per cent
Yes	70	21	91	31
No	252	76	196	66
Qualified answer	7	2	8	3
No response	2	1	1	0
Total	331	100	296	100

'(b) Why do you think this?'*

Response, where respondents answered (a) 'yes'				
Ensures marriage of all women	22	7	18	6
Has economic advantages or allows female work to be shared (often referring to village life)	21	6	38	13
Accommodates greater sexual strength of men	3	1	12	4
Solves problem of barren wife	8	2	6	2
No response	27	8	17	6
Response, where respondents answered (a) 'no'				
Emotional problems, especially those concerning wives	180	54	109	37
Divides family, especially with mention of children	19	6	11	4
Financial problems imposed by extra dependants	50	15	56	19
Religious or moral objections	14	4	23	8

* Some respondents gave more than one answer.

the polygynous husband, 'He will not be able to look after his children
properly. He may like one wife better so this will bring about envy and
hatred'. Financial problems were commonly mentioned directly, and were
almost as frequently implied when reference was made to the impossibility
of fulfilling all obligations to more than one family. Religious and moral
objections were not as frequent as might have been expected in a predominantly Christian group.

Fewer respondents put the case for polygyny and half of those who
did put the general case for Ghanaian society, stressing the possibilities in
the village of cultivating more land with the help of extra children or
sharing household and farmwork out between more wives, thus making
no claim to relate the discussion to their own way of life. Some respondents
argued that only polygyny allowed the marriage of all women, occasionally
asserting that all populations contain large surpluses of females. Frequently

this observation was coupled with the contention that only polygyny prevented many women from becoming prostitutes. A few respondents were willing to defend polygyny as proper and even necessary only in cases where the first wife was barren or subfertile. One wife, who had not been able to have children, pointed out that only the possibility of polygynous marriage had saved her from divorce and loneliness.

As expected, males are somewhat reluctant to forego their privilege of having more than one wife, and there was a significant difference (at 1 per cent) between the replies of the sexes. A higher proportion of respondents favoured polygyny in Kumasi, where the Ashanti cultural traditions still have very considerable strength, than in the three coastal cities, but the difference was statistically significant (at 1 per cent) only in the female survey. Rather surprisingly age seemed to have no consistent effect upon replies. Nor did Catholic or Protestant religious affiliation, an anticipated pattern, for the whole survey showed little cultural gap between the two groups. However, of the seven Moslems who were either wives or husbands in the two surveys, six spoke for polygyny. The replies of male respondents differed significantly (at 1 per cent) with education, 56 per cent of those with middle school education or less being opposed to the institution compared with 80 per cent of those with more extended education. Amongst females the numbers were 77 per cent and 80 per cent respectively, the greater female hostility to polygyny apparently causing the switch against traditional views to cut deeply even into the less educated group.

Unstable Marriage

Marriages have been formed and broken again fairly easily in Ghana. In the country as a whole those living in rural areas tend to marry more often than do those in urban areas. However, it is also true that it is socially more acceptable to form loose liaisons in the town than in the village. In the survey five-sixths of the female respondents had been married only once, while, if allowance is made for current polygyny, only about one-fifth of the male respondents had been married to women from whom they were now divorced.*

When asked whether they favoured stable marriage, the traditional unstable pattern was defended by no more women than had practised it and by considerably fewer men. Preferences for stable or unstable marriage could not be shown to be associated with any characteristics of the respondents, not even as might have been suspected with town of residence, sex, age, or education.

When asked to explain their views, nearly all the respondents favouring stable marriage replied in terms of the stability of home life with strong emphasis on the benefits accruing to children from such a condition. A bank cashier, whose wife was a teacher, said, 'One can be sure of a peaceful life and children with a sense of belonging'. An eighth of the respondents in each survey spoke of church teachings or moral duties. A smaller number discussed the financial problems of men having obligations to more than one lot of children, while a few referred to inheritance problems.

* Divorce is interpreted as any type of separation customarily recognised as final.

TABLE 4:3   Responses to the question, 'Do you think that it is a good thing for a man to stay with the same woman all his life?'

Response	Female survey (n = 331)		Male survey (n = 296)	
	No.	Per cent	No.	Per cent
Yes	280	85	265	90
No	41	12	23	8
Qualified answer	8	2	7	2
No response	2	1	1	0
Total	331	100	296	100

The chief case against stable marriage was its lack of variety and the difficulty of escape either from a specific spouse or marriage as such. Some felt that they should retain the right to dissolve a marriage either when the spouse ceased to have attractions or when the burden of supporting dependants became too great.

The Age Gap Between Spouses

It may well be that in traditional societies husbands tend to be relatively older than their wives than in transitional societies or in societies characterised by higher levels of urbanisation and education. It might also be surmised that a narrowing of the gap makes joint consultation on child-rearing, family size, and similar questions more likely and easier.

Accordingly, respondents were asked, 'What do you think is the best age difference between husband and wife?' The replies showed no marked desire for change from the position now obtaining and no clear evidence that a pronounced narrowing of the age gap is continuing amongst the urban elite, although the present age differences between spouses is certainly less than in traditional rural society. Median replies were four-and-a-half and five years for the female and male surveys respectively, which is less than a year below that now found between the spouses and perhaps less still below the median gap at the time of first marriage. Over half of those stating a number of years chose four to seven years, compared with about two-fifths in practice, perhaps demonstrating a growing consensus. No respondents favoured husbands younger than wives and only three females and five males suggested the same age or a gap smaller than one year. However, 9 per cent of female respondents and 5 per cent of male respondents said that it did not matter or was not important as long as the married couple was happy. Considerable numbers chose each difference between two and ten years with 22 per cent of the respondents in each survey saying five years. In both surveys a tenth replied ten years, but only negligible numbers more than that.

Most respondents justified an age gap of some years on the grounds that this is necessary if a woman is to respect her husband and do what he suggests, but it was widely suggested that a husband who is too much older becomes far too dominating. Almost a fifth argued that men need maturity in order to be able to assume responsibility. A teacher, whose husband was a personnel officer five years older, said, when advocating a four-year age gap, 'The man is supposed to take charge of the woman. This will bring about respect between them. If the man is too old, he may take over-charge of the woman. Neither must he be younger'. A clerk, seven years older than his wife, said that he needed this seniority to exercise 'control over my family from not having a good life'. He added that he did not like the traditional Ghanaian family life on the grounds that it gave other relatives the right to interfere with what his wife and children should do. A sixth of all husbands and a twentieth of all wives believed that a considerable age gap was necessitated by the fact that women age more rapidly than men.

In the male survey only, respondents were probed further on the general question of marriage ages by being asked, 'What is the best age for a woman to be married for the first time?' The replies varied little from the ages at first marriage of either the wives of the male respondents or the female respondents, suggesting a certain stability in the present practice of the surveyed group. Over two-thirds of the respondents advocated ages in the 18–21 years range and almost half favoured either 20 or 21 years. The break with traditional rural society was evidenced by only 3 per cent favouring ages under 18 years, while the contrast with some Western societies was shown by the fact that only 1 per cent stated an age over 25 years.

Change in Family Life

The central question in this section of the interviewing schedule was that on the changes in family life set out in Table 4:4. Respondents were asked to compare the life of themselves, spouses, and children with traditional Ghanaian family life. In fact, as the interviewers reported and the schedules testify, a large number of respondents compared the way they were brought up and the apparent relations of their parents with each other with what they believed to be their relations with their own children and spouses. This form of comparison was valuable and was not discouraged because it withdrew the discussion from mere speculation and allowed quite solid distinctions to be made.

As respondents often described differences at considerable length, an attempt has been made in the table to restrict replies to their main argument. Change has certainly occurred and is continuing to occur. Only a sixth of respondents attested to its absence. Furthermore, the change is persistently in one direction, towards a strengthening of relations between spouses and between them and their children, that is within the group described here as the 'nuclear family', at the expense of relations with other relatives. In one way or another 62 per cent of female respondents and 70 per cent of male respondents described this increase in the importance of the nuclear family, the difference reflecting not so much a sex difference in experience as one of ability to put it into words, for twice as many females failed to answer what was a somewhat complex, descriptive question

Replies were not markedly different by sex. Husbands were more inclined to notice matters affecting expenditure. Wives were more frequently sensitive to aspects of privacy, often about such matters as their purchases

TABLE 4:4 Responses to the question, 'In what way does your own family life (i.e. with husband/wife and children) differ from the traditional Ghanaian family life (i.e. the way families have lived in the past in Ghana, and the way they still live in many parts of the country)?'

Response	Female survey (n = 331)		Male survey (n = 296)	
	No.	Per cent	No.	Per cent
Strengthened nuclear family:				
With no particular emphasis	113	34	105	36
With emphasis on strengthened personal relations	47	14	47	16
With emphasis on increased proportion of income spent within this group	29	9	50	17
With emphasis on more seclusion and privacy, especially from other relatives	15	5	4	1
Residual answers emphasising change	27	8	14	5
No difference	54	16	54	18
No response	46	14	22	7
Total	331	100	296	100

or the right to retain food which had been seen by relatives. Otherwise replies could not be differentiated by any of the respondents' characteristics. This was somewhat surprising in the case of age and education, but interviewers and the schedules both suggested a reason. A larger proportion of the younger and also of the more educated respondents had themselves been brought up in homes where the nuclear family had already been strengthened and hence were less likely to note differences between the generations. Conversely, those with more traditional rearing were more likely to impose a traditional pattern on their families even in urban and economically improved living conditions.

A woman, who had been a typist but was now undertaking some trading, and who was married to a civil servant and had borne him four children, said, 'The children are not afraid of us as most Ghanaian children are afraid of their parents'. Closer relations between spouses were often described. One woman teacher said, 'We eat at a dining table, go out very often and we are always together', while another averred, 'My husband is not dominating and shares household chores'. Male respondents often put emphasis on their abdication of decision-making rights. An important government official attested, 'I shall allow my daughter to choose her own husband. I make my own decisions without reference to family elders, but in questions of inheritance I follow the traditional system'. A young technical school teacher, recently married and as yet without children, said, 'When a decision is being made I take my wife's opinion into account. As a Krobo [a tribe], I want my son to inherit from me. My daughter or son will have to make their own choice of husband or wife and consult me'. An agricultural officer with five children defined the position thus: 'The father should mould the children. In dispute [apparently between husband and wife] on education, control, or inheritance, the fathers of the parents should resolve it. On no account must it be referred to the opinion of an elder in the clan'. It is believed that there has also been an increasing concentration of expenditure within the nuclear family. A 50-year-old male teacher replied, 'The training of children is now the task of father and mother. One cannot add the task of bringing up the children of one's relatives. It is too expensive'. A draftsman with five children said, when commenting on the greater demands for training, 'The high cost of living and other factors make parents more responsible and family expenses are much higher than before'. A woman teacher commented that, 'Although we live in a big family house, we do not have any responsibility towards the upkeep of other members of the family'. However, the position described here is still rare; a survey of university students showed that, amongst those who had already been employed and knew the obligations imposed by earning a substantial income, four-fifths felt that they would have to provide at least a tenth of their net income in the form of assistance to relatives outside the nuclear family, the estimated number of such relatives averaging about five (Caldwell, 1965, pp. 190–3).

Household Structure

Related to the question just discussed is that of how many other relatives live within the household. The examination excludes relatives who live in nearby households, even within the same house, as long as they have separate feeding arrangements and do not share a common housekeeping fund. It also excludes non-relatives who are usually paying boarders and who are unlikely to share decision-making responsibilities.

Table 4:5 shows that about half the families examined lived alone and only a third had with them more than one other relative. Rechecking indicated that one reason for the discrepancy between the proportion of female and male respondents with no other relatives was the greater likelihood of a child from another marriage being with his mother than with his father. The question was asked in such a way that a mother would not list her child amongst other relatives while her spouse would. The suggested categories for the second part of the question did not include step-children.

The analysis of the relatives living with the family reveals a pattern very different from that obtaining in much of Western society. Parents of either wife or husband form only an inappreciable proportion of the household. Many parents live back in the native village. Even if they do live in town, or in fact live in the same town house, they almost always form a separate household as defined here. The relatives housed by the urban elite are in very great preponderance younger brothers and sisters or nephews and nieces or sometimes cousins. Their common characteristic is youth. Frequently they have come to town to be boarded and often financially supported while being educated. Often, it was discovered, this forms a kind of repayment by the urban elite for the investment which allowed them to receive their own education and reach their present

TABLE 4:5   Responses to the question, '(a) Apart from your husband/wife
and children, how many other relatives live with you?'

Response	Female survey (n = 331)		Male survey (n = 296)	
	No.	Per cent	No.	Per cent
None	180	54	132	45
One	37	11	56	19
Two	44	13	41	14
Three	27	8	37	12
Four	17	5	10	3
Five	5	2	6	2
Six to ten	9	3	9	3
Over ten	9	3	5	2
No response	3	1	0	0
Total	331	100	296	100

'(b) What relation are they to you?'

Parent(s) only	3	1	7	2
Brother(s) and/or sister(s) only	35	11	35	12
Nephew(s) and/or niece(s) only	41	12	40	14
Grandchildren only	3	1	1	0
Uncle(s) and/or aunt(s) only	0	0	0	0
Two or more of the above categories	24	7	43	15
Above categories plus more distant relatives	25	8	22	7
More distant relatives only	19	6	16	5
Respondent without relatives living with them	180	54	132	45
Respondents with relatives not identified	1	0	0	0
Total	331	100	296	100

occupational positions (Caldwell, 1965, pp. 190–3). On the whole, therefore, their presence is unlikely to affect relations between husband and
wife, although it may affect those between parents and children.

Going Out Together

Choosing to 'go out' to something is a distinctive aspect of town life. In
villages there may be festivities from time to time, but there is rarely a
choice between going to one of several cinemas, a dance, a nightclub, or
a bar. Many rural-urban migrants identify the joys of town life very
largely with these things. All the same, if the traditional gulf between
husband and wife is retained in the town, the husband may well not take
his wife out, preferring to go to a nightclub or bar, perhaps with another
male friend, to find girls there. That this annoys many wives is shown

by the frequency in the surveys with which they volunteered the information that such girls were prostitutes or something else derogatory.

Therefore, one test of changing family structure can be provided by noting the frequency with which spouses share outings. Replies to questions on the point are shown in Table 4:6. The major apparent discrepancy between the two surveys is probably more one of interpretation than of

TABLE 4:6 Responses to the questions, '(a) Do you and your husband/wife ever go out together? (b) How often?'

Response	Female survey (n = 331)		Male survey (n = 296)	
	No.	Per cent	No.	Per cent
No	54	16	17	6
Yes: More than once a week	78	24	69	23
Once a week	47	14	42	14
Less than once a week, but more than once a month	26	8	26	9
Frequently or often	53	16	67	23
Less than once a month	2	1	0	0
Rarely	55	16	74	25
Residual answers	3	1	0	0
Frequency not specified	1	0	0	0
No response	12	4	1	0
Total	331	100	296	100

fact. Interviewers observed that, when there was some dispute over whether a married couple ever went out together, wives, as the aggrieved party, were more likely to say 'never', while their husbands, somewhat defensively, replied 'rarely'. Thus, if the 'no' and 'yes: rarely' categories are aggregated, the answers of 32 per cent of female respondents and 31 per cent of male respondents are found in this new composite category.

The striking fact about the table is that there is agreement that over a third of married couples go out together at least once a week and almost a half more often than once a month. The real figures may be considerably higher, for outings were felt by some to follow no regular periodic pattern and hence they could not be more definite in their replies than 'frequently'.

No clear associations were found between any of the characteristics of respondents and the pattern of replies. However, a narrowing of the age gap between spouses may encourage closer relationships at least as measured by this kind of test. Thus, amongst female respondents, 87 per cent of those separated in age by less than five years from their husbands claimed that they sometimes went out together compared with 79 per cent of those separated in age by a greater distance. The comparative figures for male respondents were 97 per cent and 92 per cent. However, neither finding was statistically significant. These figures do suggest the apparently paradoxical finding that husbands may be less likely to take out relatively younger wives, but this jump in logic would hardly be justified, in that the connecting and causative link is the existence of such wives in the more traditional type of marriage. It is of interest to note that town of residence did not affect the pattern of replies.

When asked where they usually went on outings, two-thirds of the respondents in each survey who had stated that they did sometimes go out with their spouses, and accordingly about three-fifths of all respondents, said that they went to places of enjoyment, citing dances, cinemas, night-clubs, parties, and concerts, as well as the beach and the library. A third of the respondents in each survey said that the frequent joint outings were to such formal affairs as church or funerals and a quarter replied that they often visited relatives. Female and male responses were almost identical in distribution.

Taking Out the Children

Perhaps a more exacting test of family change is whether the parents also take children on outings similar to some of those described above. This proviso is made because traditional rural society has had long experience of some kinds of joint outing between parent and child. For instance, fishermen are proud to take their sons out in the boats to teach them the craft.

TABLE 4:7   Responses to the questions, '(a) Do you and your husband/wife ever go out with your children? (b) How often?'

Response	Female survey (n = 331)		Male survey (n = 296)	
	No.	Per cent	No.	Per cent
No	122	37	65	22
Yes: More than once a week	21	6	29	10
Once a week	37	11	35	12
Less than once a week, but more than once a month	32	10	23	8
Frequently or often	24	7	38	13
Less than once a month	1	0	0	0
Rarely	45	14	84	28
Residual answers	1	0	0	0
Frequency not specified	3	1	0	0
No response	45	14	22	7
Total	331	100	296	100

The replies to questions on this subject are shown in Table 4:7. Interviewers emphasised that we were interested in outings where both parents were present. Once again there is an apparent conflict of replies in the 'no' and 'rarely' categories, but an addition of these yields 51 per cent in the female survey and 50 per cent in the male survey, suggesting as before a difference in interpretation rather than facts. Parents certainly go out with their children less frequently than they do with each other. Nevertheless, a fifth of families claim to go out together at least once a week and almost a third once or more a month.

With the exception of the problem categories discussed above and the 'no response' category, the two surveys yielded similar patterns of answers. On this occasion town of residence did affect replies, although there was only a statistically significant association (at 1 per cent) in the male survey. In Kumasi 61 per cent of fathers claimed to go out with the whole family sometimes in contrast to 72 per cent in the other towns where the patterns were similar. In the female survey the corresponding figures were 45 per cent and 50 per cent. Education was also associated with taking the children out, although it bore no relation to the tendency for husband and wife to go out alone. This is further support for the belief that the acid test of family change is that which involves the whole family and not merely the relation between spouses. In the female survey, seven out of every ten respondents with education beyond middle school claimed such family outings compared with half that number for respondents with less education. This difference was statistically significant (at 1 per cent), but the quite marked difference in the male survey just failed to be so. However, if the male respondents are divided into those with secondary or university education and those without, perhaps a better division amongst males with their higher levels of education, the result is significant (at 1 per cent). Amongst the former four-fifths say they take the family out, while the proportion drops to two-thirds amongst the latter. The ages of the husband and wife bear no relation to the pattern of answers but, once again, the age gap between them apparently does. In the female survey, where there is a statistically significant (at 5 per cent) pattern of replies, 59 per cent of respondents with husbands no more than five years older than themselves have family outings compared with only 43 per cent of respondents with relatively older husbands. The same margin does not obtain in the male survey because of the large number of relatively older husbands who replied 'rarely' instead of 'no' thus apparently obscuring the pattern.

The broad categories into which outings fell was very similar in both surveys and did not differ very markedly from the pattern described for spouses going out together. However, although places of enjoyment still predominated as destinations, the cinema, beach, and library were conspicuous, while nightclubs and dancing were no longer of significance. In Kumasi a surprising number of families make repeated visits to the Ashanti Cultural Centre and the adjacent zoo. Visits to relatives are of greater importance than they are when the adults alone go out, and over a third of the families who take their children anywhere make regular visits to either relatives or friends. Formal outings, especially church, rank not far behind.

The Western Family

The types of change which have been described are similar to those apparently occurring amongst elites elsewhere. Nor is there any doubt about the direction of change. Whatever the basic causes, the changes themselves are tending to make the families more like Western middle-class families and to reduce those characteristics which have previously distinguished local families from families in Europe or North America.

Therefore, it seemed appropriate to describe a stereotype of a Western family as set out in Table 4:8. This description is obviously something of an overstatement and in some features, such as the stability of marriage,

TABLE 4:8   Responses to the questions, 'You have probably seen on films (or on a visit) or have heard how most families live in England or America. Usually only the husband, wife and their children, who have not yet grown up, live together in a house of their own. Most husbands and wives live together all their lives and never live at any time with another woman or man. Most families have only one, two or three children. Most families spend quite a lot of their money on these children. Often the most common type of entertainment is for the whole family to go out in their car taking their lunch with them to a beach or for a drive in the countryside. (a) What do you think is good about this type of life?'

Response	Female survey (n = 331)		Male survey (n = 296)	
	No.	Per cent	No.	Per cent
A more closely knit and happier family	184	56	164	56
Better for the development of the children	78	23	75	25
Such families are cheaper	11	3	8	3
Residual answers	33	10	18	6
Nothing good	13	4	15	5
No response	12	4	16	5
Total	331	100	296	100

'(b) What do you think is bad about this type of life?'

Dull, selfish, unsociable	59	18	52	18
Lack of mutual help	59	18	49	17
Bad for children's characters	28	8	17	6
Residual answers	26	8	25	8
Nothing bad	125	38	128	43
No response	34	10	25	8
Total	331	100	296	100

describes European and American aspirations rather than practices. However, the description did highlight the features of the Western family which differ most from the traditional Ghanaian family and so served to focus the respondents' comments. The respondents were not asked to choose between family types; they were merely asked to state what were the good things about the stereotype and then the bad things.

However, the most telling feature of the replies was just how many did insist on choosing. While only one-twentieth volunteered the view that there was nothing good about the described Western family, a startling two-fifths said there was nothing bad. The case for the stereotype is clear.

It is admired because the development of the nuclear family is quite extreme, because it is inward looking, and because there is concentration on the rearing of children. In short, because many of the changes under way in the elite families seem to have reached their logical extreme. The case against the stereotype is equally plain. It has been achieved at the expense of all tendencies towards sociability, mutual help, and unselfishness that operate outside the nuclear family and towards other relatives. It is interesting that hardly any protest was voiced about the limitation of the family to three children. The replies have in many cases been coded as comparisons, 'closer', 'better' and so on, for the answers most frequently took this form as respondents related replies, usually without specific statement of the fact, to traditional Ghanaian family life.

Rather curiously, approval or disapproval of the Western family seemed to affect respondents of all types to about the same degree. There was no suggestion of an association of replies with sex, age, education, religion, or age difference between spouses. Nor was there an association with town of residence.

Respondents praising the picture presented to them referred repeatedly to the fact that such a situation ensured 'peace in the home', largely through the lack of intervention of other relatives in family decisions and the absence of demands for financial or other assistance. However, it should not be too readily assumed that hostility to such demands is universal amongst the elite; the survey of university students indicated that it was still a minority view. The wife of a high police official said that the situation described 'would make life worth living. The children would have a good education, discipline, and affection, which they need most'. A 50-year-old father of five children commented that, 'The fatherly love for the family increases with this sort of life and children are educated by such experiences with parents'.

Those condemning the Western family pattern frequently warned of the moral and real dangers of cutting oneself off from relatives. A 45-year-old woman teacher married to an engineer pointed out that, 'The bad thing is that one tends to neglect even the parents who brought you into the world'. An administrator, whose wife was a teacher, said people 'cut off from relations get little assistance when in need. There is very little sympathy for you when in trouble'. A surveyor argued that such an independent life is 'impossible for the lower income groups'. Some thought such children 'would get too much in childhood and would become worried if they do not get it in the future'. Insecurity was also voiced by a wife, who worked with her pharmacist husband, when she said, 'If the husband or wife dies, the children become hopeless'. Finally, there were the few who were sceptical of the picture of overseas conditions. A young female civil servant commented, 'Perhaps the families may look isolated, but I am sure, when any serious thing happens, they consult older people for advice'.

Spinsterhood

If the Ghanaian elite is prepared to accept many changes from the traditional family pattern, are they prepared to accept that which is the most radical departure, the agreement that universal female marriage is not necessarily an aim of society? Continuing the Western stereotype, respondents were asked, as shown in Table 4:9, what they thought of such a situation in the West and whether they thought it could happen in Ghana.

TABLE 4:9 Responses to the questions, '(a) In these countries there are quite a lot of women who never marry and who never have any children. Some of them have interesting jobs and say that they are happy. What do you think of this?'

Response	Female survey (n = 331)		Male survey (n = 296)	
	No.	Per cent	No.	Per cent
Approval: Without qualification	9	3	1	0
Qualified—good if happy (or doing selfless work)	66	20	29	10
—good if for specific reasons (doctor's advice, disappointment in love, avoiding a specific marriage)	38	11	28	9
—residual reasons	16	5	1	0
Disapproval: Without qualification	37	11	95	33
Qualified—not congenial to Ghanaian way of life	118	35	92	31
—probably a sign of selfishness	10	3	24	8
—may be a sign of immorality	30	9	17	6
—residual reasons	2	1	0	0
No response	5	2	9	3
Total	331	100	296	100

'(b) Do you think that this will ever be the case in Ghana?'

Yes	190	57	164	55
No	105	32	109	37
Qualified answer	33	10	19	7
No response	3	1	4	1
Total	331	100	296	100

About two-fifths of the female respondents and one-fifth of the males were prepared to give some kind of approval to the position described. The higher rate of approval amongst wives was not merely the adoption of a feminist stance but the fact that many of them were justifying the unmarried English school-teachers who had come to Ghana and educated them in some of the country's most renowned secondary schools. One said, 'In these cases they have a vocation to serve mankind', but a 25-year-old woman trader, who had been married three times and had borne two children, argued, 'It is against the will of God not to marry', while a male lithographic assistant, married to a telephonist, stated, 'I feel that women who share such views are just selfish, unpatriotic, and prostitutes in disguise'. Another husband felt that 'everyone should marry to fulfil why they were created. The good things in them perish when they die'.

Women were more likely than men to see specific obstacles to marriage, but some of the reasons given pertained more to Ghanaian society and others more to Western society, especially as the latter appears as interpreted by the cinema. On the other hand, disapproval of spinsterhood was expressed almost always in terms of Ghanaian values. Unmarried women were suspected by men of being hard and selfish and by women of being immoral and a lure to husbands. A woman teacher married to an economist thought, 'They would be happy [in England] because it is not like Ghana where people would insult you and call you barren'. Another female teacher believed that the nature of single women in the West was probably much like Ghana. 'They have boy friends and engage in abortions and abominable practices'.

However, some respondents thought that there was a case even in Ghana on the grounds of sexual equality and that this case would be increasingly put. An ex-teacher, partner in a monogamous marriage but living with her six children apart from her husband, said, 'In Ghana it is the men who do not want to marry. They would rather whore with different girls'. More surprisingly a young male teacher expressed a similar view, saying, 'There are men who don't marry all their lives, so there is nothing wrong with the women doing the same'.

There is a strong feeling amongst the elite that Ghanaians will in time experience much of the economic and social conditions of the West. Thus a clear majority in both surveys felt that universal female marriage must pass, while only about a third of respondents believed that this could be avoided. A few qualified their answers by positing long periods of time before the transition or relating it to alternative paths of social, economic, or educational development. Beliefs in this matter were not associated with any of the respondents' characteristics. Even higher educational levels did not allow a clear view of the future, and indeed there can at this stage be no certainty about the extent to which universal female marriage will pass. It might be added here that in the four towns there are now women who have never married, a large number of them 'good time girls', and many more who have been married but are not currently in that state. This latter condition was not regarded as particularly surprising by respondents at least as applied to town life in contrast to life in the villages.

The Working Wife

We have seen previously in Table 2:4 that 85 per cent of the female respondents worked for a living before marriage and that 61 per cent were still doing so on at least a part-time basis at the time of the survey. Three-fifths of those previously employed in 'urban, upper' occupations still undertook some work as did over four-fifths of those who were employed in 'urban, lower' occupations. The major explanation in the latter case is that women who participated in trading usually continued to do so, although, having access to their husbands' earnings, often on an increased scale.

It was also noted that three-fifths of women in both rural and urban Ghana were in employment other than 'home duties'. This position has risen largely because women have had to share much, or even all, the responsibility for supporting themselves and their children; in return it has given them very considerable independence. The position of women in Ghanaian society and in much of tropical African society is astonishingly high compared with what it is in other poor societies found in Asia and North Africa.

This independence must affect family structure, decision-making within the family, and even the rearing of children. Although it is not suggested that most elite wives have to support themselves and their children entirely, it was believed that the extent of such support by the wives was nevertheless considerable and that no understanding of their position in the family would be meaningful unless this question was probed. Accordingly, following the question on wives' employment prior to marriage were two others, set out in Table 4:10, on the question of support for wives and children.

TABLE 4:10   Responses to the questions, '(a) If you/your wife had not married could you/she have continued to support yourself/ herself?'

Response	Female survey (n = 331)		Male survey (n = 296)	
	No.	Per cent	No.	Per cent
Yes	294	88	183	62
No	26	8	84	28
Qualified response	5	2	25	9
No response	6	2	4	1
Total	331	100	296	100

'(b) To what extent do you/does your wife support yourself/ herself and your children now?'

Not at all	93	28	84	28
Completely	10	3	0	0
Mostly	11	3	0	0
Partly	99	30	146	49
Buys clothes only	72	22	55	20
Buys some food ('chop') only	14	4	1	0
Educates children only	4	1	1	0
No response	28	9	9	3
Total	331	100	296	100

Eight-ninths of female respondents believed that they could have continued to provide for themselves if they had not married. This proportion is in fact slightly larger than the number who did support themselves before marriage, but has been raised by those who were certain that they could have done so had the need arisen. Interviewers reported that the sole reason that husbands were more sceptical of their wives' ability to have done so was their much greater tendency to regard the question as implying 'at their present standard of living, or in our way of life'. Where this rider was explicitly stated in the answer, the response is shown in the table as qualified. However, both surveys show quite clearly that Ghanaian women are not economically bound to achieving or even maintaining marriage at least in the towns. This is not equally true in the villages where society provides no real place for the unmarried woman, except in so far as she can migrate to the towns. On the other hand, social pressures, for at least a first marriage, are substantial even in the towns.

At the time of the survey, only 28 per cent of wives in both surveys were said to contribute nothing to the support of themselves and their children. The only discrepancies between the two surveys were on the degree of support and on the extent to which its nature was defined. However, it is clear that, while very few wives indeed, almost certainly fewer than among poorer town residents, entirely provide for themselves and the children, at least two-thirds contribute some support. Those who answered 'partly' or 'mostly' spent this money mainly on clothing, food ('chop'), and schooling costs in that order. Some said this extra income made it possible to continue the further education of their children. Some husbands sought to justify the position, the need itself being one sign of change. A civil servant, whose 25-year-old wife also worked for the government, approved of the joint support, saying, 'Yes, since we are all equal human beings'. The pattern of replies was not related to any of the respondents' characteristics.

Family Decisions

The kind of attitudes and the structure and changing nature of the family which must affect decision-making within the family have now been established. Accordingly respondents were asked direct questions on this matter. The investigation was difficult because people are not always very introspective, often deliberately, about such balances and clashes of domestic power. For many it was a question that they had apparently never considered, at least analytically. Thus two-fifths of the female respondents and one-fifth of the males were unable to give any answer at all. Respondents were asked to describe the kind of decisions they made themselves, those their spouses made, and those made after joint consultation.

In many ways the last question was the most interesting. Ghanaian women have never been entirely without a say, partly because they do contribute to family support, but largely because they are representatives of the family from which they come. This family, especially amongst matrilineal groups, can have a great deal to say even to the urban elite. However, the questions asked here were not intended to measure the extent to which respondents spoke for themselves rather than their families, but to gauge the roles of husbands and wives.

Over a quarter of the female respondents claimed that their husbands discussed all decisions with them, but less than two-thirds as many husbands were willing to concede this. However, there was much more agreement on joint decisions concerning children. In the surveys 35 per cent of female respondents and 38 per cent of males agreed that husbands and wives consulted each other about children's behaviour and punishment and about their education. It might be remembered that wives frequently provide financial assistance for the education. On the other hand, while a quarter of the male respondents claim to participate in decisions on running the house, fewer than two-thirds as many females agree on the point. A tenth of the respondents in each survey agreed that decisions on money matters were taken together. This does not necessarily mean that the balance of such decisions are made by one partner, for many respondents failed to provide any answers and many others neglected the listing of various fields of decision.

However, there is general agreement that most domestic matters and such family concerns as the cleanliness of the children and their clothes is decided by the wife. In most households she also controls, or in many cases is obliged to accept responsibility for, the allocation of housekeeping money so that it extends over the allotted time and buys the required amount of food and other household necessities.

In most households the husband decides, usually without a great deal of consultation, the allocation of his own income, which is normally the greater part of the household income, business matters, and questions of housing or land. Twelve men and three women reported that husbands made decisions involving sexual matters, while no-one mentioned them as matters for joint consultation or the wives' decision.

Summary

The economically better-off urban families in Ghana are in many practices and attitudes very different from the traditional family that evolved in a rural, village society practising subsistence agriculture. In Table 4:11 some of the more striking findings of this chapter have been summarised in roughly descending order of change. Factual data have been intermingled with findings on attitudinal change, for both are signs of change and, though belief and practice cannot be exactly equated, both are measures of change and do interact.

The direction of change is towards convergence with the Western family. The most distinctive features of the Ghanaian marriage, unstable marriage and polygyny, are disapproved by the great majority of respondents. Almost three-quarters of respondents realise that their form of family life is something new and two-thirds see the major aspect of newness in various changes which we can describe as fostering the nuclear family. In terms of household residence, half of them live as nuclear families. Husband-wife relations are undoubtedly strengthening as measured by the husband taking the wife out reasonably frequently, and this applies also to the children in more than a third of families. The family is certainly becoming more child-conscious. This is especially so in terms of education, for the elite family is only too aware that its children have become accustomed to enjoying a kind of life which they will, in adult life, only be able to attain themselves by securing jobs which usually demand as entry qualifications a prolonged period of education. Two-thirds of respondents already feel this kind of pressure on the large family, although other financial pressures are less frequently described. Nevertheless, such

TABLE 4:11 Summary of certain responses to questions on family change

Response	Female survey (n = 331) Per cent	Male survey (n = 296) Per cent
Unstable marriage is not a good thing	85	90
Polygyny is not a good thing	76	66
Respondent's family differs from traditional Ghanaian family	70	75
Respondent's family is closer to nuclear family than traditional family	62	70
It is difficult to train adequately all children in a large family	64	66
Husband and wife go out together at least once a month or 'frequently'	62	69
No relatives in household except spouse and own children	54	44
Spinsterhood will probably come in Ghana	57	55
Unqualified or qualified approval for spinsterhood in West	39	19
'Nothing bad' about the Western family	38	43
Husband, wife, and children go out together at least once a month or 'frequently'	34	43
It is difficult to support a large family	23	17
'Nothing good' about large families	13	21

pressures have not to date been critical for there is no evidence that elite women have substantially fewer children than do the urban poor, and both are only somewhat less fertile than are the women of rural Ghana who have families which are amongst the largest in the world. Admittedly 13 per cent of female and 21 per cent of male respondents proclaimed that they could see nothing good in such large families. It is also true that two-fifths of respondents claimed to see nothing bad about Western families, which were described as consisting of no more than three children. Certainly many members of the elite expect continuing family change, and a majority anticipate a passing of universal or near universal marriage of females. However, one should not exaggerate the extent of convergence as yet with the Western family, as is evidenced by the fact that in only a minority of families are children taken out much at all by their parents.

The new views seemed to be held rather widely. For instance there were few marked differences in outlook or experience between men and women. Change or desire for it or appreciation of it was occasionally more associated with persons of higher education or with families where the age gap between spouses was least. Similarly, respondents living in Kumasi, in close contact with the Ashanti cultural tradition, were sometimes a little more conservative than were those in the three coastal cities, but these differences should not be misunderstood. What is striking is that they were so slight, not that they existed at all. The elite is fairly homogeneous and is subject to rather similar pressures. Even the Ashanti tradition, with its conservatism in family matters and strong belief in high fertility (Lorimer, 1954, pp. 69 et seq.) provides little shielding.

5

Family Size

The aspect of family change which is most easily quantified and hence most easily identifiable over a considerable period is that of average size. Furthermore, such change in size is of very great importance. In terms of the family itself, the beginning of a decline in the number of children ever born indicates that very substantial internal change has already occurred in the relationships between husband and wife and between parents and children. Moreover, the decline in family size makes further change in relationships inevitable. In terms of the community, declining family size means a slackening of population growth rates and the beginning of the establishment of a new balance between the levels of births and deaths.

Changing Family Size

Over the last three-quarters of a century or more family size has fallen in most economically developed countries to a point where most women can expect to bear only two or three children in a lifetime. This is not yet the position in West Africa for, if current trends persist, most women will average over six births (E.C.A., 1965; Coale, 1966; Som, 1966). In macroscopic terms the difference is one between a national population growth rate of 1 per cent or less per year in the former case and a rate rising to 3 per cent or even more in the latter case.

Family Size amongst the Elite

It was noted in Chapter 2 that female respondents, although on average little more than 30 years of age, had already had an average of 3·4 children. The comparable figures for male respondents were 36 years of age and 4·4 children, who were not necessarily all by the same mother. It was also seen that those female respondents who were nearing the end of their fertile period had already averaged over six live births.

A detailed analysis was carried out of the number of children ever borne by respondents exhibiting various different characteristics. The main limitation was the small numbers of respondents of certain types. The major analyses were undertaken in terms of the parents' age, education, and religion. To overcome the problem caused by the small number of respondents in such groupings, and in view of the fact that average births by age had already been examined, average births were calculated for respondents by educational and religious subgroups only. In order to prevent distortion by random fluctuations of age, the numbers of respondents in each 5-year age group were standardised according to the total number of wives in each age group in the two surveys. These standardised averages are shown in Table 5:1.

TABLE 5:1 Average number of live births per respondent, by education and religion*

Characteristic	Female survey† (n = 331)		Male survey‡ (n = 296)	
	No. of respondents	Average No. of live births	No. of respondents	Average No. of live births
Education§:				
up to middle school	175	3·2	103	4·2
beyond middle school	109	2·6	120	3·4
Religion‖:				
Protestant	246	3·0	193	3·8
Catholic	38	2·8	30	3·4
Education and religion:				
up to middle school—				
Protestant	155	3·1	88	4·2
Catholic	20	3·3	15	4·6
beyond middle school—				
Protestant	91	2·7	105	3·5
Catholic	18	2·3	15	2·3

* Standardised for age of wife according to combined distribution in the two surveys. Standardised distribution of 1,000 respondents by age group: 18-19 years, 35; 20–24 years, 209; 25–29 years, 280; 30-34 years, 219; 35–39 years, 154; 40–44 years, 103. The only births included are those of which the respondents were the biological parents.

† Includes only 284 respondents who supplied satisfactory information on age and education and specified their religion as either 'Protestant' or 'Catholic'. Thus, 47 respondents are excluded.

‡ As above. 223 respondents are included and 73 excluded. The greater number of male exclusions arises from a greater tendency not to specify adherence beyond stating 'Christian' and a larger number in 'No religion'.

§ 'Up to middle school' includes no schooling, primary school only, and middle school but not beyond. 'Beyond middle school' includes further technical or specialised education, secondary school, and university.

‖ Includes only those specifying either Protestant or Catholic. Excludes 'Christian', 'Moslem', 'Traditional religion' and 'No religion', all of which except the first included very few respondents.

There is a persistent and statistically significant (at 5 per cent) differential in fertility by education. Respondents with higher education in each survey have been the biological parents of about one-fifth fewer children than have the lesser educated respondents. Two other points should be noted. The first is that this differential is apparently greater amongst Catholics than Protestants, although the small numbers of the former render a definite conclusion impossible. The second is that no further reduction in fertility is evidenced by isolating the university educated, for this group exhibits the same fertility as those with secondary schooling or other education beyond middle school. Thus, if the lesser educated women average about six children in the course of their fertile span, the more educated may bear only five children or slightly fewer.

It is much less certain that there is any religious differential at all. If it exists, and the best evidence is provided by the fact that it seemed to show up in both surveys, it is not that expected from Western experience, for Protestants apparently exhibit higher fertility than Catholics. However, this is so only because of markedly lower fertility amongst the more highly educated Catholics, once again found in each survey. Amongst the less educated, Catholics exhibited the more familiar higher fertility. It is quite possible that highly educated Catholics have made the greatest break with traditional society, in that they have not felt able to make much adjustment with traditional family ways and marital practices.

The sex differential, as noted in Chapter 2, arises from the fact that, whilst the female respondents have borne all the children attributed to them, in many cases more than one woman has given birth to the children attributed to a male respondent.

An attempt was made to relate to education and religion the proportion of children surviving, but no significant differentials could be established. It may well be that all the elite are sufficiently prosperous, and most hold sufficiently responsible jobs, to make them able to look after their children adequately. It is just possible that the more highly educated provided fuller information on deceased children and that this obscured any differential in the survival of children.

Children in the Household

The actual size of a household cannot be related directly to the number of live births or even to the number of surviving children. In Ghanaian society it has been common for children to live with other relatives, and, amongst the elite, a significant number have been educated in boarding schools.

The surveys showed, however, that only 24 per cent of the female respondents and 36 per cent of the male respondents had children living elsewhere at the time of the survey. Furthermore, only 18 per cent of all the living children of female respondents were living elsewhere and only 27 per cent of those of male. Some of the older children had moved elsewhere to secure employment. On average, female respondents had 3·16 surviving children of whom 2·58 lived with them, and male respondents had 3·81 surviving children of whom 2·78 were with them. The majority of children living elsewhere were those whose other parents were not the respondents' current spouses. Thus, the most common type of family was that where there were three surviving children, all of whom lived in the respondent's household.

Differential and Changing Fertility

If fertility is changing, then such changes should be measurable. So also should be the differentials in fertility caused between the different sections of society, for it is hardly conceivable that such change could affect all sections equally. In Ghana fertility change over a period of time has been difficult to estimate because of defective early censuses.

However, the surveyed group provided the means for conducting a retrospective survey, for their education and awareness of such qualities as age were far above average. Respondents were asked how many children their parent of the same sex had when she or he was the age that the respondent was at the time of the survey. The results are shown in Table 5:2. Some respondents were unable to be sure of their parents'

TABLE 5:2 Comparison of number of children born to respondents with those born to respondents' parents at the same age

	Female survey (n = 331)	Male survey (n = 296)
Respondents responding	308	243
Average number of children born to parents of same sex at same age	3·88	6·04
Average number of children born to respondents	3·16	3·81
Apparent inter-generational fertility decline	19%	37%

ages or progeny. Both problems were more acute in the case of male respondents, for fathers tended to be older, so that knowledge of parents' age was somewhat more unlikely, and there was more uncertainty about whether they had had children by women other than the respondents' mothers. The fact that the male average is over 50 per cent higher than the female average is a little surprising but probably credible. The males are older than the females, and their fathers may have been able to marry earlier than they themselves did, and certainly were much more likely to be polygynous.

If the answers are reliable, female fertility has apparently fallen by almost a fifth. The fall in individual male fertility has averaged almost twice as much, but this cannot be related directly to community or national fertility levels as it reflects a marked decline in polygyny.

The apparent fall in female fertility must be treated with some caution. It is dependent upon an accurate knowledge of mothers' children, defined here as all live births. However, errors are likely to take the form of omitting some deceased children from mothers' births and thus understating the fertility decline. Errors may well have occurred in the statement of mothers' ages, but are not particularly important if randomly distributed. More importantly, it may reflect not a decline in fertility in completed reproduction, but a decline in the children born by the mid-reproductive years due to a rise in the age at marriage and hence a delay in bearing children. This may indeed be part but not all of the explanation. If such a delay has occurred, it is quite probable that the daughters will never catch up to their mothers in the number of children borne.

If this fertility decline has really occurred, it may arise from one or more of three causes: a general fertility decline may have occurred in Ghana; the respondents may have adopted an urban fertility pattern in contrast to the rural type of fertility exhibited by many of their parents; fertility may decline with advancement up the socio-economic scale.

Confining the examination to females, it might be noted on the first points that child-woman fertility ratios indicate, if anything, a slight rise in fertility in southern Ghana between the 1921 Census and the 1960 Census. However, it is likely that the apparent movement is more a reflection of change in age misstatement than of the birth rate. On the second point, the 1960 Census yielded child-woman ratios about 12 per cent lower in the four towns than in rural southern Ghana. However, only about half the respondents come from villages or small towns, a point that may lose some of its force if the urban-rural differential has been intensifying in recent years with the growth in size of the major urban centres. On the third point, there is little evidence outside that gathered by this survey. As seen in Chapter 2, there is no certain evidence from the survey that respondents over 30 years of age had been less fertile than other urban women, but some suggestion that younger respondents may have been up to 10 per cent less fertile, possibly due to delayed marriage related perhaps to more prolonged education and other training. The Appendix indicates that by 1960 birth levels in the first socio-economic quartile suburbs of the four towns were 14 or 15 per cent below those of the fourth quartile and perhaps 20 per cent below those of the surrounding rural areas. Had it been possible to confine the comparison to elite householders, the margin might have been greater still. Thus the evidence seems to support the respondents' contention of an inter-generational fertility decline, while suggesting at the same time that there has been no general decline of the same magnitude.

Relative Increase of Surviving Children in the Family

If mortality is declining while parents continue to produce the same number of children, it is inevitable that on average a greater number of children will survive to those parents who themselves survive. This simple model ignores in its comparisons families where the parents failed to survive and the adoption of the children of relatives who died. The increases which have occurred in recent times have often been considerable and must have exerted all kinds of pressures on the traditional arrangements for housing and rearing families.

Thus, if one considers the likely fate of a family of six children born at two-year intervals and of alternating sex, one glimpses the following pictures eleven years after the birth of the first child in Ghana a generation ago and today. In 1930 the expectation of life at birth in the country as a whole may have been about 30 years while by 1960 it might have climbed to about 45 years (Caldwell, 1967a, pp. 94–5). If these dates were the central points in time for the formation of the families described above, then at the end of the periods 3·7 children could be expected on average to survive in the first case compared with 4·7 or 27 per cent more in the second.* Change amongst the elite has probably been even more dramatic. If their social origins were somewhat above average, as was shown to be the case in Chapter 2, the children in their parents' families

* These calculations are based on the 'North' set of life tables in Coale and Demeny, 1966.

might well have been subject, around 1930, to mortality approximating an expectation of life at birth of about 35 years. In their own families this expectation had probably risen by 1960 to the order of 60 years. In the first case 4·0 of the six children could be expected on average to survive and in the second 5·3, a rise of 33 per cent.

As shown in Table 5:3, respondents were asked whether they had noticed this change. Testing the original schedule had shown that the question had to refer specifically to mortality decline or become inextricably involved in speculation about fertility change.

TABLE 5:3   Responses to the question, 'In the last few years there have been big medical improvements in Ghana. This means that there are not nearly as many babies dying as there used to be, and so more children are growing up. Do you think that most families have more children in them now than used to be the case?'

Response	Female survey (n = 331)		Male survey (n = 296)	
	No.	Per cent	No.	Per cent
Yes	178	54	212	72
No	140	42	81	27
Not certain	12	4	0	0
No response	1	0	3	1
Total	331	100	296	100

A majority of respondents in each survey claimed to be aware of this phenomenon. As is usual in questions involving immutable mathematical relationships, more males had appreciated what was going on. However, what is at first sight surprising is not the awareness of change, but the large numbers who claimed not to have noticed it. The explanation here may well be the inter-generational decline in fertility between the respondents' parental families and their own. The fertility decline of a fifth claimed by female respondents would just about cancel out the effects of the mortality decrease. Furthermore, the female respondents may well have concentrated more than the males on what had happened in their own families. This hypothesis receives support from the fact that in a subsequent question, related specifically to Ghana as such, larger numbers of respondents claimed to have noticed a disproportionate rise in the number of children.

Those replying 'yes' were asked, 'What difference does this make to families?' In each survey 91 per cent of these respondents gave details of increased household expenditure, a large proportion discussing also the provision of accommodation. A market woman with nine children said, 'Bigger houses are needed and more is spent, but more is gained in the end'. This was presumably a reference to support in old age, and may have appeared of particular importance because, at 44 years of age, she was one of the oldest female respondents. A 50-year-old male teacher said, 'There is an acute shortage of housing and compound houses. Many rooms are being built and family expenditure has gone up'. Only 4 per cent of this group of respondents claimed that the increase in the number of surviving children made no difference to the household.

Relative Increase of Children in the Community

In the long run a fall in mortality without an accompanying change in fertility does not make a great difference to the relative proportions of children and adults in a society. Some rise in the comparative numbers of children does occur because the resulting climb in the rate of natural increase means that each new generation working its way up the age structure of the population is relatively greater in size than the preceding generation.

Thus, using the same kind of model as previously employed, if the expectation of life at birth in Ghana rose from 30 to 45 years between 1930 and 1960 while fertility remained constant with a gross reproduction rate of 3, the proportion of the population under 15 years of age would have risen from 40·9 to 44·0 per cent. If fertility declined the rise would have been smaller. Indeed, if the decline had been as much as 12 per cent, from a gross reproduction rate of 3·4 to one of 3·0, there would have been no rise at all (Coale and Demeny, 1966).

However, the position in most of the developing world during the last two decades has been somewhat different. Infant and child mortality has fallen quite steeply, thus reinforcing the numbers in the younger age strata of the population. There has been insufficient time to achieve any new long-term balance in the population, and, as a result, the number of children has risen disproportionately. If age reporting in the 1948 and 1960 censuses was correct or at least comparable, the ratio of the number of children, 0–15 years of age, to population over 16 years of age rose in the intervening twelve years by 14 per cent. If the ratio is confined to a comparison of population, 0–15 years of age, to that 16–44 years of age, then the rise was 13 per cent.

One would imagine that changes of such magnitude could easily show themselves in such ways as an apparent increase in the number of children and the need for making extra provision for these children. Accordingly, respondents were asked, in the form shown in Table 5:4, if they believed

TABLE 5:4   Responses to the question, 'Do you think that there are more children compared with the number of adults in Ghana now than there used to be?'

Response	Female survey (n = 331)		Male survey (n = 296)	
	No.	Per cent	No.	Per cent
Yes	198	60	222	75
No	113	34	62	21
Not certain	15	4	4	1
No response	5	2	8	3
Total	331	100	296	100

there were proportionately more children in the country. Three-fifths of female respondents and three-quarters of males did claim to be aware of an increase.

Those replying 'yes' were asked what difference this would make. Only an eighth thought it would make no difference, while nearly a third pointed out that it would inevitably increase the size of the adult population. A quarter spoke of the problems of providing schools, housing, and hospitals and of augmenting the food supply. Others struck an optimistic note. In a country of rapid social transformation, youth is often associated with such desirable characteristics as being educated in a way that is not the case in developed or slowly changing countries. The 30-year-old wife of an army officer said, 'The number of literate people will rise and this makes the country promising'.

The Possibility of Women Restricting Births

If high fertility has been, as is often suggested, an insurance against the inroads of high mortality into the family, then an awareness of declining child death rates and of increasing survival might cause introspection at least amongst the educated about the continued need for very large families. In rural southern Ghana research has shown that parents with as few as four children are no longer at all likely to be left without surviving children or even economic assistance (Caldwell, 1966a, pp. 10–18). In fact support was never directly related to family size and is increasingly less related as smaller families have more chance of educating children to a level where they can secure jobs with earnings large enough to make copious assistance possible.

Therefore, as shown in Table 5:5, respondents were asked whether they believed fewer births could achieve the same level of survival and whether they felt this to imply the need for some kind of birth restriction.

Less than half of the female respondents and just under two-thirds of the male respondents did feel that fewer births were now needed to secure the same end. Here again, there was some evidence that reluctance to agree to this proposition was related to a belief that fertility levels had fallen. Agreement to the proposition was strongly associated with the expression of the view in the earlier question that most families now have more children than used to be the case. Interestingly enough only four-fifths of the female respondents and nine-tenths of the male respondents who had expressed this earlier view now agreed that the implication was that fewer births were now needed to reach the same level of survival. Admittedly, some seem to feel, quite logically, that fewer births did not necessarily assure the same level of survival in individual cases.

A very large number—approximately nine-tenths in each survey—of those who believed that fewer births were now required went on to draw the conclusion that at least some women in Ghana would now have to find a way of restricting family size. This view was expressed by two out of every five female respondents and by three out of five males.

Replies to the question on the survival of children and its implications were not associated with any of the characteristics of respondents. However, it should be noted that the first half of the question was answered

TABLE 5:5   Responses to the question, '(a) Do you think that women have to give birth to fewer children now if they want to make sure that some grow up?'

Response	Female survey (n = 331)		Male survey (n = 296)	
	No.	Per cent	No.	Per cent
Yes	141	43	188	64
No	183	55	99	33
Not certain	4	1	2	1
No response	3	1	7	2
Total	331	100	296	100

If 'yes' for (a), '(b) Do you think that some women will now have to find some way of giving birth to less children than Ghanaian women used to?'

All responses to (a) except 'yes'	190	57	108	36
Response to (a) 'yes': (b) Yes	124	38	171	58
No	14	4	15	5
Not certain	2	1	2	1
No response	1	0	0	0
Total	331	100	296	100

'yes' by 53 per cent of female respondents with secondary school or university education compared with 41 per cent of those with lesser education.

The Possibility of State Intervention

In a country where the reduction of mortality levels is increasingly a governmental responsibility, and in the context of a developing world where a growing number of governments are intervening in the control of fertility as well, it seemed logical to follow the last questions by others on national population problems and the possibility of official action.

Respondents were asked about the eventual effects of high rates of child survival on the labour market. At the time the government had expressed no feelings but self-confidence on this score, and it was only after the survey that some apprehension was voiced in the *Seven-Year Development Plan* (pp. 5–8). Nevertheless, almost half the respondents in each survey did anticipate employment problems. Here, as frequently elsewhere in the surveys, a similar pattern of response emerged in the two surveys when questions were either factual or about the wider world. Divergence occurred chiefly when questions concerned family attitudes and views on desirable changes within the family.

In view of the government's opinions on population matters, it is not surprising that fewer respondents expected state intervention that foresaw employment problems. What is perhaps surprising is the fact that around a quarter of all respondents did expect either the governing party at the time or some future government to take at least vocal action. The male

TABLE 5:6 Responses to the question, '(a) Do you think the country will soon be getting children faster than it needs to supply enough workers when they grow up?'

Response	Female survey (n = 331)		Male survey (n = 296)	
	No.	Per cent	No.	Per cent
Yes	147	44	139	47
No	167	50	147	50
Not certain	14	5	4	1
No response	3	1	6	2
Total	331	100	296	100

If 'yes' for (a), 'Do you think it possible that some day the Government will have to ask people to try not to have so many children?'

	Female survey		Male survey	
All responses to (a) except 'yes'	184	56	157	53
Response to (a) 'yes':				
(b) Yes	94	28	61	21
No	42	13	73	24
Not certain	10	3	2	1
No response	1	0	3	1
Total	331	100	296	100

respondents, who were more intimately connected with policy making, were not unexpectedly more doubtful on this point than were the wives.

Apart from the different response by sex to the question about the probability of the government appealing for family limitation, the replies showed no association with the respondents' various characteristics. However, there was a small difference by education in the male survey. Amongst males with education beyond middle school 51 per cent foresaw employment problems compared with 47 per cent of the lesser educated, and 24 per cent thought government intervention possible compared with 17 per cent of the lesser educated. In the female survey slightly fewer of the more highly educated expected employment difficulties, but the position was reversed on the question of anticipating governmental action.

Discussion of Family Size

Change in family size is often preceded by an increasing ability of spouses to discuss the number of children they want or even to speculate on the effect on their lives of the number that they do have. The successful practice of family limitation can easily be prevented by an inability of parents to discuss such matters as optimum family size.

Respondents were asked whether they had ever had such discussions with their spouses, and those who had not were questioned further on the point. African society is essentially open and extroverted and puts few limits on discussion. As in other societies, the chief effect of cultural patterns might be that some topics might not be raised because traditionally there has been no question to be asked or decision to be made in that area. Until comparatively recently family size has certainly been in this category. It has previously been noted that sex inequality is not so great in Ghana as to forbid parental consultation, although the gap certainly widens as the age between spouses increases or with the passage from monogamous to polygynous marital state or as educational levels fall.

Table 5:7 shows that two-thirds or more of respondents claimed to have held such discussions and nearly all of them confirmed this by readily answering a subsequent question on the number of children wanted by their husbands or wives. Furthermore, before reproduction is completed

TABLE 5:7   Responses to the question, '(a) Have you ever discussed with your husband/wife how many children he/she thinks is the best number to have?'

Response	Female survey (n = 331)		Male survey (n = 296)	
	No.	Per cent	No.	Per cent
Yes: All respondents replying 'yes' (respondents stating in subsequent question number of children preferred by spouse)	219	66	213	72
	(208)	(63)	(204)	(69)
No	98	30	79	27
Not certain	0	0	0	0
No response	14	4	4	1
Total	331	100	296	100
If 'no' for (a), '(b) Why not?'				
All responses to (a) except 'no'	233	70	217	73
Response to (a) 'no':				
The need has not arisen (often in early years of marriage)	23	7	31	11
It has never occurred to me (often in early years of marriage)	36	11	17	6
These things are beyond our control, 'God's will', etc.	11	3	9	3
I do not want to restrict the number of my children	6	2	7	2
I know my spouse would not want to restrict the number of children	2	1	6	2
I am not sure of my spouse's feelings on the subject	3	1	4	1
I cannot discuss such matters with my spouse	3	1	2	1
No response	14	4	3	1
Total	331	100	296	100

many of the remainder will probably discuss the matter, for the most common reason that no discussions had been held was that the respondents were young and had as yet had few children.

As the holding of such discussions may well mark the beginning of incipient fertility decline in a society, every effort was made to distinguish those who talked about such matters from those who did not. The small sex differences apparently existing between the two surveys are probably more differences of memory and interpretation than anything more meaningful. Education is important, showing significant associations (at 1 per cent) in both surveys. Amongst respondents with education beyond middle school, 81 per cent of females and 82 per cent of males had held such discussions, while amongst those of lesser education the proportions fell to 62 per cent and 63 per cent respectively. More Protestants than Catholics had discussed family size, although in both surveys the differences between the religious groups failed to achieve statistical significance. In the female survey 69 per cent of Protestants and 57 per cent of Catholics had discussed the matter, while the equivalent figures in the male survey were 75 per cent and 65 per cent.

Type of marriage and stage of marriage is important. Communication on such matters is more difficult in polygynous marriages, although significant association (at 5 per cent) was shown only in the male survey. In the female and male surveys 70 per cent and 74 per cent respectively of monogamously married respondents had discussed desirable family size, whilst only 57 per cent and 52 per cent respectively of polygynously married respondents had done so. Discussions had also been more frequent between spouses who were closer to each other in age, although here again the margin failed to achieve statistical significance. Where the age gap was less than five years 73 per cent of female respondents and 77 per cent of male respondents claimed to have talked about family size, while the proportions fell to 66 per cent and 69 per cent respectively when the age gap was greater.

Finally, there is a complex relation between age, duration of marriage, the number of children ever born, and such discussions. In spite of the fact that a common reason given for not discussing family size was that the marriage was comparatively recent and few children had as yet been born, in the surveys as a whole it was precisely the couples with fewest children who were most likely to have talked about the subject. The association with both the number of children ever born and the number surviving is significant (at 1 per cent) in the female survey and just fails to achieve significance in the male survey. Thus, 70 per cent of females with fewer than five live births have held such discussions compared with only 61 per cent of those with more births to their credit. The proportions are 71 per cent and 59 per cent respectively for females with less than five and five or more surviving children. Amongst males the difference is small if attention is confined to children ever born, being 73 per cent for those fathering fewer than five children and 70 per cent for those fathering more. When discussions are related to surviving children, it is found that they have been held by 75 per cent of fathers of fewer than four living children and by 66 per cent of fathers of greater numbers. Many interrelations exist here. In some cases families are small because parents desired this, discussed it, and took some steps to achieve such an end; in most cases the explanation is that the smaller families have younger parents, who are likely to be less traditional in outlook and on average better educated.

Thus, parents are more likely to discuss desired family size if they are young, educated to a reasonably high level, Protestant, relatively close in age, and monogamously married. Such couples could be described as having moved furthest from the traditional behaviour patterns of West African, agrarian society.

It is particularly noteworthy that the analysis of reasons for not discussing family size reveals no major source of opposition in the society. The main effect of traditional culture patterns has been a kind of inertia, for, even amongst the urban elite, there are still respondents who had not thought of the matter. Few talked of 'God's will', a favourite and meaningful expression in the society as a whole, although one agricultural officer, a Protestant who claimed to know many methods of contraception, said, 'It is a gift of nature which we cannot control'. Few mentioned religion, but a Catholic male teacher, married to an untrained seamstress of the same religion, argued, 'It is against our religion, and she is ignorant of such things, being an illiterate woman'.

Desired Family Size

At various points in the interviewing schedule respondents were asked such questions as how many children they wanted and how many their husbands or wives preferred. In order to overcome the bias of building on an already existent family, they were also asked how many children they would recommend as best to a friend newly married or to a daughter. All these estimates have been assembled together for comparative purposes in Tables 5:8 and 5:9.

The first point to be noted is that male recommendations are in each case higher than female ones, although the margin is not very great. This is not the result of a general male preference for larger numbers, arising from a need to prove virility or explained by the fact that they do not need to bear the children. Indeed, as Table 5:10 shows, over one-and-a-half times as many males as females would advise their friends or daughters to have fewer than four children. The difference arises from two facts. Firstly, although males, like females, prefer families of four to six children, more of the former incline towards five or six in contrast to the marked peaking at four which occurs amongst female responses. Secondly, somewhat more males than females prefer very large families. This may well be associated with questions of prestige, virility, desire to establish the family line and name, and with not having to endure the necessary pregnancies. It might be argued that males, unlike females, were thinking in terms of fathering children by more than one woman as a result of polygynous marriage, unstable marriage, or both, but a check of the schedules, and the reports of the interviewers, reveals the surprising fact that almost all male respondents, even those married polygynously, assumed that their 'friends' were entering monogamous marriages. This is supported by the fact that males hoped for a slightly higher average number of children for their daughters than they were prepared to recommend to their newly married

TABLE 5:8   Recommended family size: responses to the questions, (i) 'If a friend were about to get married, and asked you the number of children to have, what would you answer?' (ii) 'How many children do you hope that your daughter will have?' (iii) 'How many more children do you want?' (iv) 'How many children does your husband/wife think is best?'

Female survey (n = 331)

Response	Recommendation to a friend		Hopes for daughter		Desired extra children plus children ever born		Desired extra children plus surviving children		Children preferred by spouse	
	No.	Per cent	No.	Per cent	No.	Per cent	No.	Per cent	No.	Per cent
0	0	0	0	0	2	1	3	1	0	0
1	0	0	1	0	1	0	1	0	0	0
2	4	1	6	2	5	2	4	1	7	2
3	21	6	18	5	21	6	27	8	16	5
4	173	52	167	51	88	27	87	26	103	31
5	47	14	27	8	53	16	62	19	31	9
6	40	12	27	8	63	19	61	18	38	12
7	1 }		2	1	22	7	15	5	4	1
8	1 }	1	0	0	19	6	17	5	4	1
9	1 }		0	0	4	1	5	2	0	0
10	2	1	4	1	11	3	9	3	5	2
11					4	1	3	1		
12					4	1	3	1		
13					1	0	1	0		
Non-numerical replies and no response	41	13	79	24	33	10	33	10	123	37
Total	331	100	331	100	331	100	331	100	331	100

Male survey (n = 296)

Response	Recommendation to a friend		Hopes for daughter		Desired extra children plus children ever born		Desired extra children plus surviving children		Children preferred by spouse	
	No.	Per cent	No.	Per cent	No.	Per cent	No.	Per cent	No.	Per cent
0	0	0	0	0	0	0	0	0	0	0
1	0	0	0	0	1	1	1	0	0	0
2	5	2	4	1	1		2	1	1	0
3	34	11	35	12	22	7	22	7	19	7
4	111	38	97	33	48	16	56	19	89	30
5	47	16	36	12	54	19	63	21	33	11
6	37	12	43	15	53	18	52	18	46	16
7	3	1	4	1	26	9	21	7	4	1
8	6	2	2	1	17	6	15	5	7	2
9	0	0	1	0	12	4	9	3	1	0
10	3	1	4	1	7	2	5	2	2	1
11			0	0	4	1	1	0	2	1
12			2	1	4	1	4	1		
13					0	0	1	0		
14					1	0	0	0		
15-19					4	1	2	1		
20 and over	1	0	1	0	2	1	2	1		
Non-numerical replies and no response	49	17	67	23	40	14	40	14	92	31
Total	296	100	296	100	296	100	296	100	296	100

TABLE 5:9   Recommended family size: average numbers of children recommended by respondents

	Respondents recommending number		Non-numerical replies and no response		Average number recommended	
	F	M	F	M	F	M
Recommendation to a friend	290	247	41	49	4·4	4·6
Hopes for daughter	252	229	79	67	4·3	4·7
Desired extra children plus children ever born	298	256	33	40	5·5	6·1
Desired extra children plus surviving children	298	256	33	40	5·3	5·8
Children preferred by spouse	208	204	123	92	4·6	4·9

TABLE 5:10   Comparison of percentages of female and male respondents recommending families of specific size.

	Family size recommended								Non-numerical, no response	
	0–3		4		5–6		7 and over			
	F	M	F	M	F	M	F	M	F	M
Recommendation to a friend	8	13	52	38	26	28	2	4	12	17
Hopes for daughter	7	13	51	33	16	26	2	5	24	23
Desired extra children plus children ever born	9	8	27	16	35	36	19	26	10	14
Desired extra children plus children surviving	11	8	26	19	37	39	16	20	10	14
Children preferred by spouse	7	7	31	30	21	27	4	5	37	31

friends. This arose partly from the fact that a handful of male respondents wanted really large numbers of grandchildren. Females, possibly extending greater sympathy to their daughters, exhibited exactly the opposite reaction.

The second important point is that the great majority of respondents have rejected the traditional aim of a very large family while not embracing Western very small family values. In both surveys, every method of measuring recommended family size produced a majority of all respondents advocating families of four to six children. In all but one case over two-thirds of those giving numerical answers chose this range, and indeed 90 per cent of female respondents' recommendations to friends were found here. Elite females are apparently increasingly coming to regard four children as the desirable number in a completed family.

However, Tables 5:8 and 5:9 show clearly that recommendations made before family formation begins are not necessarily a good guide to feelings during that formation. Once parents have had several children they may be loath to cease reproduction without another son or another daughter; they may merely want another baby. Or, in societies characterised by a good deal of unstable marriage, they may want another child by the current union.

Thus, Table 5:9 shows that the extra children still wanted by the respondents would, if added to their surviving children, bring their desired family size in each survey to about one more child per family than one might expect from their views on others' families. Furthermore, this implies average birth levels in the female and male surveys of 5·5 and 6·1 respectively, not very far below what has in fact been the completed family size amongst this group. Thus this evidence hardly supports a belief in substantial fertility decline in the near future. On the other hand, average desired family size, as computed this way, includes families which are already larger than desired, and the computation presents no way by which averages can be reduced by these negative desires.

TABLE 5:11 Responses to the question, 'how many more children do you want?'

Response	Female survey (n = 331)		Male survey (n = 296)	
	No.	Per cent	No.	Per cent
0	104	31	75	26
1	31	9	43	15
2	71	22	66	22
3	29	9	42	14
4	42	13	18	6
5	14	4	6	2
6–10	13	4	7	2
'What God brings', not certain	9	3	14	5
No response	18	5	25	8
Total	331	100	296	100
Average desired by those stating number	1·9		1·8	

On the other hand, the question about the desired extra number of children did elicit the fact that almost a third of the female respondents and a quarter of the males wanted no more children at all. It was later shown that a substantial number of this group would welcome advice or assistance in achieving that end. Most respondents were fairly sure about exactly how many more children they desired, averaging in each survey about two extra.

An examination of respondents desiring no more children revealed no discernible patterns except in terms of existing family size. In both surveys the respondents' number of children ever born and number of surviving children showed strong negative association with the numbers of extra children wanted. Thus, it can be seen in Table 5:12 that, while few Ghanaians want less than three children, substantial numbers of women are satisfied with their existing family in each family size group from three

TABLE 5:12   Respondents wanting no more children, by number of surviving children

Number of surviving children	Percentage of all respondents with this number of children wanting no more	
	Female survey	Male survey
0	7	0
1	3	0
2	5	2
3	22	7
4	52	23
5	62	40
6–10	74	74
11–15	100	80

up, and substantial numbers of males are satisfied in each group from four up.

Males are certainly less easily satisfied by small families than are females. However, it should be noted in passing that the female respondents who claim to be satisfied with having no children or one child are probably convinced that they are sterile. No male takes this position because even the childless are usually convinced that they could and might father a child by another wife.

Women in this socio-economic group are certainly coming increasingly to regard four children as constituting an adequate family. Thus a majority of females with four surviving children want no more. Amongst males the same degree of satisfaction is not reached until they have six children.

Another point established by Tables 5:8 and 5:9 is that there is a strong correlation between the number of children respondents believe their spouses to desire and the number they want themselves. Thus, although males desire more children than do females, their estimates of their wives' desired numbers is above the female respondents' estimates of the number wanted by their husbands.

However, in each case the estimate of the number desired by spouses is close to the number of children respondents would recommend to others and is well below the implied desired family size computed by adding the number of extra children wanted to current family size.

This adds weight to the previous suspicion that there is in many families real conflict between the desire to have for one reason or another a certain number of extra children and views on the optimum size of the family. If the former provides the strongest motivation, and it might well as it has a certain immediacy, then achieved family size might remain persistently above advocated size.

Education appeared to have a slight effect in lowering recommended family size. In the female survey respondents with middle school or lesser education recommended an average of 4·6 children for a friend, while those with more extended education would advise only 4·4. In the male survey the former group recommended 4·7 children and the latter 4·8, but it should be noted that respondents with secondary schooling or university education advised only 4·4.

Religion had no clear effect, possibly once again because of the small number of Catholics, which rendered no differential statistically significant. Thus, while in the female survey Catholic respondents recommended 4·7 children compared with 4·5 for Protestants, the position was reversed in the male survey with Catholics and Protestants advising 4·4 and 4·7 respectively. No other characteristics were found to affect measurably the respondents' replies.

Where comments were made, for this series of questions asked essentially for quantitative answers, they were mainly justifications for advising small families because of the problems of the modern world. A graduate teacher, himself father of five children, said that he would prefer his daughter to have less than this number because 'you can't afford to educate them without great strain'.

The Possibility of Planning Family Size

It is sometimes claimed that traditional societies regard such fundamental matters as reproduction as being essentially in the province of nature and outside the sphere in which human decisions determine events. Furthermore, it is suggested that societies often take a long time to shake off such beliefs and adopt more scientific viewpoints.

In the survey a handful of people had argued that family size was not a subject for discussion in that these things were beyond human control or were decided by God's will. Subsequently they were asked directly whether they believed that the number of children in a family was largely a matter of fate.

Table 5:13 shows that almost two-thirds of the female respondents and half the males thought that this was in general true. This does not

TABLE 5:13   Responses to the question, 'Do you think that the number of children a person has is mostly decided by fate (or "God's will")?'

Response	Female survey (n = 331)		Male survey (n = 296)	
	No.	Per cent	No.	Per cent
Yes	206	62	139	47
No	109	33	146	49
Not certain or qualified response	13	4	4	2
No response	3	1	7	2
Total	331	100	296	100

mean that the majority believed that reproduction was controlled by occult powers, but it does mean that most felt that it was either a sphere in which divine wishes and decisions counted or more commonly that control of family size was so complex that the size of the completed family was largely a matter of luck or ill luck. The latter was expressed in completely down-to-earth terms by the woman school-teacher who pointed out that fate, in the form of disease, can cause sterility.

What is more important than the number agreeing to the proposition is that a third of the females and half of the males rejected it. Every effort was made to identify this group.

Firstly, rejection of this concept of fate or luck was associated with sex (at 1 per cent level), in that many more males rejected it. It was rather surprisingly not shown to be associated with education. However, only 60 per cent of females with education beyond middle school believed in fate compared with 68 per cent of those with lesser education, while the equivalent figures from the male survey were 47 per cent and 51 per cent. Religion did not appear to be related in any way to the pattern of replies; nor was the age or type of marriage.

Some respondents qualified their replies, as did the male graduate teacher with five children, who said his answer was, 'Yes for the un-educated and no for the educated class'. A female clerk, who was a Catholic and opposed the use of contraceptives while approving *coitus interruptus* (withdrawal), said that the number of children was decided by 'God's will with the co-operation of the married couple'.

Further questioning of the respondents showed that many who replied 'yes' meant in the existing circumstances in Ghana and were not necessarily describing their own marriage. This is also borne out by an examination of the schedules. Thus, although replies are associated (at 1 per cent) with the use of contraception, the correlation is not as close as might be expected. In the female survey 42 per cent of respondents who had ever practised contraception somewhat surprisingly said 'yes', compared admittedly with 74 per cent of those who had not. Comparative figures in the male survey were 25 per cent and 64 per cent. However, we shall see later that most of the respondents who had practised contraception had done so without marked success, and this experience may have confirmed in many of them a belief in fate.

In order to isolate those who believed that family planning was impossible from those who merely thought it not very successful in Ghanaian conditions, respondents were asked whether some people could carry out accurate planning. It might be noted that the question set out in Table 5:14 asks not only for a belief in such planning but also in its efficacy and so might compel the sceptical or unsuccessful family planners to reply 'no'.

The replies show that two-thirds of the respondents believe such planning to be possible even if they were dubious about it succeeding in their own case. This time female and male replies converged and the difference only just bordered on statistical significance (at 5 per cent).

This time the division between respondents who believed family planning possible and those who did not was clearer. Education certainly played a role, showing significant association in both female (at 1 per cent)

TABLE 5:14 Responses to the question, 'Do you think that some people can decide exactly how many children they want and then plan things so that they have only that number?'

Response	Female survey (n = 331)		Male survey (n = 296)	
	No.	Per cent	No.	Per cent
Yes	203	61	206	69
No	110	33	85	29
Not certain or qualified response	12	4	2	1
No response	6	2	3	1
Total	331	100	296	100

and male (at 5 per cent) surveys. Only 55 per cent of females with middle school education or less believed such planning to be possible compared with 73 per cent of those with more extended education. The comparative figures in the male survey were 64 per cent for respondents with lesser education and 75 per cent for those with more education. Thus, in each survey three-quarters of all respondents with education beyond middle school believed that it was possible to control accurately family numbers.

Belief in the possibility of family planning was greatest amongst partners in stable, monogamous marriages. In the female survey 64 per cent of respondents who had been married only once believed such planning to be possible while only 50 per cent of those credited with a greater number of marriages held this view. In the male survey the proportions were 75 per cent and 57 per cent respectively, a significant association (at 1 per cent). Of course, it may well be the case that the kind of co-operation and mutual understanding necessary to the successful limitation of family size can be achieved much more easily within stable, monogamous marriage. This association is not one which arises from the fact that younger couples have had fewer marriages and are likely on the whole to be more attracted by 'modern' viewpoints. As a matter of fact, age showed no significant association with replies, although in the male survey 71 per cent of males with wives under 30 years of age said 'yes' compared with 67 per cent of respondents with older wives.

Religion did not appear to affect male replies, but in the female survey 67 per cent of Protestants said 'yes' compared with 51 per cent of Catholics.

Those respondents who did believe that some people could decide their family size were asked how they did it. The international nature of the present discussion of family limitation is shown by the fact that over nine-tenths of these respondents in each survey used some general term such as 'family planning', 'birth control', or 'contraception'. Often replies went no further. The wife of a public servant commented, 'I have heard of this but I don't know how successful they are'. Two respondents talked of 'God's grace'. Nine females and eight male respondents referred to sexual abstinence. A 44-year-old woman teacher with five children explained, 'They do not have sexual connections after they have had the number of children they want'. One respondent, interestingly enough a drug-store keeper, referred to indigenous womb-turning to produce sterility. However, many made vague statements about doctors knowing about such things, and the wife of a clerk said, 'I understand they use some kind of medicine'.

Summary

Most members of the Ghanaian elite have probably been the parents of fewer children than their ancestors had been at the same age, although they may well have more surviving children. It is just possible that they have been affected by some general decline in fertility as the pressure upon tropical Africans to populate or perish has diminished, but most of their fertility decline can be explained by the fact that birth rates are lower in the towns and somewhat lower still amongst the economically better-off in these towns. In addition male fertility has fallen markedly with the movement away from polygyny and, at least in this socio-economic class, towards stabler marriage. Even amongst the elite, the more highly educated are a fifth less fertile than the lesser educated, and this is evidence that some fertility decline is likely to continue. However, there is no equivalent fertility differential by religion. Catholic families are not larger than Protestant families, as experience in some Western countries would have led us to suspect. The reason may be that Catholicism as a whole has found it more difficult than Protestantism to accommodate itself to traditional marital practices, especially polygyny and unstable marriage. Certainly some Protestant churches have been just as rigid in outlook, but other sects have risen with more accommodating attitudes.

However, even the families of the urban elite are still very large by world standards. They may not continue to be so, for times are changing, and the elite are under considerable pressure, specifically of the types examined in the next chapter. Their awareness of national and domestic high fertility problems and some of their reactions are summarised in Table 5:15.

On the whole a greater number of males believe in the possibility of controlling family fortunes, at least as far as size is concerned, while more females hope for a relatively small family or for the immediate curtailment of its growth. The least traditional views and actions, that is the belief that fertility may be too high, the discussion of family size, the recognition that some people can successfully plan family numbers, and so on, are most strongly associated with extended education. There are weaker associations with the existence of stable, monogamous marriage and with a relatively small age gap between spouses. Neither age nor religion affect the position very greatly. Certainly, there is a relationship with the practice of contraception, but it is far from absolute, suggesting that many who have tried contraception are far from sure that it is very successful while some who have not practised it think it might work.

Substantial numbers of respondents in each survey had noticed changes in the country's population patterns. Two-thirds had taken part in one significant social change by discussing desirable family size and over a quarter by being satisfied with the existing size of their families. Two-thirds

TABLE 5:15 Summary of certain responses to questions on family size

Response	Female survey (n = 331) Per cent	Male Survey (n = 296) Per cent
Children now form a larger proportion of the population	60	75
Most families now have a larger number of children in them	54	72
Fewer births are now needed to secure the same number of surviving adult children	43	64
Some women will have to find ways of having fewer children	38	58
Present fertility levels may cause future employment problems	44	47
The government may some day appeal for lower fertility	28	21
Discussions have been held with spouses on family size	66	72
Respondents want no more children	31	26
Family size is mostly decided by fate	62	47
Some people can successfully plan family size	61	69

also believe that it is possible, at least for some people, to control family size successfully. Perhaps the most remarkable feature is the growing consensus among wives in this socio-economic group that four children is enough.

6

The Growing Needs of Children

We have seen in Chapter 5 that the majority of the respondents probably had fewer children than did their parents at the same age. Yet, while most Ghanaians believe that their parents' generation uncritically, and usually thankfully, accepted large families, such a viewpoint is no longer universally held. In Chapter 4 it was recorded that only 4 per cent of male respondents and 7 per cent of females failed to list at least one bad aspect of the large family, and in Chapter 5 it was shown that preferred family size is generally lower than that which has hitherto been achieved.

The increasing awareness of the problems of the large family is not then primarily the product of greater numbers of surviving children. In the responses to the question analysed earlier two-thirds of all respondents complained of the growing costs of education and lesser numbers spoke of general support costs.

These are not problems which are the exclusive concern of the urban elite. Another research project showed that only in rural areas which are still very largely within the subsistence economy and where schooling has not penetrated do large families now fail to impose upon parents extra financial strain. Such areas are now found on a large scale only in northern Ghana. Even in rich rural areas of the south with still plentiful supplies of land, the existence of a cash economy meant that questions of choice in spending were part of everyday life. Money spent on children could not be spent in other ways; the need to spend money on children became more acute with the availability of schooling.

Nevertheless, such strains are more severe in the fully cash economy of the towns than they are in rural areas, where food and housing are less likely to demand regular, large-scale expenditure. Furthermore, the magnitude of the expenditure and savings arising from economic choices of one kind or another are greater among the wealthier. So, often, is the pressure to train children to a point where they can earn the same kind of income as their parents could provide.

It is precisely in this area that the kind of critical pressures arise which may become intensive enough to instigate considerable fertility decline. Accordingly, a series of questions was framed to probe the respondents' feelings and extra care was taken to examine the exact nature of the personal responses.

Change in Treatment

As shown in Table 6:1, respondents were asked to discuss the differences between their own upbringing and that received by their children. Over three-fifths of female respondents and three-quarters of the males did

TABLE 6:1   Responses to the question, 'In what ways do you treat your children differently from the way you were treated yourself as a child?'

Response*	Female survey (n = 331)		Male survey (n = 296)	
	No.†	Per cent†	No.†	Per cent†
Live or act as a nuclear family, go on outings together, etc.	91	27	66	22
Give them the best, more love, better education	82	25	85	29
Allow them more freedom and independence	41	12	45	15
Don't use corporal punishment	21	6	25	8
Residual reasons	8	2	17	6
No difference	60	18	23	8
No response	69	21	43	15

* Response is main argument in a given reply; only occasionally were two arguments thought to be distinct and listed accordingly.
† Adds to more than survey numbers and 100 per cent because of listing of more than one response in some cases.

name at least one difference. Most felt strongly about the matter, attributing the changes not merely to rise in the socio-economic scale or expected inter-generational changes, but to fundamental alterations in the whole Ghanaian way of life. Amongst many there was more than a mere note of bitterness as they surveyed their own childhood.

Many respondents are strongly conscious of a strengthening of the nuclear family, of a more confined family area within which pleasures are shared and affection exchanged more intensely. Many are equally conscious of a greater freedom, especially for children, and an associated decline in strictness and corporal punishment.

Perhaps the most striking feature of the pattern of responses was the fact that, while only 23 per cent of males either failed to respond or saw no change, 39 per cent of females were found within these two categories. Observations during interviewing and a subsequent attempt to investigate this question at greater depth both suggested the same explanation. Female respondents tend to discuss the role of mothers and male respondents that of fathers, and it is the position of the latter which has changed most radically in terms of outlook and action.

Some of the respondents, almost always second generation members of the urban elite, quite correctly pointed out that in their own cases no marked change in the pattern of upbringing had occurred. One such woman who, as the wife of a driver, was clinging precariously to residence in a wealthier suburb, said, 'I was pampered when I was a child. My father could buy me two tins of sardines, which I could eat in a matter of minutes, but I cannot do the same for my children because the cost of living has gone too high'. Others, a small minority, denied that changed expenditure patterns were in themselves signs of radical change. A high civil servant commented, 'I look after my children better than I was because I am relatively richer, but at the same time the training I give them is not much different from what I received when I was young'.

In Table 6:1 an attempt has been made to make the responses quantitatively meaningful by selecting the central arguments and aggregating them into groups. These arguments can be subdivided, and different arguments were supported by the same kind of observation. In what follows an attempt has been made to single out the persistent types of supporting observations and to quote them in the context in which they were given.

For instance, many respondents pointed to the increasing residential importance of the nuclear family or alternatively to the greater love felt within tightly knit family groups and made the point that their children were now free to discuss problems. In traditional village life children, it appears, frequently bottled up concrete or emotional problems for very long periods and were not expected to resolve them with the help of adults. The wife of a civil servant said, 'My children are now more close to me. There was a feeling of apartness in the way I was treated. We converse a lot and they are ready to ask about many things'. Nor were such improvements in communication merely with mothers. A male teacher pointed out, 'I am very free with them; I can sit down and discuss their needs and how best we can meet them'.

Often related to this lessening fear was a reduction in punishment, although only in the few cases listed in Table 6:1 was it said to have disappeared. Many respondents commented, 'I beat them less'. The wife of a senior civil servant remembered, 'When I was a child, I used to be beaten up and never given money to spend on my own; I do not beat my children'. One woman teacher claimed, 'I make them feel ashamed rather than punish them'. While another made the point more thoroughly, 'I avoid corporal punishment. I advise them against any amount of misdemeanour. I often reprimand and scold them whenever they default. In short I use the psychological way'. Even an illiterate wife, who remained a part-time farmer, was able to say, 'I don't beat my children as much as I was and also I encourage them to discuss things they do not understand'.

Such views were expressed as frequently by males as females. A headmaster commented, 'Discipline was harsher than now. I am now lax and tolerant'. A surveyor believed, 'Now it takes persuasion and discussion to correct child offences, whereas in other times the cane did most of the persuasion'. A technical officer in the party youth movement (The Young Pioneers) analysed his role as a father and observed, 'I tend to pamper them; I find out why problems they become involved in arise without molesting them'.

Coupled with these views was a growing belief in the need for greater childhood freedom. A district commissioner, father of 'about eight children' by four different women, pointed out that the children he was currently rearing were subject to 'less regimentation and more freedom than I was allowed as a child'. This loosening up was not confined to those who had broken most with traditional marital patterns. A civil servant who had been married successively to five different women and who had nine living children, attested, 'The slavery and rigid training are gone forever;

for instance, my children decide which school to attend, the wife or husband they want and so on—things I could not do as a child'. A woman baker, married to a bar-keeper, said, 'My children are allowed to choose what they want to do, and, except when the business is considered bad, they are allowed a free hand'.

Increased affection within the circle of parents and children was often stressed, sometimes with the added rider that it was the parents who were undertaking the care of the children. A seamstress married to a civil servant related, 'I lived with a harsh stepmother—I give my children every affection they need'. A woman teacher said, 'I stayed with my aunt. My children enjoy motherly and fatherly love and enjoy the company of their brothers and sisters'. The wife of a clerk stated, 'More patience is exercised for my children and I care for them more than I was cared for'. The growth in affection was often related to the confinement of family size, which was sometimes felt to be really astonishing. 'I live with them like they are my little sisters and brothers' was one mother's comment. Frequently, actions were cited as evidence of change and greater love. An agricultural officer's response was, 'I try to let them feel happier by providing their needs', while that of a male cashier was, 'I play with them when I am free'.

Again and again these changes were related to a strengthening of the nuclear family as a residential unit, a child-rearing organisation and as a group which often sought entertainment together. An accountant's wife stated, in spite of the fact that her father had been a school-teacher, 'I depended on my father, mother, grandmother, and grandfather, but my children depend on their parents'. A teacher, wife of a meteorological observer, described their family life in terms which illustrated why she had seen nothing wrong in the stereotype of the Western family. 'My children go out with their parents. They are free with me and are never afraid to tell me their troubles. Parties are called at their birthdays. They go to the cinema once a week'. Similar notes were struck by a woman teacher, who said, 'We eat together, while I never ate with my mother; they can ride in a car, while I had to walk', and by a female lecturer in a teachers' college, who answered, 'My children are taken to cinema shows once a week and we all eat together at the table'.

Going out together was considered important and was often placed first in lists of changes. For instance a woman teacher married to another teacher replied, 'I go out with them; I answer all their questions; I supply them with their needs; if they misbehave, I punish them'. Another mother, also a teacher, pointed out, 'My children attend film shows and plays for entertainment; I was entertained with folk songs and Ananse stories'. One contrast, inherent in many replies, but specified by the wife of a college lecturer, was, 'My children are allowed to go to cinemas and are sent to school by compulsion'. Other entertainment took place in the home. A photographer with one young child said, 'I buy him toys; of course, I can't tell whether I ever used toys at all'.

The more formal obligations of child-rearing were equally stressed, with repeated references to schooling, dressing, and care of health, the first two often interrelated. It was in connection with these things that climbing costs were frequently mentioned.

Sometimes there was a note of bitterness about the past. The wife of a high civil servant replied, 'My children are all at school, but when I was young I was not allowed to finish elementary school because my parents thought it was a waste training a woman'. Sometimes the bitterness extended to the present. The mother of six children, herself still a part-time farmer in a marriage where the couple were struggling to remain in the wealthier part of Sekondi, complained, 'My children are all grown-ups and so they do not want to work on the farms any longer, and, if I had foreseen this in the past, I could have made it but for them'. Usually only praise was lavished upon education, and the point was often made that daughters as well as sons were being sent to school. Sometimes the expense extended beyond day school, for the most prestigeful schools of Ghana are the large, well known, and long-established boarding schools. A dispenser with three children said, 'I send them to boarding school at a very early age for their elementary education so that they can get into good secondary schools easily'. Sometimes the process of schooling went beyond the normal span or hours. A stenographer, married to a nurse and with one young son, pointed out, 'At four he goes to day nursery, which I never attended', while a mother, who was a teacher, explained that she added to her children's schooling by teaching them more in the evenings.

The question of dress was raised more frequently than we had expected. Many respondents felt that there was a particular need to see that children were sent to school in reasonably presentable clothes and with shoes on their feet. A postal officer, considering the nature of change, remarked, 'The main difference is that I find it is obligatory that I buy my child clothes and send her to a secondary school, but my father did not do all these things and he felt he was not obliged'. A large number of answers hardly varied even in word order from the civil servant, married to a salesgirl with two children, who said, 'I don't want them to go bare footed and naked and we always keep them well dressed'. The wife of a manager in a business pointed out, 'I have provided them with footwear though I never had it at this age'.

Much of the explanation for the low mortality amongst the elite children was explained by the earnestness with which respondents described their efforts to look after the children's health. Many of the comments were reminiscent of those found in the letter columns of newspapers in Australia, and presumably elsewhere in the now developed world, a century ago when the middle classes were becoming increasingly sure that they could preserve the lives of all their children if only they exercised enough care and adopted cautious and regular habits of child-rearing. This was especially the case with young children. A woman teacher with a young baby said, 'I feed him from a bottle and boil all drinking water', while another explained, 'I teach my children right from their infancy how to use the chamber pot. I have hours for feeding the children whereas I was fed any time during my infancy'. The same belief in care and regularity was found also in attitudes to older children. A lithographic assistant with one young son reported, 'I see that my child puts on suitable clothing each time. I also see that he eats nutritional food'. A business man said of his four children, 'I plan their daily activities for them; they go to bed at fixed times', while an educational officer reported of his two in comparison with his own upbringing, 'I am keener about what they eat and when they eat; they are better clothed and get medical attention'. There was also the assurance that they would receive modern medical treatment if needed. The wife of an accountant pointed out, 'I take them to hospital when sick instead of taking them to native doctors'.

Sometimes change in activities, especially that resulting from schooling or urban living, was mentioned. A newspaper proof-reader, with a wife who worked in a factory, said, 'At least they don't do any strenuous work, as I used to do on my father's farm, and are never naked'. Sometimes evidence of more privacy was cited, as in the case of the wife of a Kumasi timber contractor who reported, 'They have a room to themselves; I used to sleep with my mother when I was young and even when I grew older'.

Some respondents generalised about the transformation which had occurred. Most were well aware that some of these changes made the support of children much more costly, that going to school instead of farming, wearing clothes and shoes, going to the cinema, visiting the doctor, having a separate room, and so on had not been achieved except at very considerable cost. Surprisingly few attributed any of the changes to movement from rural to urban areas. For instance, none drew attention to the fact that 'going out' is largely an urban activity and is pointless in a village where there is usually nothing in this sense to go to. However, many did regard the differences in upbringing as the result of changing times—many more indeed than regarded them as stemming from a rise in socio-economic class. Some attributed this to external influences or examples. A female tutor in a college said, 'I treat my children like Europeans', while an agricultural officer remarked, 'The Western type of treatment is in vogue now'. Occasionally the term 'civilised' was used to describe the new way of life, perhaps a suitable term in view of the relation of the process to urbanisation.

Finally, it should be noted that these quotations are a balanced selection of views expressed, but they are necessarily the views of the majority who did attest to change. Those failing to answer the question obviously cannot be quoted, and even the smaller number who saw no intergenerational differences rarely went into further explanation. A few, usually second generation elite, merely asserted that they had been treated in much the same way as they handled their own children.

Spending on Children

Many of the respondents had already volunteered the information that such changes in way of life had disproportionately raised the expenditure upon children. However, they were all asked, as shown in Table 6:2, whether the fraction of income spent upon children had risen, and, if so, why this had occurred.

As nearly all respondents attested that the fraction spent on children had risen, no associations between this answer and other characteristics of the respondents could be determined. The main reason given by the greater number of respondents was the expenses of the kind already discussed, schooling, clothing, entertainment, and a more spacious way of life. However, almost as many spoke of the rising cost of living, thus

Population Growth and Family Change in Africa

TABLE 6:2 Responses to the question, '(a) Are families spending a bigger or a smaller fraction of their money on their children than they used to do?'

Response	Female survey (n = 331)		Male survey (n = 296)	
	No.	Per cent	No.	Per cent
A bigger fraction	311	94	276	93
A smaller fraction	14	4	5	2
No difference, the same	0	0	4	1
No response	6	2	11	4
Total	331	100	296	100

If 'A bigger fraction' for (a), '(b) Why do you think this is so?'*

All responses to (a) except 'A bigger fraction'	20	6	20	7
Response to (a) 'A bigger fraction':				
More money spent on schooling, clothing, entertainment etc.	178	54	125	42
Cost of living higher	136	41	138	47
More money spent within the nuclear family	4	1	15	5
No response	7	2	13	4

* A few respondents are listed as giving two main arguments.

raising the question whether some of them had fully understood that the first part of the question referred to proportional and not absolute expenditure. If there was confusion, it was apparently a little greater amongst female respondents than males. There had certainly been distressing inflation prior to the survey, often reducing the spending power of the elite to a level well below that which their new high salaries had seemed to promise. Part of the reason for this inflation was undoubtedly the unprecedented expansion in numbers of available urban elite jobs. In the two years before the survey, the Accra Retail Price Index had risen almost 20 per cent and the Accra Index of Local Food Prices and Other Items by a little more (Killick, 1966, pp. 414, 416).

Perhaps the most remarkable feature of Table 6:2 is that no respondents explained the greater expenditure upon children in terms of the larger number of surviving children. Although this factor is certainly of importance for the community as a whole, it is difficult for the individual family to face the fact that their spending pattern would have been different if one of the children now living had died instead.

Some respondents saw changed expenditure patterns as an inevitable part of progress or, in the words of several, 'civilisation'. A business man, whose wife was a teacher, believed 'the present standard of living demands that', while an accounts clerk put the matter on a slightly different plane by saying, 'Fashion demands that'. A young stenographer, married to a nurse and with one child, attributed the change to 'awareness of the consumption patterns of Europeans'.

Half of all respondents had something to say about training or education. Many referred to the general preparation, social as well as specific schooling, for the new world which their children would enter, a world very much like that currently enjoyed in developed countries. Some took it as the only way of ensuring continued development to that state. The wife of a clerk, mother of four surviving children from eight births, supported greater expenditure upon children, saying, 'Yes, because they want better progress than there used to be'. A 30-year-old male teacher with three children maintained that, 'Parents have realised that they have to give their children better treatment so that they might grow up to live in a new world'. Sometimes it was a case of maintaining or improving the standard of living to which their parents had already accustomed them. A civil servant pointed out that, 'Now parents want their children to have better opportunities than they had', while the wife of another argued, 'A better future is sought for children so they will have a better place in life'.

Far more comment was made directly on the need for schooling and its financial demands. A woman teacher, wife of an engineer and mother of five children, pointed out, 'Families are spending a bigger fraction of money this way because everyone wants to give their children a higher education than he or she had'. A cashier felt, 'Parents are becoming more enlightened and realise children need training', while a young technician believed that, 'Nobody can neglect the education and appearance of a child as in former times'. A businessman, father of four children, said, 'Parents now feel obliged to set their children on their feet when they grow up, so they are prepared for professions or business when young'. Education is certainly costly, as was pointed out by a polygynously married businessman with five children when he said, 'Children are now better prepared for their future life and it is expensive to do this'. On the other hand, as will be discussed later, education is an investment from which there may be returns. A woman teacher, married to another teacher, explained climbing expenditure, saying, 'Because people now see how good it is to look after children; they see that every good investment yields huge fruit'.

A somewhat smaller group commented generally on the changing expenditure pattern without making schooling costs their major theme. A civil servant's wife claimed, 'Families are buying more children's clothing and accessories, prices have increased. On the other hand parents are spending little on themselves and keep up with fewer family responsibilities in the absence of increased income'. One male teacher felt that, 'Parents now want their children to have the best of what they didn't get even', while another elaborated, 'There is a bigger amount, because children are now being fed on milk, not breast milk, pretty clothes are bought, medical attention is more frequently sought, and so on'. Again and again changing obligations were stressed. A radio programmer explained, 'Parents are obliged to buy many things for their children which were formerly not available or considered luxuries'. More detail was provided by an audit examiner, who said, 'Parents are obliged to provide their children with education, clothing, pocket money which all other responsible parents now do'. The same theme of responsibility appeared in the reply of a shopkeeper, who pointed out that, 'No responsible person can allow his children to go naked as in former times'.

Finally, inflation was frequently mentioned, a phenomenon incidentally which makes people conscious of expenditure patterns which they might otherwise have taken for granted. Often the view was expressed that rising prices should not be allowed an easy victory. A young seamstress, monogamously married to an old man believed to be fifty years her senior and comfortably off because of his income from farms and other property, maintained that, 'Prices are very high these days, but civilisation demands that people should live comfortably'.

The Impact of Schooling

Preliminary investigations had shown the key role that schooling costs played in making urban elite parents, and almost certainly others as well, conscious of the problems of the large family. The main survey substantiated this. Accordingly specific questions were framed to probe the matter.

The 1948 Census revealed that 5½ per cent of the population over ten years of age had reached at least Standard III at school. By 1960 25 per cent had done so. In the former year 164,000 people over ten years of age had either been at school or were still there. By the latter year this number had swollen almost sevenfold to well over a million, and in the population of all ages was nearing one-and-a-half million. By 1960 two-thirds of the children, 6–14 years of age, in Accra were at school, and in the country as a whole the fraction did not fall below two-fifths. The education of girls still lagged but there had been relative improvement in the preceding twelve years. The post-war period has witnessed a startling educational revolution, and it is the very speed of the process which has made parents so conscious of where their extra money is going (Hurd, 1967).

Table 6:3 shows that in each age group about one-and-a-half times as many children were being kept at school in 1960 in the four towns as in Ghana as a whole. For comparison with the general urban figures, Osu, Kokomlemle, and Adabraka in Accra have been chosen. All are solid middle-class to upper-middle-class suburbs (assuming that 'class' is meaningful in the Ghanaian context), following in the socio-economic scale the very elite suburbs where the British administrators used to live (see Appendix). Osu is probably marked by a net inflow of children into boarding schools, but the other two suburbs may well have a net outflow at least of the children of the elite at secondary school age. It can be seen that in these three Accra suburbs school attendance rates were one-and-a-half to twice those found in the country as a whole. In the 6–14 age range between two-thirds and four-fifths of all children were at school, and perhaps nearly all those of the urban elite, for, as discussed earlier, even the wealthier suburbs contain poorer people either in substandard houses or living as servants or sub-tenants in larger houses. What is particularly striking about the three suburbs is that from 70 to 90 per cent as many 15-year-old girls are at school as are boys of that age. The

TABLE 6:3   School attendance in Ghana, 1960

(a) Percentage of children at school in Ghana, the Four Towns and three Accra suburbs, by major age groups

Residential area	Age groups (years)*			
	6–11	12–14	15–19	20–24
Ghana	39	42	24	3
Four Towns†	61	60	33	5
Osu‡	81	78	46	5
Kokomlemle‡	71	64	35	6
Adabraka‡	70	64	33	5

(b) Examination of 15-year-old children

Residential area	Percentage at school		Sex-ratio of children at school§
	Boys	Girls	(males per hundred females)
Ghana	48	22	249
Four Towns†	62	38	162
Osu‡	82	60	110
Kokomlemle‡	63	37	124
Adabraka‡	60	39	143

* Age groups have been selected so as to approximate to various types in schooling in Ghana and elsewhere.
† Accra, Kumasi, Sekondi-Takoradi and Cape Coast Municipal Areas.
‡ Suburbs of Accra, as defined in *Special Report 'A'* on towns in 1960 Census.
§ Computed from enumerated numbers attending schools and not calculated by comparing percentages.
Source: 1960 Population of Ghana Census, Vol. III and *Special Report 'A'.*

attendance rates of children of this age must be accepted with caution because of the movement of considerable numbers of students from their home areas to boarding schools where they were frequently enumerated.

Table 6:3 demonstrates the very high school attendance rates in Ghana, the highest in tropical Africa. It also shows the high retentive power of the schools, so high indeed that there is a greater proportion of children in the country as a whole at school in the 12–14 age group than in the 6–11 group. This is not a sign that a decline in school enrolment has begun. To a slight degree it is probably more apparent than real in that advance in age statement to census enumerators has had some effect. It is largely a product of the fact that Ghanaians start school late, especially in rural areas far from schools, reaching maximum attendance (in 1960) only at eleven years of age, and of the fact that subsequent attendance, especially among the poor, is often intermittent. If insufficient money is available, a child will often leave school, only to return when relatives or others have found some money or when the child himself has earned some (Hurd, 1967, pp. 226–8; Caldwell, 1967a, p. 51).

There is in Ghana a respect for education and a determination to keep children at school despite fearful financial sacrifices that is astonishing to most Western observers. A survey of students in the University of

Ghana showed that 88 per cent of them had only been able to continue through secondary school because of assistance from relatives or other private individuals and that half continued to receive substantial outside help while at university (Caldwell, 1965). Parents formed over half of all named sources of financial support.

This educational fervour is not all misdirected sentimentality. Up to the present schooling has subsequently brought financial returns, as a result of the occupational success so achieved, greater than the initial investment in it. This position may not continue, for children are flooding through the schools at a faster rate than a developing economy is able to create jobs in its modern sector. Furthermore, there have been strong pressures on the educated to return the money invested in their education. Indeed the pattern has in fact been to return a substantial surplus. In another survey 70 per cent of aged persons in urban areas and 53 per cent in rural areas said that they had received more back from educational investment in their children than they had put in, compared with 18 per cent and 35 per cent respectively who said they had not, the balance being those who had made no such investments (Caldwell, 1966a). Two-fifths of all respondents averred that they had received a 'much greater' return. One should not overstate the 'financial bargain' side of such arrangements for much of the emotion involved is not overt and arises from the structure of obligations built into the Ghanaian family system. Thus, although 84 per cent of students at the University of Ghana expect when earning to help support relatives other than their own spouse and children, only 53 per cent of all students, and 60 per cent of those who had received considerable financial assistance, regarded these expenditures as the repayment of a moral debt. Furthermore, interviewers gained a strong impression, especially in the case of the female respondents, that the children of the urban elite felt less moral obligation and were in fact less likely to be giving much financial support to relatives beyond their own nuclear families. Admittedly, this might be largely a reflection of the fact that their parents were less in need of such assistance.

Finally, and briefly because we are here anticipating the respondents' own replies, why is schooling, fee-free at primary and middle school levels, expensive at all? In rural areas it results in at least the partial withdrawal of children from such economic activities as farming and from ancillary tasks like housework and the carrying of water and fuel. One investigation in the various rural areas of Ghana showed that children attending school do no more work than children five years younger who do not go to school. In the towns the position is different, but some withdrawal from petty trading and other activities does take place, largely because of a reduction in available labour time, but partly because of a greater disinclination of school-children to undertake such tasks. Then there are the direct costs of education. Day secondary schools do charge fees and boarding schools at all levels do so. Although a free textbook scheme had been announced at the time of the survey, it had not come into effect. School uniforms are also expensive. Preliminary investigations left no doubt that there were costs of a less obvious nature, arising primarily from the extra awareness that schooling imparts of possible means of consumption and a more intense feeling that one should enjoy some of these things.

Earlier interviews had shown that the whole question of the extra cost of school-children was not a simple one of merely having to pay more fees or buy uniforms. Much that was pertinent was bound up with the change that education had wrought on the place of children in the family, their parents' attitudes to them and their ability to exact expenditure other than school fees. Accordingly, the four questions set out in Tables 6:4 and 6:5 were asked, thus raising the more general problem first.

TABLE 6:4 Responses to the questions, 'Many more children are going to school now than used to be the case. (a) Do you think that this makes any difference to parents' attitudes to their children (i.e. do parents treat children who are going to school or have been to school differently than they treat children who did not go to school)?'

Response	Female survey (n = 331)		Male survey (n = 296)	
	No.	Per cent	No.	Per cent
Yes	198	60	178	60
No	108	32	96	33
Cannot tell, qualified response	13	4	13	4
No response	12	4	9	3
Total	331	100	296	100

If 'yes' for (a), '(b) What difference does it make?'*

All responses except 'yes' for (a)	133	40	118	40
'Yes' for (a):				
Educated children are treated better	155	47	157	53
Parents look down on illiterate children	24	7	104	35
Residual responses	9	3	4	1
No response	15	5	29	10

* Numbers total to more than survey numbers and percentages to more than 100 because some respondents gave two major responses.

There is little doubt that schooling does profoundly modify relations within the family. Only a third of respondents said that this was not so, and even many of this group went on to argue that it should not be so rather than was not so. Educated children achieve the same kind of advancement towards more equality with their parents that educated wives do in relation to their husbands. Thus, in the course of a generation or more the spread of schooling can profoundly alter the two most fundamental relationships within the biological family. Half of all respondents, and well over three-quarters of those who maintained that parental attitudes changed, agreed that educated children were treated better. Some respondents, curiously enough many more males than females, went on to make a second comment that parents look down on illiterate children, but others may have thought that this was already implied by the first response.

The supporting explanations given by respondents to explain or amplify their answers show just how deep differences and bitterness can go in a society suddenly divided by rapid educational changes into the educated and uneducated, literate and illiterate. Furthermore, only a small minority of parents protested about differential treatment for the educated and uneducated; most regarded it as inevitable and even desirable.

The differences in treatment spring basically from the fact that in a society where education has come to most children only very recently parents genuinely admire the prowess of the educated. A graduate teacher, married to a primary school teacher, noted, 'Those who attend schools are given special respect'. A civil servant explained, 'Parents are not ashamed to present children who have been to school to friends and visitors because of their neatness'—a neatness incidentally which has obviously been achieved only at a price. The benefits are not merely for external show, for in the words of a nurse, married to an accountant, 'School-children make the family more buoyant and lively and interesting'. There is substance in the pride. One woman school-teacher pointed out that, 'School-children's views are now respected when discussions are being held', and another that, 'The children are left to make decisions which otherwise would have to be made for them'. In fact these decisions do not always determine only their own actions. The wife of a businessman attested, 'Parents often seek advice from their educated children', and a woman teacher explained, 'Children who have been to school are sometimes consulted for advice but this would never be the case for an illiterate child'. Another reported, 'The educated child educates the helpful and willing uneducated parent, and there is greater understanding in the home'.

It was commonly agreed that many parents looked down upon their children who had not been to school. A railway storekeeper reported, 'Children who do not go to school are contemptuously treated', and a woman teacher felt, 'Some parents who are uneducated tend to serve their children who attend school and look down on those who do not go'.

This leads almost inevitably to differential treatment. The wife of a shopkeeper noted that, 'Those who do not go to school are made to do all the housework, whereas the school-children sit idly at home or attend school'. This was supported by the young wife of an old, polygynously married man, when she said, 'School-children are treated more tenderly and therefore all work is left for the uneducated'. One civil servant reported that children were 'more cherished when educated' and another that 'parents are more gentle to those who have been to school', while a businessman thought it sensible that 'they are valued more and hence parents are more liberal to them'. A woman school-teacher also took this very common view: 'They respect their [educated] children and treat them accordingly'. The wife of a clerk explained, 'It makes them more proud of the children and therefore more of their wants are met unlike the case where the children do not go to school'. There were a few protests, such as those voiced by a doctor's wife, 'Many parents give extra care to the school-going children; I personally feel it very bad'.

As the uneducated are less likely to be providing future assistance, they must work for their keep now, and in an urban area housework is an important part of such work. A clerk's wife said, 'The unfortunate children who do not go to school do all the housework'. School-children of course have less opportunity. A male school-teacher pointed out, 'The only chores these children can do is before they leave for school at 7 a.m.' But this is not the basic reason for the different work loads. An official in a party organisation reported, 'The non-school-goers slave at home; the school-goers usually do not do menial work', and a high official in the judicial system went further: 'The non-school-attender becomes the servant of his or her brothers and sisters attending school'. The mother of five children, herself still undertaking part-time farming, had found, 'Children who go to school do not want to work on farms, and so they are not made to'.

Such variations in treatment are not unnoticed by the children themselves. A woman teacher had noticed that, 'Those going to school are respected more, and this makes them look down upon the others not going to school', resulting, in the words of a clerk's wife, in 'enmity between the two sets'.

However, pride and joy are not the only emotions parents feel towards their school-going children. There are worries. School-children, partly because of their long absences from home and partly because they have learnt to be more sceptical of traditional restraints, can present control problems. Secondary schoolgirls, as we will note again later, may consort with men whom their parents would not approve and may endanger their successful education by becoming pregnant. A clerk with three children reported, 'They always try to keep those who attend school under proper control'. Furthermore, educated children might show less respect for traditional obligations, especially with a strengthening of ties within the nuclear family. A teacher, married to a businessman and mother of three children, stated, 'Parents now realise that after a child has left school he will use his earnings on his wife and children and not on them'.

Even in this discussion references were made frequently to the inevitability of greater spending on school-children. A post office official believed it natural for parents to be 'fond of children who go to school and spend lavishly on them'. One businessman reported, 'Parents trouble themselves about the appearance of those going to school', and another that 'they provide those who have been at school with many things which they would never buy for those who have never been to school'. Not all this expenditure is spontaneous. Many parents come to feel, not only that school-children expect more, but that they will be so resentful if they do not get it, that they may not give their parents some assistance from later earnings. There is often an element of apprehension in the better treatment of school-children.

The question of expenditure was pursued further, as is shown in Table 6:5. Five-sixths of male respondents and three-quarters of females asserted that schooling was an item in raising the cost of rearing children. The greater number of costs described were direct ones, compulsory fees and required uniforms, but associated extra clothing and pocket money needs were frequently mentioned. They must be dealt with here in one group because so many respondents listed them together, as if one followed from another. Smaller numbers specifically mentioned textbooks or writing

TABLE 6:5 Responses to the questions '(a) Does it (i.e. the fact that more children are now going to school) make any difference to the amount of money that has to be spent on children?'

Response	Female survey (n = 331)		Male survey (n = 296)	
	No.	Per cent	No.	Per cent
Yes	240	72	254	86
No	52	16	29	10
No response	39	12	13	4
Total	331	100	296	100

If 'yes' for (a), '(b) What is the extra money spent on?'*

All responses to (a) except 'yes'	91	28	42	14
Response to (a) 'yes':				
School uniforms and fees, other clothing, pocket money, etc.	174	53	181	61
Textbooks and writing materials	59	18	90	30
Luxuries, frivolities etc.	20	6	38	13

* Numbers total to more than survey numbers and percentages to more than 100 because some respondents gave two major responses.

materials, while only a minority insisted on labelling the kinds of extras desired by school-children as luxuries.

Interviewers did not receive the impression that the majority of respondents, who denied that school attendance was now raising costs, or who failed to answer the question, were in fact disputing that schooling was costly. Rather were they arguing that they were not now burdened by an extra load, because they were the kind of parents who would always have sent their children to school no matter what the sacrifice. Furthermore, this kind of somewhat illogical response was markedly commoner amongst female respondents. Sometimes the need for providing luxuries or even pocket money was illuminating. The wife of a civil servant, with four children, listed her expenses of this type as 'equipment for school, transport and a few pennies to persuade the children to go to school regularly'.

Living with Children

At all times during the research, both during preliminary investigations and in the main survey, frequent mention was made of such practices as eating with children or sleeping in the same room. Often they were used as indicators of whether a break had been made with traditional family ways or not.

This is an appropriate point to examine the matter more closely, for in one way it forms a bridge between the aspects of family life considered so far and those we are about to examine. Sleeping apart from children and eating with them can be used as indexes to measure the extent of change in family life and the degree to which the respondents' ways approximate to those towards which the urban elite seem to be moving. On the other hand the extent of privacy in husbands' and wives' sleeping arrangements can have a pronounced effect on the ease with which at least some family planning methods can be used. Thus the question has implications for the argument in the next two chapters.

In Table 6:6 it can be seen that the Ghanaian urban elite family still exhibits distinctive differences from the Western family described earlier. Just over a third of male respondents claimed to eat at the same time and in the same room as their children. This is a fair measure of the number of families where the parents and children sit down to eat together.

TABLE 6:6   Responses to the question, 'Do you eat meals with your children?'

Response	Female survey (n = 331)		Male survey (n = 296)	
	No.	Per cent	No.	Per cent
Yes	148	45	107	36
No	124	37	161	55
Qualified response, sometimes	7	2	1	0
No response	52	16	27	9
Total	331	100	296	100

The fact that nearly half the female respondents eat with their children is not evidence of discrepancies between the surveys but merely confirmation that in some families the children eat with their mothers but not fathers. Nevertheless, in probably half of all elite families the children eat with neither parent.

One sign of social change is that the question proved embarrassing to a surprisingly large number of respondents, who were forced to reply differently from the way they felt they ought to have replied or the way they thought university students might expect them to reply. This was the explanation for the high failure to respond to a simple factual question.

The question on sleeping with children evoked some of the same kind of embarrassment—a disinclination to agree that traditional ways were still being approximated—that was revealed by the preceding one. However, it does appear from Table 6:7 that a third of elite couples sleep with no children at all and over half with none above three years of age. This, as many respondents pointed out, does mark a break with the past. Only one in seven males admit to sleeping in the same room as any child over seven years of age, and even if nearly all those failing to respond in the two surveys are hiding such a condition, in fewer than a quarter of all families must parents sleep in the same room as any children except young ones.

Even where parents do sleep with children the average number is only two, and few sleep with more than three. Thus the pattern is not one of a single large family bedroom. Nor is it one where the mother is more likely to go to another room to sleep with her children, for the pattern

TABLE 6:7   Responses to the question, '(a) Do you sleep in the same room
as any of your children? If so, what are their ages?'

Response	Female survey (n = 331) No.	Female survey (n = 331) Per cent	Male survey (n = 296) No.	Male survey (n = 296) Per cent
No	125	38	101	34
Yes:				
Only babies and infants under 3 years	71	21	59	20
One or more children 3–6 years (and possibly younger ones)	55	17	67	23
One or more children 7 or more years (and possibly younger ones)	25	8	42	14
No response	55	16	27	9
Total	331	100	296	100

if 'yes' for (a), '(b) How many of them?

All responses to (a) except 'yes'	180	54	128	43
Response to (a) 'yes':				
One	72	22	67	23
Two	47	14	57	19
Three	16	5	29	10
Four or more	16	5	15	5
Total	331	100	296	100

Average   number   of   children   sleeping   in   same   room   as
respondents

	Female survey	Male survey
All respondents	0·9	1·1
All respondents claiming to sleep in same room as any children	2·0	2·0

of female and male responses does not significantly differ except in the
cases of failure to reply and sleeping with older children. Interviewers
suspected that these categories overlapped and that the real difference
was largely one of greater male candour.

Summary

One aspect of social modernisation, or at least of partial social Westernisation, is the relative improvement in the status within the family of wives
and children. Such improvements probably increase the proportion of
both emotion and expenditure that is concentrated within the nuclear
family and this increase in turn strengthens the tendencies towards change
from traditional patterns. Such movements are related to the spread of
education, and the interrelation is complex and ramifying.

The balance within the urban elite family in Ghana has moved rapidly and significantly. Children are securing more parental attention and understanding and are certainly incurring a larger share of family expenditure. This expenditure itself buys them schooling and clothing which earns them more respect and more expenditure. The process can hardly be halted. The single greatest proponent of change is the spread of education, partly a political decision, partly a necessity if the process of economic development and the provision of adequate employment, especially urban employment, is to continue.

Table 6:8 shows that most of the Ghanaian elite are well aware of these changes. They are also aware of the social revolution which is being

TABLE 6:8   Summary of certain responses to questions on the growing needs of children

Response	Female survey (n = 331) Per cent	Male survey (n = 296) Per cent
A bigger fraction of income is being spent on children	94	93
Sending children to school affects expenditure	72	86
Respondents treat their children differently from the way they themselves were treated as children	61	77
Parents treat children going to school differently from those who did not go	60	60
Respondents do not sleep in same room as any children over 3 years	59	54
Respondents do not sleep in the same room as any children	38	34
Respondents eat with children	45	36

achieved by the spread of schooling facilities. Such a rapid revolution can be searing, and some of the effects manifested during the transitional period to universal education within both individual families and the society as a whole are disquieting, but such manifestations are probably the best guarantee that the society will insist that the process must continue until the goal of universal education is reached.

Growing expenditure upon children is causing strain among the families of the urban elite. This growth in expenditure is not a product of increased family size. The respondents almost certainly had had fewer children than their parents, and were probably even rearing fewer surviving children. The rising costs of children comes from a change in attitudes and living patterns. The children of well-off persons living in the major towns should go to school, be reasonably well dressed, be regularly fed, and their health should be adequately cared for. Some of these feelings arise from urban residence and the sheer march of time, but there are other factors. Communication between spouses and between parents and children is improving. The children, especially the educated ones, can exert pressure to see that at least some of their wants are satisfied. The urban elite are aware of the living standards which their children have enjoyed and of the prolonged education they will need to ensure that they can secure the kind of job necessary to guarantee the same level of living during their adult life. Indeed, most parents assume, almost certainly correctly, that even more education will be needed to achieve such occupational success in the years ahead.

Thus large families, even though average family size may have declined somewhat, are giving rise to increasing, or at least increasingly felt, economic pressures. In some countries such pressures have led to attempts to reduce family size and eventually to success in this objective. Family size fell in the late nineteenth century in countries of north-western and central Europe and English-speaking countries of overseas European settlement. One of the pressures in these countries at the time was the spread of universal schooling. Initially, the most marked reduction in family size was amongst the wealthy of the towns.

The same pattern may not be repeated in Ghana. Nor may the critical social changes necessary to achieve a falling birth rate operate for a long time to come. But this can to some extent be tested. It is possible to discover whether the better-off urban families have found that rearing children is increasingly expensive. That they have we have already established. It is also possible to find whether they have tried to limit the size of their families, if these attempts have been successful, and whether such attempts are likely to occur on a greater scale in the future. The next two chapters examine these matters.

7

Pregnancy: Occurrence and Prevention

The Childless

Being pregnant has traditionally been a common condition of Ghanaian women. In the twenty-five year span from some age between 15 and 20 years to perhaps something over 40 years they have on average spent over five years in pregnancy and ten to fifteen years or even more in a pregnant or post-pregnant condition which prevented conception.

This is not the case in most economically developed countries, where women on average give birth to fewer than half the children borne by Ghanaian women. However, such small families have only become a normal pattern during the course of the last eighty or ninety years. During that time birth rates have been reduced in the richer countries by women spacing pregnancies further apart and becoming pregnant for the last time at an earlier age. The failure of some women to bear any children at all has played a role in reducing birth rates; thus, in the United States 10 per cent of women, 45–49 years of age, had borne no children in 1910, while the proportion had risen to 16 per cent by 1955 (Freedman et al., 1959, p. 5).

Accordingly, there was some point in inquiring of the survey respondents about childlessness and its cause. Three questions covering the matter are set out in Table 7:1.

The number of female respondents eligible to reply to question (a) in Table 7:1 was the same as those previously reporting no live births, but in the male survey the number was slightly smaller because of respondents currently married to an infecund wife although they had fathered children by some woman.

The survey found that 7 per cent of urban elite women were biologically infecund,* a figure which evidence from elsewhere suggests is probably about what could be expected. The lower male figure apparently arises from several causes. A childless male will usually look for another wife, either to supplement or replace his sterile one. A few husbands seemed to the interviewers to be optimistically explaining quite lengthy periods of sterility in second wives as due to insufficient time since marriage. Finally, we did hear it rumoured that a childless wife, who suspects the cause might lie with her husband, will sometimes seek secretly to become pregnant by some other man.

---

* In the following discussion the biological ability to bear children is referred to as 'fecundity' and the inability as 'infecundity'. Childlessness, regardless of cause, is described as 'sterility', while those who are biological parents are described as 'fertile'.

115

TABLE 7:1   Responses to the questions, '(a) Why have you/your wife not had a baby?'*

Response	Female survey (n = 331)		Male survey (n = 296)	
	No.	Per cent	No.	Per cent
Respondent ineligible (a birth has been reported)	289	87	268	90
Respondent eligible:				
Insufficient time since marriage	14	4	14	5
Cannot tell, apparent infecundity	24	7	6	2
Intentional sterility (family planning etc.)	2	1	6	2
No response	2	1	2	1
Total	331	100	296	100

'(b) Would you like/like her to have one?'*

Respondent ineligible	289	87	268	90
Respondent eligible:				
Yes	36	11	23	8
No	2†	1	4	1
No response	4	1	1	1
Total	331	100	296	100

'(c) What have you done to try to make it possible to have a baby?'‡

Respondent ineligible	303	91	286	97
Respondent eligible:				
Medical treatment, unspecified or both Western and indigenous	9	3	2	1
Medical treatment, Western only	12	4	1	0
Medical treatment, indigenous only	0	0	0	0
No response	7	2	7	2
Total	331	100	296	100

* Asked only where a female respondent or a wife of a male respondent has not had a birth.
† Includes one very qualified response.
‡ Asked of respondents replying 'yes' for (b) and not replying 'insufficient time' for (a).

There seems to be fairly conclusive evidence that the great majority of even those respondents who claim to have employed family planning methods have not done so in order to remain childless either throughout married life or for a substantial time after marriage. The latter aim was reported by a handful of respondents. A typist, who had been married to a teacher for three years, both of them Protestants, attributed her lack of children to the practice of contraception, necessary, she said, 'Because I want to work for some time'. The desire to have no children at any time was reported by only 1 per cent of the respondents in each survey, and the suspicion remained that several of these persons believed their current marriage to be infecund and really meant that they would prefer to remain childless rather than break up the marriage, especially as there could be no guarantee that the new marriage would prove fruitful.

Infecundity is regarded in Ghana as a very serious problem, both because it leaves married couples without children and because it threatens the stability of marriages. Thus, three-quarters of the female respondents who were almost certainly infecund admitted to having sought treatment. In addition several of those not responding had probably employed indigenous treatments only and were diffident about saying so to university interviewers. Some of the male respondents were genuinely uncertain whether their wives had been treated. Many of the sterile wives talked seriously and at great length about their childlessness, sometimes treating the interviewers, somewhat to their surprise, as close and understanding confidants if not as confessors. Certainly every avenue of cure had often been investigated. The 33-year-old wife of a pharmacist explained, 'I have been to Germany for medical treatment, but I have not as yet had one'. Although more faith may be pinned by the elite on modern medical techniques, infecund women are likely to try traditional methods as well. It is the very great provision for traditional treatment that serves as a measure of the horror of childlessness. Every fetish shrine has a section, often an important one, set aside for treatment, and here, as elsewhere, traditional religion and traditional medical practice blend. A common type of response was that of the wife of an army officer. She had been educated to beyond secondary school level, and had since participated in a childless, monogamous marriage for over five years. Her story was, 'I have been to a gynaecologist and a fetish priest with no success'. Often less moderation was shown. The wife of a sales manager complained after nine sterile years of marriage, 'I have seen so many surgeons and fetish priests'.

Attitudes to Pregnancy

Attitudes to pregnancy are likely to vary according to whether wives are pregnant at the time of interview or not. With this in mind, female respondents were first asked, as shown in Table 7:2, whether they were pregnant, and male respondents were asked whether any wife was pregnant. One-sixth of female respondents agreed that they were. There is certainly no evidence from this figure of the beginning of fertility decline. If all these pregnancies were to result in live births, the incidence of pregnancy taken together with the age distribution of the respondents would imply a total fertility rate (i.e. approximately the size of the completed family in conditions of unchanging fertility) of about seven. This is close to the national rate and above the urban one. The extra margin of pregnancies reported by male respondents of their wives above that reported by female respondents is the exact amount one would expect from the incidence of polygyny.

TABLE 7:2   Responses to the questions, '(a) Are you/any of your wives pregnant (i.e. having a baby) now?'

Response	Female survey (n = 331)		Male survey (n = 296)	
	No.	Per cent	No.	Per cent
Yes	55	17	63	21
No	257	77	214	72
No response	19	6	19	7
Total	331	100	296	100
If 'yes' for (a), '(b) Are you pleased?'				
All responses to (a) except 'yes'	276	83	233	79
Response to (b) 'yes':				
Yes	51	16	54	18
No	4	1	9	3
Total	331	100	296	100
If 'no' for (a), '(c) Would you like (her/them) to be pregnant?'				
All responses to (a) except 'no'	74	23	82	28
Response to (b) 'no':				
Yes	93	28	77	26
No	146	44	121	41
Not certain, don't know, qualified	3	1	5	2
No response	15	4	11	3
Total	331	100	296	100

Note: In Tables 7:2 and 7:3 percentages have been made to total 100, and this accounts for apparent differences of 1 per cent in places between these figures and those published in Caldwell, 1966b.

Once the wife is pregnant, few Ghanaians are regretful. Only one pregnant female respondent in fourteen was not pleased about her condition and even amongst male respondents the proportion did not rise above one in seven. The proportions are almost certainly very low compared with the position in the contemporary West.

This cannot be accepted as it stands as evidence of a continuing maximum fertility tradition. At the most it is a reluctance to curse fate. For, in each survey in the case where the wife was definitely not pregnant, only 36 per cent of respondents would wish it otherwise while 57 per cent were satisfied that pregnancy should for the time being at least not occur.

Sometimes the desire not to become pregnant in the immediate future was explained in terms of family plans. A civil servant's wife married for fourteen months and with a young baby, desired her next child 'after my baby is at least one year old'. A lithographic assistant, father of one child, felt, 'I would like her to be pregnant at a time suitable to us'.

It is possible to summarise these responses, as in Table 7:3, in terms either of satisfaction with the existing condition or of desire for pregnancy. Thus, of the eight-ninths of respondents who replied to all questions, two-thirds were satisfied and one-third were not. The greatest source of dissatisfaction arises from the absence of pregnancy and not from its presence. However, only half the respondents did in fact desire pregnancy at the

TABLE 7:3   Satisfaction with condition of pregnancy or desire for pregnancy
(a) Percentage of respondents satisfied with existing condition

Respondents	Female survey	Male survey
Where pregnancy exists:		
Satisfied	16	18
Dissatisfied	1	3
Where pregnancy does not exist:		
Satisfied	44	41
Dissatisfied	28	26
Residual (i.e. no definite response at some stage)	11	12
Total	100	100
Summary:		
Satisfied respondents	60	59
Dissatisfied respondents	29	29
Residual	11	12
Total	100	100

(b) Percentage of respondents desiring pregnancy

	Female survey	Male survey
Where pregnancy exists:		
Desiring pregnancy	16	18
Not desiring pregnancy	1	3
Where pregnancy does not exist:		
Desiring pregnancy	28	26
Not desiring pregnancy	44	41
Residual (i.e. no definite response at some stage)	11	12
Total	100	100
Summary:		
Desiring pregnancy	44	44
Not desiring pregnancy	45	44
Residual	11	12
Total	100	100

time of the survey, and even this number was raised to this point by the large number of persons who accepted pregnancy as desirable when it occurred even though many of them almost certainly did not desire it before its occurrence.

The Deferment of Pregnancy

If over half of couples where pregnancy does not at any given time exist do not wish it to occur in the immediate future, is there any evidence of steps taken successfully to defer pregnancies? To test this respondents were asked, as shown in Table 7:4, to calculate the longest period between pregnancies in their marriage and to account for the length of this period.

TABLE 7:4   Responses to the questions, '(a) What is the longest time that has passed between any of your/your wife's (wives') pregnancies?'

	Female survey (n = 331)		Male survey (n = 296)	
Response	*No.*	*Per cent*	*No.*	*Per cent*
One year or less	14	4	11	4
Two years	75	23	81	27
Three years	61	19	55	19
Four years	26	8	18	6
Five or six years	14	4	15	5
Seven years or more	7	2	9	3
Not applicable because respondent or wives have had less than two pregnancies	77	23	51	17
No response	57	17	56	19
Total	331	100	296	100

'(b) Why was it so long?'

	Female survey		Male survey	
Responses not analysed:				
No response to (a) or not applicable	134	41	107	36
Response to (a) but not to (b)	4	1	1	0
No period between pregnancies of 3 years or more	88	27	92	31
Responses analysed (in all cases at least one period between pregnancies of 3 years or more):				
Don't know, just no pregnancy	40	12	36	12
Separated from spouse, no spouse at the time	27	8	14	5
Ill-health	21	6	18	6
Family planning—contraception etc.	13	4	22	8
Family planning — indigenous methods or *coitus interruptus*	2	1	0	0
Family planning—not sleeping together	1	0	5	2
Family planning—abortion	1	0	1	0
Total	331	100	296	100

In about a fifth of cases the question was not really relevant because the female respondents or the wives of the male respondents had not yet had two successive pregnancies. The case has already been investigated where this itself may be the result of deliberate action. In the remaining cases the exercise was difficult, and it is not surprising that another fifth of the respondents felt incapable of calculating the period. Few respondents had borne babies every year, but even without restricting births this is rare. A teacher, with three children after five years of marriage, pointed out, 'It is normal for women to give birth at two-year intervals'. And, in fact, only a third of the respondents in each survey, or about half those responding, claimed to have passed even once a period of three years or more without a pregnancy. Of those respondents who replied, the great majority have had a pregnancy about every two years, with the interval sometimes being a little shorter and occasionally rising towards three years. Perhaps an even higher proportion of those who failed to respond follow this pattern. This does not mean that they are likely to have eleven children between say 22 and 44 years of age for the inter-pregnancy interval tends to lengthen in the later years of the reproductive span. Those who had gone three years or more between pregnancies for no apparent reason were in general the older respondents.

It was quite clear from the respondents' observations that a period of two years between pregnancies was quite normal and hence could in no cases be taken as evidence of successful interference with conception. Thus examination was necessarily confined to the third of the respondents in each survey who calculated that at least one pair of successive pregnancies had been separated by three years or more.

In about two-fifths of these cases the evidence was that the gap between pregnancies was just an unusually long natural one for which respondents could provide no explanation. In other cases spouses had been away, or there had been a gap between marriages in a pattern of unstable marriages.

Ill-health was mentioned by a number of respondents, and in some cases even repeated questioning failed to ascertain whether it was supposed to lead to infecundity or a reduced level of sexual relations. The 43-year-old wife of a teacher who had borne his seven children explained, 'Because I was sick and thought I had come to my menopause'. Certainly, it seemed sometimes to be assumed that a husband's absence or a restriction of sexual intercourse followed on ill-health. A teacher, wife of an engineer, said of a four-year interval, 'It was because of ill-health and the absence of my husband'. An illiterate petty trader related, 'There was some abdominal trouble that demanded medical care', presumably having learnt the term 'abdominal' as a result of the trouble.

The view had apparently long been held in the society that a further pregnancy quickly following a birth could easily jeopardise the safety of the baby especially by reducing at an early stage the amount of breast milk available for feeding. This is certainly more the case in village society than it is amongst the urban elite. However, amongst the latter the point was often mentioned, serving less as an explanation of pregnancy post-ponement than as a justification of why such postponement had been attempted. The wife of one civil servant said, 'In order to devote more time to the caring of the children', and the wife of another, 'So that the baby grows up stronger'. Sometimes such precautions were related to the ill-health of a wife after pregnancy, a high civil servant saying, 'Because of the ill-health of my wife and the desire by us to postpone another pregnancy', and sometimes to the sickness of the baby, a clerk reporting, 'The child took a long time to walk and my wife had to look after him'. A technician felt, 'There should be enough time for the first child to grow well'.

For these reasons or others 5 per cent of the female respondents and 9 per cent of the males claimed to have employed deliberately some method with sufficient success to postpone pregnancy by three or more years. Part of the reason for the difference between the two surveys was that polygynous males were often having no sexual relations or only irregular ones with a wife other than the one in his urban elite household, the former being the kind of wife unlikely to be reached by the female survey. These respondents form only a small fraction of those who claim to have used some method of family planning, and are a testimony to the low rate of success of such methods. In fact they amount to only one-seventh and two-sevenths respectively of the female and male respondents who claim to know and have used a method for preventing or deferring pregnancy. They also form an equally small proportion of respondents claiming at least one inter-pregnancy gap of three years or more, again amounting to one-seventh and two-sevenths respectively of such persons in the female and male surveys. Of those methods which achieved success, modern family planning methods made up over four-fifths of the cited cases in each survey.

The Prevention of Pregnancy

(a) Knowledge

Amongst the urban elite some knowledge of family planning methods is much more widespread than the preceding examination of its successful use might indicate. Thus Table 7:5 reveals that more than half the respondents in each survey claim to know some method and almost as many can name some recognised method if answers such as 'contraceptives', 'family planning', 'things that can be bought from the chemist', and the like are accepted as establishing the point.

The major determinants of knowledge of contraception are education and background. The former showed significant association with such knowledge in both surveys (at 1 per cent) and the latter in the case of the male survey (at 1 per cent) and just failed in the female survey. Table 7:6 shows that, whereas fewer than half of the respondents with middle school or lesser education knew of any way of preventing pregnancy almost two-thirds of those with more advanced education did. In fact four-fifths of males who had been to university knew some method. The small margin between female respondents with training beyond middle school but lacking university education and those who did experience the latter can probably be partly explained by the large number of nurses in the former group. Urban background also played a role, for appreciably more respondents of urban than of rural birth knew something about family planning.

TABLE 7:5 Responses to the questions, 'Some people know a way to stop themselves/their wives having a baby (i.e. becoming pregnant), (a) Do you know a way?'

Response	Female survey (n = 331) No.*	Per cent*	Male survey (n = 296) No.*	Per cent*
Yes	172	52	163	55
No	146	44	126	43
Qualified response	2	1	0	0
No response	11	3	7	2
Total	331	100	296	100

'(b) What is the way?' (asked of respondents answering (a) 'yes')

	Female No.	Per cent	Male No.	Per cent
All responses to (a) except 'yes'	159	48	133	45
Response to (a) 'yes': Contraceptives, family planning, materials from the chemist, etc.	138	42	116	39
Condoms	12	4	5	2
Tablets (i.e. foaming tablets)	8	2	5	2
Jellies	0	0	2	1
Diaphragm	1	0	0	0
Rhythm	12	4	19	6
Coitus interruptus	4	1	0	0
Indigenous medicines	4	1	0	0
Not sleeping together	5	2	14	5
Sterilisation	0	0	10	3
Abortion	0	0	6	2
No response	2	1	0	0

* Numbers add to more than survey numbers and percentages to more than 100 because in some cases two answers were given.

TABLE 7:6 Percentage of respondents claiming knowledge of some method of preventing pregnancy, by education and birthplace

Survey	Highest level of education			Birthplace	
	Middle school or less	Above middle school*	University	Small town or village†	City or big town
Female	44	65	67	46	56
Male	48	62	78	50	65

* Includes university, although this category is also shown separately.
† I.e. rural.

The role of religion and age was far less clear. Religion showed significant association (at 5 per cent) only in the female survey, where 57 per cent of Protestants knew of a method compared with only 41 per cent of Catholics. Age just failed to show significant association (at 5 per cent) in the female survey, where the older females appeared more likely to have heard of a method, perhaps because they and their friends were faced by greater problems. Thus 57 per cent of women over 30 years of age had heard of a method compared with only 46 per cent of younger women. The gap becomes even greater if the effect of education is removed by standardising it for age. Age, like religion, appeared to play no equivalent role amongst males.

Knowledge of some method of preventing pregnancies is surprisingly widespread, being claimed by slightly over half the respondents in each survey. Furthermore, in a society which has been traditionally orientated towards very high fertility, knowledge of indigenous methods of contraception is rare. Where methods were known they were almost always modern methods. Respondents agreed on this point. The wife of an army officer felt that knowledge was extensive 'especially among young men and women', although, as we have seen, the evidence does not seem to bear her out on the last point. A pharmacist and his wife, the latter having been included in the female sample, claimed from their own experiences that 'a lot of women in Ghana use contraceptives'.

The large number of respondents merely answering 'contraceptives' or 'family planning' rendered the examination of the responses according to the respondents' backgrounds hazardous. The only data which appeared to present some pattern were responses according to education. This analysis showed an even greater preponderance of the more educated naming specific means of contraception, which implies that the gap between the more and less educated in terms of knowledge might be even greater than that set out in Table 7:6. The analysis also revealed two-and-a-half times as many lesser educated respondents employing either indigenous methods or continence as did the more educated, but these proportions were exactly reversed for the use of rhythm methods.

It is possible that the large 'Contraceptives, family planning, materials from the chemist etc.', section in Table 7:5 can be largely broken up into condoms, foaming tablets, and jellies, the only contraceptives which in 1963 apparently came into the country under the import control regulations, probably in that order of frequency as is suggested by the specific answers. It has been suggested to the writer that the purchases from the chemist also include various patent medicines, labelled as being for 'feminine hygiene', which have been manufactured in England for a century or more (D. I. Pool, personal communication). Diaphragms have to date been little used.

Respondents frequently coupled replies by saying one can use contraceptives or alternatively not sleep together either all the time or periodically. Various attempts at continence were reported. An accountant's wife in her early thirties, already the mother of three children, reported, 'I don't have sexual intercourse'. She said abstention had worked at an earlier stage of her marriage for three years and soon after resuming sexual relations she had borne twins. She had since refrained from sexual relations but would certainly 'use a better method from a doctor or clinic' if told how. A teacher, wife of a scientific technician, said women could prevent pregnancy 'by not being together with their husbands, but I will not use this method again as my husband doesn't approve'. A storekeeper replied, 'Yes, refrain from sex, but also contraceptives'.

Rhythm methods were frequently mentioned, proportionately no more by Catholics than their numbers in the surveys. A bar-keeper's wife, in her early forties and mother of eight children, said that pregnancy could be prevented by going without sex 'two weeks after the menstrual period. Occasionally it does not work, but I will use it in future—it is a widespread method—if a doctor told a better way I would use it'. Various husbands referred to the need for 'knowledge of one's wife's periods' and 'restraint at fertile periods'. A civil servant, with four children from his 28-year-old wife advocated 'refraining from sex at dangerous periods, but it didn't always work'.

Occasional references were made to operations on the womb, possibly occasionally to attempts to displace it, but at other times the responses were probably mistaken descriptions of sterilisation. A female teacher, married to an engineer, said, 'The womb is removed'.

(b) Action

Knowing a method of pregnancy prevention is not the same thing as employing it. In fact, when those who had stated a method of prevention were asked whether they had ever employed it, fewer than two-thirds of them in each survey said that they had. Thus, as shown in Table 7:7, one-third of all respondents in each survey claimed to have tried at some

TABLE 7:7 Responses to the question, 'Have you ever used it (i.e. the method named for preventing pregnancy)?'

Response	Female survey (n = 331)		Male survey (n = 296)	
	No.	Per cent	No.	Per cent
All responses in Table 7:5 except naming a method	159*	48*	133	45
Method named in Table 7:5:				
Yes	109	33	97	33
No	63	19	60	20
No response	0	0	6	2
Total	331	100	296	100

* Two respondents who did not name a method in Table 7:5 did answer this question and hence are not included in this figure.

time to prevent pregnancy. At the same time it should be recognised that this proportion is higher than speculation before the survey had suggested.

In each survey there was a clear association (significant at 1 per cent) between the use of methods for preventing pregnancy and both education and birthplace. This was not solely a product of the greater knowledge of methods for preventing pregnancy possessed by the more highly educated or those born in the larger towns. Table 7:6 showed that each of these groups was more likely to know about family planning, while Table 7:8 shows

TABLE 7:8 (a) Percentage of respondents claiming knowledge of method of preventing pregnancy who have ever used a method, and (b) Percentage of all respondents who have ever used a method, by education and birthplace

| Survey | Highest level of education | | | | Birthplace | | | |
| | Middle school or less | | Above middle school | | Small town or village | | City or big town | |
	(a)*	(b)*	(a)*	(b)*	(a)*	(b)*	(a)*	(b)*
Female	60	27	67	44	56	26	68	38
Male	51	24	66	41	53	26	65	42

* (a) and (b) are the two percentages of respondents described in the heading of the table.

that they are also more likely to act upon such knowledge. The combined effect of differentials in both knowledge and action is that whilst two-fifths of the better educated respondents are likely to have tried to prevent pregnancy only a quarter of those with lesser education are likely to have done so. Similar differentials separate respondents born in the cities and large towns from those of more rural origin.

The only other characteristic of respondents which apparently played a role was religion, and once again the relationships were more complex than those found when examining education and birthplace. It was seen earlier that only amongst female respondents were Catholics significantly less likely than Protestants to know about family planning. However, it is amongst male respondents, and such respondents only, that Catholics are significantly (at 5 per cent) less likely than Protestants to put such knowledge to use. The combined effect of these differentials is that more Protestants than Catholics are likely to be practising family planning. How-ever, the margin was appreciably greater in the female survey, a fact which prompted an examination of mixed Protestant-Catholic marriages. This

TABLE 7:9 (a) Percentage of respondents claiming knowledge of preventing pregnancy who have ever used a method, and (b) Percentage of all respondents who have ever used a method, by religion

| | Religion | | | |
| Survey | Protestant | | Catholic | |
	(a)*	(b)*	(a)*	(b)*
Female	64	38	47	19
Male	61	33	41	26

* (a) and (b) are the two percentages of respondents described in the heading of the table.

revealed that family planning was more likely to be employed by couples in such marriages when the wife was the Protestant than when she was the Catholic.

Sometimes a sex difference in replies occurred because, although a couple had used a contraceptive device, only one spouse had been responsible for its procurement and use. A radio mechanic said, 'I can't describe it, but she has used it'.

(c) Success

The respondents were asked, as shown in Table 7:10, whether the method for preventing pregnancies always worked. Two-thirds of those who had used a method claimed that it always had worked. Those claiming success made up about a fifth of the respondents in each survey. This can be

TABLE 7:10 Responses to the question, 'Did the method always work?'

Response	Female survey (n = 331)		Male survey (n = 296)	
	No.	Per cent	No.	Per cent
All respondents who had never used a method	219*	66*	194*	65*
Respondents who had used a method:				
Yes	72	22	62	21
No	37	11	38	13
Qualified, not certain	2	1	2	1
No response	1	0	0	0
Total	331	100	296	100

* The slight discrepancies between this table and Table 7:7 are explained by respondents who answered this question although they had failed to name a method for preventing pregnancy.

compared with the 5 per cent of female respondents and 9 per cent of males shown in Table 7:4 as having explained a gap of three years or more between pregnancies in terms of successful family planning. The difference is not necessarily attributable to excessive optimism. The 3-year test applied is severe, especially in the case of those younger respondents who might not at the time of the survey ever have desired such a long gap between their children.

One method of testing the apparent optimism was by asking whether the respondents intended to use the family planning method in the future. In fact this question was asked of all respondents claiming knowledge of a method for preventing pregnancy. The results, as shown in Table 7:11, contained some surprises.

In each survey, almost nine-tenths of all respondents who had ever employed a family planning method intended to use it again. Not only was this the case amongst nearly all those who claimed success for their method but even amongst the majority of those who admitted failure. The

TABLE 7:11   Responses to the question, 'Do you think that you will ever use this method in the future?'

Response	Female survey (n = 331)		Male survey (n = 296)	
	No.	Per cent	No.	Per cent
All respondents except those stating in Table 7:7 whether they had used a method known to them	159	48	139	47
Response in Table 7:7 'no':				
Yes	96	29	86	29
No	13	4	10	3
Not certain	0	0	1	0
Response in Table 7:7 'no':				
Yes	26	8	32	11
No	28	8	19	7
Don't know, not certain	6	2	4	1
No response	3	1	5	2
Total	331	100	296	100

general attitude was that of the bar-keeper's wife, quoted above, who preferred rhythm, with its occasional failings, to nothing at all.

More interesting still was the finding that half the respondents claiming knowledge of a method but not yet having employed it asserted that they would do so at some time in the future. Thus, 71 per cent of females and 73 per cent of males claiming knowledge of a method asserted either that they had already used it or intended to do so.

(d) Approval

There are two types of approval which are important in the use of family planning methods, that of one's spouse and that of the community.

The responses to the question about spouses' approval, set out in Table 7:12, are instructive. All but 18 per cent of females and 14 per cent of males claiming knowledge of a family planning method believe that they know what their spouses' attitudes to the use of such methods would be. Once again there is clear evidence of fairly open communication in such marriages. There is also strong evidence that the approval of spouses sets a ceiling on the likelihood of employing any means of family planning. One should, of course, be very cautious about placing too much faith in such data, for the responses may reflect the views of the respondents even more than those of their spouses. Nevertheless, it might be noted that the 122 female respondents who have either used family planning methods or anticipate their use at some time are the same 122 respondents who believe that their husbands would approve such methods. The position is very similar in the male survey. Eight respondents who did not expect approval from their wives anticipated using family planning methods, but they may have expected that such use would occur with subsequent wives or other women.

TABLE 7:12   Responses to the question, 'Would your husband/wife approve [of the use of a method for preventing pregnancy]?'

Response	Female survey (n = 331)		Male survey (n = 296)	
	No.	Per cent	No.	Per cent
All respondents except those stating in Table 7:5 that they knew a method of preventing pregnancy	159	48	133	45
Respondents knowing a method:				
Yes	122	37	126	43
No	22	7	14	5
Qualified, not sure, can't tell	20	6	10	3
No response	8	2	13	4
Total	331	100	296	100

Finally in this part of the interviewing, an attempt was made to see whether respondents, who knew about family planning methods or used them, felt isolated. Did they regard themselves as a very small, atypical group? The replies to the question in Table 7:13 showed that most respondents who knew a method for preventing pregnancy, and nearly all those who used such a method, felt that the use of family planning methods were reasonably common. Subsequent discussion revealed quite clearly that respondents were not under the impression that contraception extended far into rural Ghana or even down the social scale. Often, indeed, they referred to people learning such things from necessity while at secondary or middle schools. But they did not regard themselves as amongst a handful of persons practising family planning in Ghana, as some people consulted before the survey had supposed they would feel.

TABLE 7:13   Responses to the question, 'Do you think that there are many people in Ghana who now use such methods?'

Response	Female survey (n = 331)		Male survey (n = 296)	
	No.	Per cent	No.	Per cent
All respondents except those stating in Table 7:5 that they knew a method of preventing pregnancy	159	48	133	45
Respondents knowing a method:				
Yes	143	43	107	36
No	15	5	29	10
Qualified response	3	1	12	4
Not sure, cannot tell	10	3	13	4
No response	1	0	2	1
Total	331	100	296	100

More males than females qualified their original reply by defining the area of the population in which the use of family planning methods was reasonably well known. As noted before, this greater awareness of statistical truths or of the general nature of the population was a feature of male responses, perhaps arising from the administrative responsibilities experienced by many of the men.

Summary

Two things have been clearly established. The first is that family planning methods are more extensively known and even practised among the urban elite than many outsiders would have predicted. The second is that much of the family planning practice has not been very successful.

The urban elite are not, of course, typical Ghanaians (in rural surveys we even heard them described on occasion as 'black Europeans' and once as 'black whitemen', but their number is increasing rapidly. More importantly, they are important catalysts of cultural change. Many non-traditional aspects of living, which ten or twenty years ago were confined to a very small urban elite, are now found much more widely throughout the country.

Table 7:14 shows that the fact that most of the Ghanaian elite are still happy enough when pregnancy occurs is no longer a measure of their desire for pregnancy. Hardly more than a third of non-pregnant women or husbands of such women desired that pregnancy should take place. There is presumably a strong possibility that the remaining two-thirds will have some interest in methods for preventing or deferring pregnancy.

In fact over half of the respondents claimed knowledge of some method of preventing pregnancy and the proportion rose towards two-thirds amongst respondents with extended schooling or urban birth. Almost three-quarters of the respondents who knew of a method, forming two-fifths of all respondents, felt there was a certain respectability and normality about pregnancy prevention, in that they believed such practices were common, that their own spouses would approve, and that the methods would be practised within their own marriages if in fact they had not already been practised.

A third of the respondents had in fact already used such methods and the proportion rose to two-fifths amongst respondents with extended schooling or urban birth. Two-thirds of them, or a fifth of all respondents, claimed success in preventing pregnancy. The evidence, however, did little to bear out any contention of sustained success. The proportion of female respondents who were pregnant at the time of the survey did not suggest a level of fertility significantly below the Ghanaian norm, especially that found amongst town population. Although a third of respondents or their wives had passed at least one 3-year period between successive pregnancies, the evidence was that this was largely the result of chance or sub-fertility, the latter frequently associated with increasing age. In fact, only 5 per cent of female respondents and 9 per cent of males explained a gap of three or more years between pregnancies in terms of family planning, but some of those who explained the gap in terms of ill-health, may have meant that pregnancy was intentionally prevented in view of the wife's sickness.

TABLE 7:14 Summary of certain responses to questions on pregnancy occurrence and prevention

Response	Female survey (n = 331) Per cent	Male survey (n = 296) Per cent
Where pregnancy has occurred, proportion of respondents happy	93	86
Where pregnancy has not occurred, proportion of respondents with any reaction other than desiring pregnancy soon	64	64
Knowledge of a method of preventing pregnancy:		
All respondents	52	55
Respondents with education beyond middle school	65	62
Respondents born in city or big town	56	65
Knowledge of a method and belief that many people use such methods	43	36
Knowledge of a method and belief that spouses would approve use	37	43
Knowledge of a method and either have already used it or anticipate using it	37	40
Have used a method of preventing pregnancy:		
All respondents	33	33
Respondents with education beyond middle school	44	41
Respondents born in city or big town	38	42
Have passed at least one period of three years or more between pregnancies	33	33
Claim successful use of method preventing pregnancy	22	21
Passing of period of three years or more between pregnancies attributed to family planning	5	10
Desiring no children at all	1	1

Two findings have very significant implications for the future. One is that knowledge of family planning and its practice increases with education and urban birth. To some extent these two are interrelated, because the standards of education were somewhat higher amongst the urban-born, but, when responses were standardised so as to nullify this interrelation, both could still be shown to be potent factors. As the coming generation of parents contains a much higher proportion of highly educated and urban-born persons than was found amongst their parents' generation, it seems likely that the use of family planning will extend to a point where it does have a demonstrable effect in lowering the birth rate.

The other is that, at least among the elite, knowledge of methods of preventing pregnancy was very largely a knowledge of modern family planning methods. The evidence seems to be that high fertility has been accepted so much as a good thing in traditional Ghanaian culture and religion, arising doubtless largely as a response to the very high death rates of the past, that no widely known traditional methods of contraception have arisen. As will be seen later, there probably has been some abortion; but certainly amongst the urban elite, and probably amongst other groups, there has been no competition between indigenous and imported methods of birth control.

8

Family Planning

It was seen in the last chapter that a third of the respondents in each survey had employed a method which they believed would prevent pregnancy. Furthermore, two-thirds of these respondents claimed to have achieved success with their efforts.

Subsequently an effort was made to examine more closely the incidence of use of modern contraceptives. Table 8:1 confirms the earlier finding that the great majority of those who have tried to prevent pregnancy have used modern contraceptive methods for the purpose.

The Practice of Contraception

(a) The respondents

Just over a quarter of all respondents claim to purchase contraceptive materials from doctors or chemists. Moreover, nearly all respondents who had ever bought contraceptives claimed still to be doing so, although

TABLE 8:1 Responses to the question, 'Some people already get such materials (i.e. to prevent pregnancy) from doctors or chemists. Do you?'

Response	Female survey (n = 331) No.	Per cent	Male survey (n = 296) No.	Per cent
Yes	88	27	81	27
Not now, but at some time in the past	3	1	0	0
No	218	66	200	68
No response	22	6	15	5
Total	331	100	296	100

perhaps intermittently, at the time of the survey. Those who had temporarily stopped because of pregnancy or desire for pregnancy are included in the 'yes' responses.

The attempt to identify the users of contraceptives proved so fruitful that it is easier to begin by stating who they were not. No correlation existed between the number of children ever born to respondents, or indeed the number of those children still surviving, and the use of contraceptives. It is possible, of course, that there are tendencies here which neutralise each other when the data is presented in this way. In some cases large families may imply an aversion to contraception while in others they may provide the motive for the use of such methods.

The use of contraceptives is related to origin, circumstances, marital history, views on population growth, and desire to limit family size. Birth-place plays a role, at least partly because contraception is commoner in the towns, especially the larger centres, and those born there are more likely to be acquainted with it. They may even have parents, or more likely older brothers or sisters, who have practised it. The relation between town life and contraception was mentioned frequently. A typical, if rather more sophisticated, response to the subsequent question about whether many people in Ghana employed contraception was that of a barrister who said, 'Yes, in the urban areas but not in the rural ones'. Thus, while 29 per cent of town-born females used contraceptives only 23 per cent of those from the villages did so. The association with birth-place was even more striking in the male survey (significant at 1 per cent), almost certainly because husbands' attitudes are more decisive than are those of their wives in deciding whether contraception should be employed within the family. While only 18 per cent of males born in rural Ghana used contraceptives, 40 per cent of those originating in the towns did.

The part played by religion in making the use of contraception within the marriage possible was largely that suggested by earlier findings. The decision to use contraceptives is much more likely to depend on the views of the husband than those of the wife, but, where one partner is adamant that contraception should not be used because it contravenes religious teachings, that partner is much more likely to be the wife than the husband. Thus in both surveys the use of contraception was significantly associated with the wife's religion, but in neither case was it associated with the husband's religion. In each survey 32 per cent of Protestant wives were using contraceptives, while in the female survey only 11 per cent of Catholic wives and in the male survey 16 per cent of the husbands of Catholic wives said that they were using such family planning methods.

A more important determinant is education. The use of contraceptives increased with level of education in each survey (significant in each at 1 per cent). In each survey only 20 per cent of respondents with education not extending beyond middle school used them, while 36 per cent of those with more extended education did so.

Age and occupation do show some association with the use of contra-ceptives, but in each case this may largely reflect educational levels. Far more of the young have received extended education, and certainly the degree of education is strongly reflected in occupational success. Dividing the marriages into those where the wife was under 30 years of age and those where she was older, it might be noted that only in the male survey was the association statistically significant (at 5 per cent), 32 per cent of the younger couples using contraceptives compared with 22 per cent of the older ones.

Contraception was more widely practised with rise in the occupational scale, no matter whether the occupations of husbands, wives, or respon-dents' parents were examined. Just as the second generation urbanites are more likely to use contraceptives, so are those who were brought up in middle- or upper-class homes. Where the father was a 'white-collar' worker, a third of his children used contraceptives; where he was not, only a quarter of the children did so. Rather curiously, in each survey the strongest association with the use of contraceptives was with the spouses' occupation. The division was clearest in the female survey, where almost half the wives of men with 'white-collar' jobs claimed to practise contraception, compared with less than a quarter of the wives of men with lesser jobs.

The structure of the marriage strongly influences the use of contraceptives. They are most likely to be used in stable, monogamous, first marriages. There are statistically significant associations (at 1 per cent) not only between the practice of contraception and participation in both stable and monogamous marriages, as shown in Table 8:2, but also between its practice and the approval of such marriages. As observed before, male polygynists are much more likely to be traditionalist in outlook and opposed to innovation than are their wives, some of whom may well be participating in polygynous marriage without feeling the

TABLE 8:2 Percentage of respondents using contraceptives by type of marriage and marital history

	Percentage using contraceptives	
	Female survey (n = 331)	*Male survey* (n = 296)
Type of marriage:		
Monogamous	28	29
Polygynous	17	4
Marital history:		
Married once	29	31
Married more than once	8	19

slightest approval of the institution. However, the number of partners using contraceptives in polygynous marriages must approximately balance, whatever their views. The differences between percentages in the table arise partly from the small numbers of polygynous respondents, partly from a sex differential in the 'no response' rate, and partly from the difference noted before in what constitutes another 'wife'. The male respondents who agreed that they were polygynists were usually traditionalist indeed. The opposite may well be the case in unstable marriages, as gauged by repeated marriage and divorce or separation. Survey findings indicated that unstable marriage was more common amongst males, but marriages were perhaps most frequent amongst the smaller number of females who did undertake it. This group may differ most from the earnest wives attempting to hold together an existing marriage and rear their children to educational and occupational success. Some of them were certainly more akin to temporary mistresses. Yet the fact that only a quarter as many practised contraception as did the wives in stable marriages showed that the charge frequently heard that contraception is employed by women of loose morals to protect themselves from pregnancy may in Ghana be wide of the mark. The imbalance between the percentages using contraceptives in this case is not surprising and merely reflects a differential by sex in the incidence of instability.

Other aspects of family life are also important, especially the existence of a nuclear family, at least as measured by residential condition. In each survey a third of all couples, who lived with no other relatives except their own children, used contraceptives, while less than a quarter did so in households which included one or more other relatives. Similarly contraception was more likely to be employed by parents who took their children for outings. An existing pregnancy at the time of the survey showed no association with the usual use of contraceptives, perhaps a measure of the ineffectiveness of that use.

The use of contraceptives is strongly associated with personal philosophies about both the public and private weal and with attitudes towards pregnancy. For instance, of those respondents who believed that rapid population growth was a bad thing for the country, 37 per cent of the females and 51 per cent of the males used contraceptives compared with only 24 and 22 per cent respectively of those who held other views about such growth. Less than a sixth of respondents who felt that family size was decided largely by fate or God's will employed contraceptives but almost half of those disagreeing with this assertion used them.

As might be expected, a particularly close association could be shown with attitudes towards family limitation or even its consideration. Discussion between spouses of whether contraceptives should be used usually preceded such use, and in each survey almost half the couples who had ever discussed the matter had subsequently gone on to practise contraception. Nearly all respondents using contraceptives believed that family planning clinics should be established in Ghana and agreed that they would use them. However, only a third of those not using contraceptives were opposed to the setting up of clinics. In fact over half the non-users would expect to use such clinics, and described their present failure to practise contraception as arising primarily from the lack of knowledge or difficulty of obtaining the means.

When the analysis is extended further to include an examination of the interaction of the various characteristics of the respondents, a clearer appreciation is possible of the influence of both education and religion. Table 8:3 shows that the use of contraceptives continues to increase with more extended education in the case only of Protestant females. No Catholic female with secondary education or more admitted to their use. Furthermore, an examination of the schedules shows that it is precisely this group who do have strongest religious objections to contraception although in each cell of the table fewer Catholic than Protestant females use contraceptives. Their Catholicism is very much the kind met in the West, partly because most of them have received their secondary education in five elite schools, all but one boarding schools, with definite religious affiliations. There is no evidence of a similar reaction among males, where the usual West African pragmatism seems to have exerted itself.

(b) Others

However, in spite of this frequently described lack of knowledge, many more respondents know of at least someone who buys contraceptives

TABLE 8:3 Respondents purchasing contraceptives by sex, religion, and education*

| Sex | Religion | Education (highest level reached) | | | | | |
| | | Primary school† | | Middle school | | Secondary school or further | |
		No. in cell	Per cent purchasing	No. in cell	Per cent purchasing	No. in cell	Per cent purchasing
Female	Protestant	42	21	123	25	92	48
	Catholic	9	11	11	18	18	0
Male	Protestant	19	26	74	19	108	36
	Catholic	6	33	9	22	18	33

* Excludes 'no response' at any stage and other religious categories.
† Respondents with no schooling were combined with those with only primary schooling because their numbers fell below the minimum per cell we were willing to analyse.

than employ them themselves. This can be seen by comparing Tables 8:1 and 8:4. This margin is especially great in the case of women, for, although necessarily approximately the same number of wives practise contraception as husbands, considerably more women know someone who buys contraceptives. Women's talk more frequently touches on such matters than does men's.

TABLE 8:4 Responses to the questions '(a) Some people in Ghana already get such materials (i.e. contraceptives) from doctors or chemists. Do you know anyone who does?'

| Response | Female survey (n = 331) | | Male survey (n = 296) | |
	No.	Per cent	No.	Per cent
Yes	162	49	121	41
No	147	44	163	55
Very qualified response	3	1	2	1
No response	19	6	10	3
Total	331	100	296	100

'(b) Do you think many people in Ghana do?'

Yes	164	50	136	46
No	126	38	131	44
No response	41	12	29	10
Total	331	100	296	100

Evaluating the spread of contraception was for most respondents merely a case of knowing that they were used in one's own marriage or by one's friends. If they were, most respondents said that contraceptives were used by many people in Ghana. Comparatively few respondents who did not have personal knowledge of such use felt the practice to be at all widespread even amongst their own socio-economic group.

Some respondents qualified their replies. The most frequent qualifications were that contraceptives were used by townspeople and not villagers, by the educated or rich, by women who had been to secondary school or girls who were still there, by men who had been to university, and by prostitutes or women of loose morals. All assertions but the last are undoubtedly correct, and the last was not a matter which the surveys were competent to judge.

The Desire for Advice

While the survey was proceeding it became clear that there was a wide margin between the number of respondents who were practising family planning and those who claimed that they would like to do so. In order to measure this margin respondents were asked whether they would follow medical advice on contraception. Over half the female respondents and almost two-thirds of the males said that they would. In the case of females the proportion was double that of current users of contraceptives, and in the case of males double the proportion claiming to have used any method to prevent or postpone a pregnancy.

In addition a considerable number of respondents replied with a qualified 'yes'. Many more females than males did so, because considerably more answered along similar lines to the civil servant's wife with four children who said, 'Yes, if my husband is ready for it'. Apart from doubts about spouses' attitudes, most qualifications took the form of provisos about health or family size. One woman teacher said, 'On health grounds, yes—on other grounds, no', while another replied, 'If my life is in danger I will use it'. The daughter of a chief and wife of a civil servant answered, 'If it is not for health reasons, no'. But many more gave responses which were not fully explained such as, 'If it is necessary', or 'If the need arises', or 'If there is no alternative'. Some spoke in terms of expense, such as the wife of an army officer, who said, 'Our using of any new method depends on how much we can afford to spend'. Others spoke of the needs of some members of society only; a female clerk pointed out, 'Not all people would like to have children, and if they could be helped in this it would save many unwanted babies and will stop illegal abortions'.

However, the easy acceptance of hypothetical nostrums can hardly be equated with the real problems of everyday life, especially in the matter of family planning, for some forms of contraception can be awkward, inconvenient, and troublesome. To probe this, these problems were put to the respondents, and they were asked whether they would be prepared to accept complicated, troublesome methods. Probably we overstated the case, for the number who remained interested in family planning was reduced approximately to those respondents who were already practising contraception. This group remains the hard core, strongly motivated to limit family size; outside them is found an equally large group who could be interested if only matters were simple enough. In terms of the prediction of fertility change or of a transition to smaller sized families, this group must be regarded as marginal, although possibly subject to the effect of change in social attitudes, contraceptive technology, or the role of the

TABLE 8:5   Responses to the questions '(a) If you were told by a doctor some other way (or a better way) to avoid having a baby, would you use it?'

Response	Female survey (n = 331)		Male survey (n = 296)	
	No.	Per cent	No.	Per cent
Yes	180	54	192	65
Qualified yes	36	11	22	7
No	99	30	70	24
No response	16	5	12	4
Total	331	100	296	100

'(b) If it were complicated and took quite a lot of trouble, would you still use it?'

	Female survey (n = 331)		Male survey (n = 296)	
All responses to (a) except 'yes' or 'qualified yes'	115	35	82	28
Response to (a) 'yes' or 'qualified yes':				
Yes	77	23	86	29
Qualified yes	8	2	20	7
No	115	35	108	36
No response	16	5	0	0
Total	331	100	296	100

state in such matters. Some of them did question the degree of trouble. The young wife of a civil servant, mother of one child, said, 'If reasonable trouble, yes, but otherwise no'.

The analysis of this question in terms of the other characteristics of the respondents is in many ways more revealing than the examination of those actually using contraceptives. Between them the two questions

TABLE 8:6   Family planning practices and attitudes

	Female survey (n = 331) Per cent	Male survey (n = 296) Per cent
Respondents who have used a method for preventing pregnancy	33	33
Respondents who buy contraceptive materials	27	27
Respondents who would employ contraceptive method recommended by a doctor*	54	65
Respondents who would use recommended method even if complicated and troublesome*	23	29

* Includes only 'yes' responses and not 'qualified yes'.

provide a very clear insight into the process of family limitation in Ghana and likely future developments.

For instance, education, though significantly associated with the use of contraceptives in both surveys, is not so associated in either with willingness to use such methods. The chief effect of education in this regard is merely to increase the ability to cope with innovations, especially in a country where the government showed no enthusiasm for making access to such innovations easy. Perhaps education also led to a slightly greater interest in innovations and a reduction in apprehension of them, for in the female survey 65 per cent of respondents with education beyond middle school would use a method revealed by a doctor compared with 60 per cent of those with lesser education, while the comparative numbers in the male survey were 74 per cent and 70 per cent respectively.

Similarly, age and place of birth showed no significant association with readiness to use a method. The greater use of contraceptives by second generation urbanites arises largely from the experience and sophistication that town-rearing brings. Even with regard to this question, sophistication probably leaves a small margin between the groups, for 65 per cent of town-born females would follow such advice compared with 57 per cent of the village-born, comparative figures in the male survey being 75 per cent and 70 per cent.

Nor did pregnancy conditions result in a significant differential in answers, although where a pregnancy condition currently existed 67 per cent of females would accept advice compared with 60 per cent in the case of the non-pregnant, the margin falling to 75 per cent and 73 per cent in the case of males.

The effects of religion, family size, and marriage structure are rendered markedly clearer, for attitudes towards contraception are no longer obscured by the large numbers of respondents who favour family planning but do not know how to set about it.

Religion is significant in the case of both wives (at 1 per cent) and husbands (at 5 per cent). In the female survey 67 per cent of Protestant wives would accept such advice compared with only 46 per cent of Catholic wives. In the male survey the margin was smaller but it still stretched down from 75 per cent for Protestant husbands to 59 per cent for Catholic husbands.

Family size, measured either in terms of children ever born or of those surviving, is clearly positively related to willingness to use contraception amongst females (at 1 per cent) but not amongst males. Only a minority of childless women expect to be interested in contraception, but the number climbs to 59 per cent for all women with less than five children and to 69 per cent for those with larger families.

This analysis also confirms earlier suspicions that it is the husbands and not their wives in polygynous marriages who are the real traditionalists. There was a strong association (significant at 1 per cent) between monogamy and willingness to practise contraception amongst males, where three-quarters of those monogamously married would do so compared with less than half of those polygynously married. The corresponding figures for females were 62 per cent and 60 per cent and even that margin was explained solely in terms of greater caution about their husbands' views.

The same position held in the male survey with regard to stable marriage, where there was a significant association (at 1 per cent) between having been married only once and willingness to use family planning methods. Where respondents had not been divorced or separated almost four-fifths would use them, but amongst those exhibiting an unstable marriage pattern the fraction fell to three-fifths. Interestingly, this was not the case amongst female respondents. Fewer females experiencing successive marriages used contraceptives than the stably married but on the other hand more of them would like to, 72 per cent compared with 62 per cent of the women who had been married only once. Thus, even if contraceptives were not used to the extent stated, the desire to do so appears to be there.

If respondents are examined in terms of grouped characteristics, once again the most interesting pattern is that demonstrated by the interaction of education and religion, age playing no significant role. The pattern noted amongst females in the examination of the use of contraceptives is found again, but this time it can be detected amongst the male respondents as well. Desire to employ contraception increases amongst Protestants with education, but amongst Catholics there is a fall in the most educated, and perhaps 'most Catholic' groups; indeed the fall amongst males is continuous with increasing education. It is this interaction which partly explains the

TABLE 8:7 Respondents who would use a method told by a doctor for preventing pregnancy, by sex, religion, and education*

		Education (highest level reached)					
		Primary school		Middle school		Secondary school or further	
Sex	*Religion*	No. in cell	Per cent purchasing	No. in cell	Per cent purchasing	No. in cell	Per cent purchasing
Female	Protestant	40	60	123	65	92	74
	Catholic	6	50	13	54	18	44
Male	Protestant	19	63	73	80	108	80
	Catholic	4	75	7	71	18	56

* Excludes no responses at any stage and other religious categories.

lack of association between education and willingness to use family planning methods, but it should be noted that such willingness does not increase steeply even amongst Protestants.

The Cost of Children and of Contraception

Respondents frequently raised questions not only about the difficulty of contraception but also its cost. Those who were judged sufficiently serious about the question of pregnancy prevention, selected by their willingness to persevere even with complicated and troublesome methods, were questioned about cost along the following lines. 'It might cost quite a lot of money. What would be about the most money per month that you (or you and your husband/wife) would be prepared to spend on such things?'

In the female survey the median amount was just under £2 10s. with half the respondents suggesting amounts between 15s. and £5. In the male survey the median amount was about £1 5s. with half the respondents suggesting amounts between 15s. and £2 10s. The lower figures for male respondents probably arise largely from the fact that more males replied, thus making them a less selective and perhaps less desperate group. Whilst almost a quarter of all males were willing to use complicated and trouble-some methods for preventing pregnancy and to cite a maximum cost, only a little over a sixth of the females fell into this category. In each survey only about 4 per cent of all respondents either quoted amounts of about £5 or stated that they were prepared to spend any amount.

These amounts of money may be large in terms of the Ghanaian population as a whole, but in terms of whole families and more particularly of the urban elite they are not large. The median male figure probably amounted to a fifth of the national income per head at the time of the survey. The median male amount, £18 per annum, would be less than 2 per cent of the net family incomes of most of the respondents. The stated amounts may be depressed by attitudes towards medical costs in a country where much treatment is free or nearly so.

It is possible to argue that the cost of contraception either is or should be regarded as a substitute for the cost of rearing one or more extra children and hence that its limiting cost should bear some relation in the user's mind to the maintenance costs of children. Accordingly those respondents who had suggested a maximum cost for preventing pregnancy were further questioned about how much child-rearing cost at different ages.

Nearly all the respondents questioned on this point managed to estimate the cost of bringing children up, and most of them put a con-siderable amount of effort into constructing the estimates. On average, female respondents suggested higher figures than did the males, and perhaps were nearer the truth because in the great majority of cases it was the wives who were responsible for the housekeeping costs. In the female survey the median estimate for the monthly expenditure on a baby was just under £3 10s. and half of all respondents suggested amounts between £1 10s. and £4 10s. For a child of a few years of age the median was about £5 10s. and half of all estimates fell in the range from £3 10s. to £7 10s. Thus a baby might cost about 5 per cent of net family income and an older child about 8 per cent. In the male survey the median estimates for a baby and an older child were about £2 5s. and just under £4 respectively and the ranges into which half the estimates fell were £1 10s. to £4 10s. and £2 10s. to £5 respectively.

The theory that the most people are willing to spend on contraception bears some relation to the expense of child-rearing was well substantiated. A high correlation existed in both surveys between the two groups of answers, and as the estimated cost of child-rearing rose so did the maximum

TABLE 8:8   Median estimates of maximum desired expenditure per month on pregnancy prevention, cost of keeping a baby, and cost of keeping an older child*

	Female survey	Male survey
Maximum desired expenditure on pregnancy prevention	just under £2 10s.	about £1 5s.
Cost of keeping a baby	just under £3 10s.	about £2 5s.
Cost of keeping an older child	about £5 10s.	just under £4

* All money expressed in Ghanaian currency, at the time of the survey at par with sterling.

amount which might be spent on contraception. This might, of course, merely mean that the richer are willing to spend more on everything.

No support was received for the view that the amount which might be spent on contraception can be equated with the cost of rearing one, or even more than one, child. In the female survey the median amount which might be spent is little more than two-thirds the cost of a baby and less than half the cost of an older child, while in the male survey it is little over half the cost of a baby and about a third the cost of an older child.

On the other hand the respondents may well have been influenced by their knowledge of contraceptive costs, for the median amounts are sufficient to cover most contraceptive costs, even, in the case of the female survey, oral contraceptives.

The Discussion of Family Planning

Earlier it was suggested that little change in family size can be expected in society unless husbands and wives have begun to discuss that topic. One could go further and argue that little is likely to be done about the prevention or postponement of pregnancy unless that subject is one that can be discussed at least between spouses.

The findings from a series of questions probing into this matter are shown in Table 8:9. Over two-fifths of all elite couples have already discussed contraception. The fact that about nine-tenths of all these discussions have resulted in agreement demonstrates either the ease with which one spouse, probably the wife, gives in to the other or more likely that such discussions become possible when spouses sense from remarks or reactions that they are thinking along the same lines.

Furthermore, three-quarters of the respondents who had not discussed the prevention or postponement of pregnancy felt that they could do so. Many of them said that they would probably do so in due course. They are probably correct, for many of them still had small families at the time of the survey.

Ghanaian society is open and frank and most subjects can be discussed both within the bounds of family and outside. If a subject is not discussed it is less likely to be because of taboos than because the matter has never concerned the society and does not appear to be relevant. In parts of

TABLE 8:9 Responses to the questions: '(a) Have you ever discussed this kind of thing (the prevention or postponement of pregnancy) with your husband/wife?' If 'yes' for (a) '(b) Does he/she agree with you?' If 'no' for (a) '(c) Do you think you could discuss such things with him/her?'

Response	*Female survey* (n = 331)		*Male survey* (n = 296)	
	No.	*Per cent*	*No.*	*Per cent*
Yes:				
Agrees	121	37	119	40
Disagrees	13	4	8	3
Not sure or qualified	3	1	0	0
No response	1	0	0	0
No:				
Could discuss it	119	36	114	38
Could not discuss it	41	12	32	11
No response	5	2	2	1
No response	28	8	21	7
Total	331	100	296	100
Summary:				
All respondents who have discussed	138	42	127	43
All respondents who have not discussed	165	50	148	50

Ghana where most adults are still illiterate and where the usual form of livelihood is subsistence agriculture this is undoubtedly still the case with regard to contraception. The fact that less than an eighth of respondents felt that pregnancy prevention was a subject that could not be discussed within their marriage was certainly testimony to the ease of communication in the society and perhaps particularly amongst the urban elite.

The pattern of response is on the whole one which previous analysis has made familiar. Age seems to be of little importance; even amongst those who could not discuss the matter there is only a slightly greater proportion of older than younger couples. Nor is the number of children, either as measured by births or survivors. However, the position is somewhat different if attention is focused on the couples who could not discuss pregnancy prevention. In the female survey 16 per cent of those with five children or more could not discuss the matter compared with only 11 per cent of those with fewer children, while in the male survey the comparable proportions were 18 per cent and 7 per cent. Those with larger families may contain a larger number of traditionalists. At least part of the explanation of the larger families may be the inability to discuss or implement any form of birth control. Indeed, such respondents may exhibit the same level of fertility as traditional rural society.

Once again background is important. In both surveys almost half the town-born have talked about such matters, but discussions amongst the village-born fall to two-fifths in the male survey and a third in the female survey (significant at 1 per cent). More marked still is the rural-urban birth differential amongst those who could not discuss such matters. Where the husband comes from a village failure to discuss is up to one-and-a-half times more likely than when he comes from a town; where the wife comes from a village the male and female surveys suggested that it was twice and thrice respectively as unlikely as when she comes from a town.

The most marked influence is that of education (significant association at 1 per cent in each survey). In each survey only 33 per cent of respondents with education not extending beyond middle school had held such discussions, but where education had been more extensive the proportions rose to 55 per cent and 53 per cent in the female and male surveys respectively. In a quarter of all cases where the wife had had no schooling it was felt that discussions could not be held, but with increased education the proportion fell until discussion was impossible for only a tenth who had been to secondary school and none who had attended university. The fall amongst husbands was similar, but discussion was impossible for an even higher proportion of the relatively few who had never been to school or had not proceeded beyond primary school.

Religion is again of importance but, as might be expected, the religious differential in the discussion of contraception is not as great as in its practice. In each survey discussions had been held in 46 per cent of the cases where the respondent was a Protestant, but in only 41 per cent where the husband was a Catholic and 30 per cent where the wife was. Amongst female respondents such matters could not be discussed in 24 per cent of cases where she was a Catholic compared with only 11 per cent where she was a Protestant; the margin amongst males was very much smaller.

Family planning is more likely to be discussed by those reared in middle-class homes. Where the father had a 'white-collar' job 52 per cent of female respondents and 45 per cent of males had discussed pregnancy prevention, compared with 38 per cent in each survey where he had not.

The respondents' own occupations were also of marked importance. The likelihood of discussion increased with rise in the respondents' occupational status, especially that of wives. Where the female respondent held an upper status job at the time of the survey, she reported discussions in 55 per cent of all cases, compared with 38 per cent of all other female respondents. Part of the explanation lies in the educational differences, but there may also be a strong temptation to keep wives in such lucrative positions and a very real fear of the consequences of pregnancy.

The structure of the marriage is the other major determinant of communication between spouses. Unstable and polygynous marriage certainly make such communication more difficult. Table 8:10 shows that the proportion of respondents in these categories who feel that discussions would be impossible is double that found amongst stably or monogamously married respondents. The age gap between spouses, perhaps greater amongst the unstably or polygynously married, also plays a role, especially in rendering discussion impossible.

TABLE 8:10   The discussion of pregnancy prevention, by sex and marriage structure

	Female survey Per cent	Male survey Per cent
Discussions have been held		
Number of marriages:		
One	46	46
More than one	19	39
Number of wives currently possessed by husband:		
One	44	44
More than one	34	35
Discussions could not be held		
Number of marriages:		
One	12	8
More than one	22	20
Number of wives currently possessed by husband:		
One	11	10
More than one	23	17
Age gap between spouses:		
Less than five years	8	8
More than five years	16	13

Further probing was carried out to find the causes of disagreement among the small number of respondents reporting discussion but disagreement. The numbers were small but they did bring out one point clearly. The discussions were almost invariably initiated by the spouse who wanted to limit the size of the family, and where disagreement did occur it was usually in the form of a reaction against the idea. The fact that more females than males reported this may show that more wives than husbands readily agreed to their spouses' wishes.

The most common reason given by spouses for raising the matter was that of financial pressures, amounting to three-quarters of all cases listed. The grounds for disagreement were much more varied. Less than a third of the reasons given were specific religious objections, although these, together with the assertion that such activities were 'unnatural', made up about half. Of the balance of reasons, one-third claimed that contraception was dangerous or unwise, and two-thirds cited the desire for a larger family or at least a family larger than that existing at the time when the suggestion was made.

An attempt was also made to discover on what grounds it was believed that the discussion could not take place. It might be noticed that about half the specific replies given by women refer to their husbands' likely reactions rather than their own, while only a quarter of the men's answers refer primarily to their wives' feelings.

Some of the respondents who did not discuss such things amplified their replies. A woman teacher, ten years younger than her husband, said, 'We should be prepared to care for every child that God puts in our charge', while a woman baker, mother of seven children and twelve years younger than her retired husband whom she was helping to support, added, 'We feel the children come and so must be supported just like that'. The 35-year-old mother of four children justified the lack of discussion, 'Because I like to have many children around me'.

Others explained their feelings about their spouses. A Grade I drafts-man discussed his wife, eleven years younger, mother of four children, and like himself a Jehovah's Witness, 'She might not understand or refuse'. However, he did add that they might eventually find contraception to be necessary, but, if possible, he would prefer the stress to be on self-control.

TABLE 8:11 Responses to the question, 'Why couldn't you discuss such things (the prevention or postponement of pregnancy) with your husband/wife?'

Response	Female survey (n = 331)			Male survey (n = 296)		
	No.	Per cent	Percentage of those who could not discuss	No.	Per cent	Percentage of those who could not discuss
All respondents except those who could not discuss	290	88	—	264	89	—
Respondents who could not discuss:						
We don't discuss such things	9	3	22	10	3	31
I know spouse would not agree	4	1	10	3	1	9
Spouse would not listen	6	2	15	2	1	6
It would hurt spouse	6	2	15	1	0	3
It has not occurred to me	8	2	19	11	4	35
I am not sure	0	0	0	1	0	3
Residual responses	7	2	17	4	2	13
No response	1	0	2	0	0	0
Total	331	100	100	296	100	100

Summary

Amongst Ghana's urban elite the purchase of contraceptives is no longer a practice either known only to a very small minority or undertaken by very few, which was probably the position a generation ago. The position by 1963 was very different in spite of the pro-populationist attitude of the government and a total absence of any publicity about the retailing or distribution of contraceptives. In fact, communication on the subject seems to have been largely by word of mouth between relatives or friends, more often from woman to woman than from man to man. Thus, as can be seen from Table 8:12, beliefs about the extent of the practice of

TABLE 8:12   Summary of certain responses to questions on family planning

Response	Female survey (n = 331) Per cent	Male survey (n = 296) Per cent
Would use a method to prevent pregnancy:		
Unqualified and qualified	65	72
Unqualified only	54	65
Believe many people buy contraceptives	50	46
Know someone who buys contraceptives	49	41
Currently buying, or have in the past bought contraceptives	28	27
Currently buying contraceptives	27	27
Would use a method to prevent pregnancy even if complicated and troublesome:		
Unqualified and qualified	25	36
Unqualified only	23	29
Have discussed or could discuss contraception with spouse	78	81
Have discussed contraception with spouse	42	43

contraception rested largely on whether one was either practising it personally or knew someone who was. Unlike some other parts of Africa, such matters were never discussed in the press or on the radio.

The salient facts were that over two-fifths of all respondents had discussed the possibility of contraception with their spouses, over a quarter were actually purchasing and presumably using contraceptives, and perhaps two-thirds would be prepared to do so, at least at some stage such as on the attainment of the desired family size, if the suggested contraceptive methods were simple enough. Such findings confirm the earlier observations that there are considerable inducements to the urban elite to limit the size of their families.

In matters of action, far more than in matters of desire, the urban elite is not homogeneous. Both the discussion of contraception and its practice is greatly facilitated by education. Moreover, in a group where most males have necessarily acquired a considerable degree of education in order to achieve their occupational success, the decisive factor is often the educational level and occupational experience of the wife.

However, the conditioning of the new elite and their social readjustments is not merely the product of their schooling. Life in the big towns and an upbringing in an urban, economically well-off household are experiences which must affect attitudes towards traditional social patterns very profoundly indeed. That this is so has been borne out by the analysis described in this chapter. Contraception is much more likely to be considered and used by urbanites of two or more generations and by the occupationally upper classes in the modern sector of the economy of the second or more generations.

Probably social change, especially as it is manifested in alterations to the family structure, is self-reinforcing. Certainly the behaviour patterns of families which are least like the traditional forms are the most radical.

The discussion and use of contraception is much more likely to occur in monogamous, first marriages. Other facilitating factors seem to be residence as a nuclear unit and a relatively small age gap between husband and wife. In fact, any change away from traditional patterns, such as closer relations between husbands and wives or parents and children, as evidenced here by joint outings for instance, may well accelerate tendencies towards family limitation.

Personal beliefs also play a part. Catholics are less likely than Protestants to discuss contraception and less likely still to practise it. However, it should be noted that almost half of all Catholic wives and three-fifths of Catholic husbands would accept advice on how to prevent conception. The position is complicated by education, for these proportions fall amongst the most highly educated Catholics who have received their education in a few prestigeful schools and are likely to be more Westernised than their co-religionists in the sense that their values are closer to those of Catholics in European culture areas.

In another sense beliefs are also important. As noted before, there is an association between being apprehensive of too rapid national population growth and personal use or willingness to use contraceptives. The process is probably circular, each view interacting on the other and strengthening both aspects of belief and behaviour. Similarly, personal use of family planning methods strongly influences views on the desirability of governmental intervention in the population field.

These patterns should not obscure the general picture. The greater discussion and use of contraceptives among the town-born, the better educated, and the children of the old urban elite is more a sign of ability to cope with the mechanics of social change than with a much greater willingness to go the way of that change. In fact the lesser educated and rural-born are almost as keen to limit family size; they are just much less equipped to do anything about it, either by way of obtaining contraceptives or even knowing how to discuss the matter with their spouses.

The new social upper strata of Ghana's towns are adaptable and are willing to adapt. Within them there is not a pronounced conflict of the generations on the question of preserving traditional practices. Thus age is not a determinant of any real importance in the adoption of family planning. Social traditionalists are marked less by age than by their greater adherence to polygyny, unstable marriage, or a wide age gap between husband and wife, although it should be noted that all these characteristics are to some extent positively associated with age.

The husband's views are more likely to be of importance than are the wife's in adopting family planning methods. Nevertheless, it should be noted that communication in the Ghanaian family, especially as it exists in the wealthier areas of the towns, is relatively free. Wives do express their views and these are often influential. This is particularly the case when the wife is a well-educated Catholic, but it may also increasingly be the case when she has borne a large number of children. For wives, much more markedly than husbands, become more interested in the possibility of contraception with increase in family size.

The differentials noted in this chapter between various groups in the use of contraceptives make it inevitable that the practice of contraception, and possibly its effectiveness, will increase. As educational levels rise, the size of the town population grows and its links with rural life weaken, and, with the continuation of the apparently existing trend towards monogamy and stable marriage amongst the urban elite, a greater proportion of the town population will acquire those characteristics which are most strongly associated with the use of contraception. Against this is an unwillingness to spend as much on family limitation as on the cost of rearing a single baby but, nevertheless, the amounts quoted would in most cases cover the cost of contraceptive materials likely to be used.

9

Population Control

The evidence of the largely spontaneous spread of birth control ideas and practices amongst the urban elite, without governmental assistance and indeed with some discouragement, raises the question as to what the effect of governmental intervention or of large-scale intervention with governmental approval would be. What would be the effect on contraceptive practice within the family, indeed what would be the effect on population growth, if information about contraceptives and even their supply became not difficult but easy to acquire?

In many developing countries questions of this sort are very relevant for the future projection of population and economic growth. Governments may well provide family planning facilities, indeed in some countries are already supplying them, and may use their influence and information services to make the use of such facilities 'respectable', in the sense of fitting in with national policies.

Such actions are hardly properly described as 'population control' or even 'population planning', but such terms have been widely used and their meaning is understood. In reality this chapter will attempt to assess whether large-scale intervention in the family planning field would be likely to have any considerable effect upon the size of families among the economically better-off classes of Ghana's major towns.

The Establishment of Family Planning Clinics

The nature of such clinics was explained to the respondents and they were asked, as shown in Table 9:1, whether they favoured the establishment of institutions of this type.

Three very interesting points emerged. The first is that nearly all respondents had views on the matter; failure to respond and even qualified answers were rare. The second is that more females than males apparently believed the suggestion to be a good one, but this impression may not be wholly correct. In the course of the survey work we came to feel that it was not the establishment of clinics, but the possibility of a clash with what appeared to be existing government policy, that made the males cautious. After all many of them held positions of considerable authority in the governmental system. Thirdly, the proportions favouring clinics were very large, almost three-quarters of the wives and even more than two-thirds of the more cautious husbands.

The pattern of replies was not affected at all by age, number of children, or the wives' pregnancy condition. The older Ghanaian males, at least in the urban setting, are as radical as the young. Nor apparently were opinions suddenly changed or sharpened by the onset of an un-

151

TABLE 9:1   Responses to the question, 'In some countries clinics have been
set up where doctors can tell women how not to have the
babies that they do not want, and can supply the materials (i.e.
preventing the women from becoming pregnant—not causing
abortions by removing unborn babies from pregnant women).
Do you think that it would be a good idea if this were done in
Ghana?'

Response	Female survey (n = 331)		Male survey (n = 296)	
	No.	Per cent	No.	Per cent
Yes	237	72	198	67
Qualified yes	4	1	3	1
No	82	25	86	29
Qualified no	0	0	2	1
Don't know, not certain	4	1	1	0
No response	4	1	6	2
Total	331	100	296	100

expected pregnancy or the arrival of more children than had perhaps
once been anticipated or desired.

Birthplace and education bore rather similar relations to the responses.
In each survey clinics were desired by a somewhat greater proportion of
respondents with town birth or extended education, but in no cases were
the margins considerable, never of the same order as those discovered
when considering the current use of contraceptives or the holding of
discussions on contraception. However, it should be noted that almost as
many town-born males as females, approximately three-quarters in each
case, wanted clinics. The differentiation between the sexes arises partly
from the larger number of village-born males. Amongst those with
education beyond middle school almost three-quarters approved of the
establishment of clinics compared with two-thirds of the respondents with
lesser education.

Occupation and religion do demonstrate important, if different, trends,
and help to illuminate the whole question of communication between the
spouses.

As seen before, the majority of respondents had not discussed
pregnancy prevention with their spouses even though most of them believed
that they could do so. In the event many of them seemed to find it hard
to believe that their husbands or wives could adapt to innovation as easily
as they themselves could. This was especially the case where the spouse's
occupation and background were such as to make it appear improbable
that he or she would approve of innovation, an effect compounded by
the fact that more respondents with spouses in this category had held no
discussions. Thus, as can be seen in Table 9:2, the respondents' opinions
about the desirability of clinics (opinions naturally affected by whether
it was felt agreement could be reached within their own marriages about
using them) vary little with the respondents' own occupations, but are
markedly associated with those of their spouses. Many more respondents

TABLE 9:2   Respondents   approving   the   establishment   of   clinics   by
            occupation

Occupational category	Occupational status	Female survey Per cent	Male survey Per cent
Own occupation	High	74*	66
	Low	71*	69
Spouse's occupation	High	77	82*
	Low	62	63*

* Working wives only.

with spouses employed in upper status jobs are convinced that they would be able to use them and hence that their establishment would be well worth while. The greatest approval came from husbands whose wives were currently employed in high status employment, perhaps a sign that they hoped such employment would continue. In both surveys the children of fathers with high status positions showed somewhat greater approval of clinics, but the margins were not great.

The effect of religion is twofold. First, both surveys established that it was the wife's religion that was of greater importance. In each survey its association with views on clinics was statistically significant (at 5 per

TABLE 9:3   Respondents approving the establishment of clinics by sex,
            religion and spouse's religion

Spouse	Religion	Female survey Per cent	Male survey Per cent
Wife	Protestant	76	70
	Catholic	57	56
Husband	Protestant	76	69
	Catholic	61	59

cent) while in neither case were those of the husband. Secondly, the gap between the views of persons of different religions, whether themselves or their husbands, is greatest when seen through female eyes.

Once again marriage patterns and family way of life were of very great importance. Table 9:4 shows that respondents who had engaged in only one marriage were almost one-and-a-half times more likely to favour clinics than were the more unstably married. It also gives further support to the view that, while the husband in a polygynous marriage is likely to differ markedly in social outlook from the husband in a monogamous marriage, the wives in the two types of marriage are not so differentiated. Where the nuclear family was the residential unit husbands and wives were more likely to approve of clinics. This was also the case where a pattern had been established of taking the children on outings.

TABLE 9:4   Respondents approving of the establishment of clinics, by sex and aspects of family life

Aspect of family life	Condition of respondent	Female survey Per cent	Male survey Per cent
Number of marriages	One	73*	72*
	More than one	53*	55*
Nature of current marriage	Monogamous	71	69*
	Polygynous	68	39*
Relatives beyond nuclear family living in household	None	75‡	61
	One or more	66‡	53
Taking children on outings	Sometimes	75†	68
	Never	63†	62

* Difference within the survey between the dichotomous divisions significant at 1 per cent.
† Significant at 5 per cent.
‡ Just fails significance at 5 per cent.

Attitudes and actions are also of importance. Where respondents believe that family size is largely decided by fate or God's will far fewer favour clinics than do respondents believing otherwise (significant in both surveys at 1 per cent). Nevertheless, it might be noted that even in the first category a majority feel clinics should be established. Where respondents have not discussed contraception only three-fifths approved the establishment of clinics, but, where they have, three-quarters of the males and almost nine-tenths of the females approved (significant at 1 per cent). Respondents who consider high rates of population growth to be bad for the country are more likely to favour clinics, but the difference was statistically significant (at 1 per cent) only in the male survey.

When responses were subdivided by both religion and education, the now familiar pattern was observed. Approval rose slightly with education amongst Protestants of both sexes, and this time amongst Catholic males as well, but did so in the case of Catholic females only as far as middle school education, falling sharply amongst those with more extended education. Thus, only half the Catholic female respondents with further education desired clinics.

Considerable effort was expended in eliciting the reasons for the respondents' attitudes on this question, and the major reason given by each is set out in Table 9:5.

It is a measure of the respondents' understanding of the issues involved in the questions about family planning clinics, and perhaps also of the relevance of the whole matter to their own lives, that so few non-responses are reported in Tables 9:1 and 9:5.

TABLE 9:5   Responses to the question, 'Why do you think this?' (following the question on whether the establishment of family planning clinics would be a good idea)*

Response	Female survey (n = 331)		Male survey (n = 296)	
	No.	Per cent	No.	Per cent
No response or 'don't know' to question of clinics	8	2	7	2
In favour of clinics:				
To instruct about contraception	46	14	108	37
To prevent birth of unwanted children	61	18	31	11
To reduce abortions	57	17	29	10
To relieve the financial strains of large families	54	16	21	7
To protect the country from too rapid population increase	17	5	9	3
No response	6	2	3	1
Against clinics:				
Ghana needs children	41	12	45	15
Immoral, not right	23	7	26	9
Against God's laws	6	2	5	2
Dangerous, unpleasant, dislike such things	2	1	7	2
Killing of innocent children	2	1	0	0
Children are a source of happiness	1	0	1	0
Children are a source of wealth	2	1	0	0
No response	5	2	4	1
Total	331	100	296	100

* The major reason only is listed for each respondent.

Women were far more vocal than men in explaining just why they desired clinics. Many more male respondents just assumed that there were obvious problems about very large families and matter-of-factly explained the need for clinics merely in terms of required advice and instruction. Most respondents wanted clinics both for their own further guidance and to serve what they believed to be a widespread need, but there was some dispute on both points.

The most common viewpoint on need was that of the Radio Ghana announcer, who said, 'Because we know little or nothing of such things', but he admitted that many of the younger men seemed much better informed than he himself was. A surveyor's assistant, whose wife had borne him nine children before becoming infecund, related, 'We don't need them now', but he favoured their establishment, 'Because most people here are ignorant on such matters'. The view was supported by a wife who was a petty trader and who asserted, 'Such clinics would be of immense help to ignorant folk'.

Sometimes the emphasis was on the safety or efficiency of methods which would presumably be offered by such clinics. A reporter with a government newspaper, nine years older than his wife, who was in her later twenties and had so far borne three children, replied, 'Because most of us do not know safe ways of restricting or controlling births'. A storekeeper with five children argued, 'Because most of us have not had any specialised advice on the issue and people use whatever means are available; this could be dangerous'. This remark and others implied more resort to indigenous methods than had the responses to direct questions on the prevention of pregnancy. A 19-year-old wife, who had not yet had a child nor used contraceptives in spite of a willingness to do so if she could find out about them, favoured clinics, 'So that people need no longer consult fetish priests'.

Some respondents saw the need for family limitation but could not understand why anyone, or anyone except 'the ignorant and foolish', would need clinics. A wife in her early forties, in spite of having borne seven children, argued that contraceptives were now readily available and that clinics were completely unnecessary, although she did add the remark, 'If you don't want the baby, why become pregnant?' A woman teacher, whose husband was also a teacher, conceded with some impatience that clinics were necessary, 'Because some cannot do it themselves'.

There was a cleavage in a number of cases between what were felt to be personal needs on one hand and national on the other, but the division was not a simple one. A high party official, seeing that, largely because he was already rearing five children, his private needs were at variance with governmental policy, said, 'Personally yes, because I want no more children'. A technician in government service, father of eleven children of whom ten were surviving, put the case for providing clinics even though he personally would not want the facilities: 'There is nothing wrong in that; people who need such advice should have it; we wouldn't use it because we would like nature to have its own course'.

Finally, there were provisos about the service. A barrister who believed that 'once a person decides not to have any more children it becomes purely a medical matter and the best advice can be sought in a clinic', nevertheless advocated their establishment only, 'if it is limited to wives or at least grown ups'.

In spite of the high fertility traditions of the society, the problem of unwanted children was a persistent theme. An ex-typist, married to a civil servant and mother of his four children, felt 'clinics should be set up, because there are too many people having babies through accidents, so children are not well cared for'. A teacher, wife of an electrician, said, 'To stop so many people bringing forth', while a civil servant's wife believed, 'A baby must be born only when the two parties concerned are both ready to welcome the baby'. Sometimes it was suggested that only wanted babies were likely to receive first class care. A polygynist, father of seven children but now using contraceptives at least in his relations with his junior wife who had borne him one child, advocated clinics because 'it will give us healthy children'.

The major problem was that of extra children and not of illegitimacy, although admittedly the position might have been somewhat different if we had been interviewing women who were not currently married. Even so, illegitimacy is hardly the problem in Ghana that it is in many other societies. A shopkeeper, whose 30-year-old wife had already borne him five children, said, 'It will help those who are sexual maniacs not to have babies outside marriage'.

The physical strains of child-bearing were not mentioned nearly as frequently as the financial pressures, but occasionally the matter was raised. A wife, who had borne nine children in twenty-three years of marriage and explained the fact by pointing out that she knew of no method of avoiding pregnancy, desired clinics, 'So that parents could be released from child-bearing'. A civil servant's wife who had three children by the time she was in her late twenties, wanted clinics, 'Because producing many children is very bad'.

It was the cost of rearing large families which dominated the personal reasons. One woman teacher with five children recommended clinics 'to stop people who cannot afford to bring up children from having them', while another, who had borne six children by her middle thirties, said, 'It is very expensive nowadays to bring up a big family'. The theme of increasing expense, admittedly in a period of sustained inflation and increasing commodity shortages, was common. An army officer's wife with seven children advocated clinics, 'Because people are finding it more and more difficult to support a large family'.

The difficulties of the improvident were frequently described. A Methodist accountant, father of four children, felt clinics to be necessary, 'Because some have too many children than they can care for'. While a midwife married to a public servant felt that, if facilities were provided, 'The size of family will be limited and parents won't have children who will be a burden'. One male graduate working with a party organisation advocated clinics 'to avoid future expenses', while another, teaching in a secondary school and father of five children by his 30-year-old wife, said, 'Yes, this will limit the families and raise the standard of living'. Sometimes feelings were mixed. A seamstress, wife of a clerk, and mother of only two children at 30 years of age, pointed out, 'Limitation of family is necessary because children are now beginning to become a liability to parents economically [but] this [the establishment of clinics] would be too much—nature should not be disturbed to that extent'. The couple were apparently using rhythm methods, abstinence, *coitus interruptus,* or possibly all three, to keep down their own family size.

Besides this concern for the family, and related to the pressures to take action to prevent large families, was a concern about the dangers of abortion, which certainly supported those respondents who were later to attest that it was common. Some of the respondents seemed to be talking about dangers to others and some to themselves. Certainly women were far more worried than men on the point.

A nursing sister, apparently in a position to know, argued that, 'This would prevent many of our people from having abortions', while a shopkeeper's wife felt, 'It would save many people from dying of abortion'. Other cases were put for reducing abortion. One young Protestant wife urged clinics 'to stop the young girls from having abortions', while another felt similarly because, 'It is better to prevent pregnancy than have abortions. This in the first place is a sin and secondly may cost her life'. A high public servant was convinced that, with the provision of clinics, 'The abortion rate will come down'. A public servant's wife believed they were necessary 'to put an end to the practice of abortions in this country', as did an army officer's wife 'so as to promote better home planning and to stop people having to remove unborn, unwanted babies'.

Fewer respondents supported the case for clinics with arguments on national welfare. A scientist, who had been born and partly brought up in Britain did, 'Because it will limit population increase and enable Ghana to keep pace with economic development'.

However, the case against clinics was frequently argued on such grounds, often in the spirit and even the words of the newspapers and pronouncements by leading politicians. A female public servant, married to a lawyer and mother of four children, opposed the establishment of any clinics on the grounds that, 'Population will decrease and at present manpower is needed'. Elements of both national competition and defence were also present; a woman teacher with four children felt against clinics, 'Because our population is very small compared to other countries'. Sometimes national need and personal morality were intermingled; the Methodist wife of a headmaster opposed clinics, 'Because we want to have the increase in population; they will decrease our population and kill innocent children'.

The moral case against clinics, and indeed against contraception, was usually not related directly to religious views, though admittedly they may often have formed their basis. However, a woman teacher, married to a personnel officer, both of them Catholics and parents of four children, argued, 'It is not good; God said, "Increase and multiply", so I see no reason why such things should be carried on'.

The Use of Family Planning Clinics

Respondents were then asked whether they would use such clinics if they were established. The replies set out in Tables 9:6 and 9:7 show that about two-thirds of them agreed with or without qualification that they would. The usual qualifications were 'when we have enough children' or 'if we need to', but some were of the type 'if my husband agrees'.

The fact that fewer respondents expected to use clinics than recommended their establishment, a phenomenon found mainly amongst female respondents, was explained chiefly by the number of women who expected to complete their reproductive span before such facilities were likely to be available. The decline in male interest from that shown for a pregnancy prevention method recommended by a doctor is mainly a reflection of the continued greater concern amongst some of them over the political implications of clinics.

The pattern of responses according to the other characteristics of the respondents was in the main almost identical with that already found in the question about establishing clinics. Once again age and number of children were of little importance. Small margins in favour of the use of clinics were found with extended education, urban birthplace, middle- or

TABLE 9:6 Responses to the question, 'If such clinics were set up, would you/your wife/your husband ever use them?'

Response	Female survey (n = 331)		Male survey (n = 296)	
	No.	Per cent	No.	Per cent
Yes	184	56	182	61
Qualified yes	26	8	17	6
No	98	29	84	28
Qualified no	3	1	0	0
Don't know, not certain	7	2	2	1
No response	13	4	11	4
Total	331	100	296	100

TABLE 9:7 Comparison of respondents favouring use of pregnancy prevention method suggested by doctor, establishment of clinics, and use of clinics

Respondents favouring*	Female survey (n = 331) Per cent	Male survey (n = 296) Per cent
Use of pregnancy prevention method suggested by doctor	61	72
Establishment of clinics	73	68
Use of clinics	64	67

* 'Yes' and 'qualified yes' responses have been aggregated.

upper-class background, and residence in nuclear families, but they were never great enough to achieve statistical significance. With higher status occupations use of the clinics became more likely, but the decisive margins (significant at 1 per cent in both surveys) once again were associated with spouse's occupations. Stable marriage and monogamy were both associated (at 1 per cent and 5 per cent respectively) in the male survey with willingness to use clinics. However, amongst females the margin of likely users between the stably and unstably married was smaller, ranging from 64 per cent to 56 per cent, and at 63 per cent to 60 per cent all but disappeared between the monogamously and polygynously married. Females residing in nuclear family households numbered 69 per cent of likely users compared with 57 per cent of those living with more distant relatives as well. There was still a strong association (at 1 per cent) between the discussion of contraception and willingness to use clinics.

However, some interesting changes did occur in the pattern of response by religion. The number of Protestants wishing to use clinics was substantially less than the number advocating them, because of nearness to the end of the reproductive period, insufficient numbers of children and so on; all Catholics in such conditions were against clinics. Every Catholic respondent in the two surveys who favoured the establishment of clinics also intended to make use of them. Thus, although some margin in willingness to use clinics was recorded between Protestants and Catholics, 67 per cent to 57 per cent in the female survey and 68 per cent to 59 per cent in the male survey, it was statistically significant in neither survey.

As would be expected, there was a strong association (significant at 1 per cent) between advocacy of clinics and willingness to use them, but it was not absolute, as is disclosed by Table 9:8. It has been seen above that some Protestant respondents favoured clinics even though they did not expect to use them. There were other respondents, some of whom believed that the existing distribution of contraceptives through doctors and chemists was sufficient, who would certainly use clinics if they were

TABLE 9:8 Comparison of views on the establishment of clinics with willingness to use their services

Respondents' views on the establishment of clinics	Percentage of respondents with specified view on establishment of clinics expressing willingness to use clinics					
	Female survey			Male survey		
	Yes and qualified yes	No and qualified no	No response or not certain	Yes and qualified yes	No and qualified no	No response or not certain
Yes and qualified yes	79	17	4	94	4	2
No and qualified no	22	72	6	11	85	4

established. Just as Catholics had religious reasons for tying their general views to their specific needs, males had political or administrative reasons for doing so.

Once again an analysis subdivided by both education and religion shows that Catholic willingness to use clinics does not continue to rise with education beyond the middle school level and that the greatest gulf between Catholic and Protestant views occurs amongst the most educated groups.

An attempt was made to probe further into reasons for not wishing to use clinics, partly in the belief that these might not be identical with the reasons given for opposing the establishment of clinics. This was in fact the case in that most respondents who were unwilling to use clinics now gave personal reasons for this decision. It is possible that the asking of two similar questions forced many respondents into a second response, but, nevertheless, the diminution of responses in terms of political or moral philosophies is striking.

Table 9:9 suggests that some of the women who wanted many children probably should have responded in Table 9:6 with a qualified yes, meaning 'not yet'. However, it does appear that the traditional desire for children and the reaction against the unfamiliar and strange are stronger forces militating against contraception than are specifically religious objections.

TABLE 9:9   Responses to the question, 'Why wouldn't you use these clinics?'

Response	Female survey (n = 331)		Male survey (n = 296)	
	No.	Per cent	No.	Per cent
All respondents except those replying 'no' or 'qualified no' in Table 9:6	230	70	212	72
'No' or 'qualified no' in Table 9:6:				
Desire for many children	44	13	13	4
Dangerous, unpleasant, dislike the idea	21	6	34	11
Children needed to develop or populate Ghana	15	5	17	6
Such things are against God's law	9	3	5	2
Such things are immoral or not right	4	1	6	2
Such things would mean the killing of innocent children	1	0	0	0
No response	7	2	9	3
Total	331	100	296	100

Abortion

It was originally planned that the surveys should secure information on the incidence of abortion but, just before preliminary field tests began, cabinet announced that the death penalty would be imposed for its practice. The news, as printed and broadcast, left some doubt as to whether capital punishment would be inflicted on the practitioner or patient. Rather than jeopardise the success of the whole survey, we reduced our questions to the single one presented in Table 9:10 inquiring about the prevalence of abortion and not relating it to personal experience. We felt it necessary to protect the survey by being the first to point out that abortion was illegal but, by so doing, we may well have deterred some respondents from admitting knowledge of the practice.

The 'no response' rate was relatively high amongst women, and some interviewers gained the impression that it was particularly high where the woman had herself had an abortion. It is possible that this was the somewhat fanciful interpretation of the embarrassment caused by a rather awkward question. Even if this was so, the fact remains that only about two-fifths of the respondents regarded the practice as very common, although much admittedly depends on the definition of 'common'. Beyond this vague term we concluded we could not go without causing some official disquiet.

The identification of respondents by response could hardly be said to locate the groups with the highest incidence of abortion but merely those groups within society who were most likely to come in contact with it. Even this search was rather unfruitful. All that can be said definitely is

TABLE 9:10   Responses to the question, 'In some countries the number of babies being born is much smaller than it would otherwise be, because many women have abortions (if necessary, explain that "abortion" means removing the unborn child). This is not legal in Ghana. Do you think that this way of stopping having a baby is very common in Ghana?'

Response	Female survey (n = 331)		Male survey (n = 296)	
	No.	Per cent	No.	Per cent
Yes	100	30	128	43
Qualified yes	16	5	6	2
No	151	46	129	44
Qualified no	15	4	3	1
Not certain, don't know	13	4	18	6
No response	36	11	12	4
Total	331	100	296	100

that the town-born seem to know more about it than the village-born (statistically significant only in the male survey, at 5 per cent), thus suggesting that the practice is not widespread in rural areas, and that males, perhaps with more pressure upon them to exhibit sophistication, claim to know more of it than do females. Only amongst town-born males did as many as half the respondents claim definitely that abortion was very common.

A doctor's wife, who was in the sample, said, 'It is not very common but we often hear of people dying as a result of abortion'. A senior civil servant believed, 'It is common in the cities'. Some qualified their answers, often with specific reference to secondary schoolgirls. One woman teacher replied, 'Yes, especially among the young girls', while another said, 'No, it's common only among the schoolgirls'. Others believed that the government moves had already reduced its incidence. A party organisation official claimed, 'It used to be, but now it is uncommon because of the attitude of the government towards it', and a telephonist, married to a police officer, said, 'It used to be until the government made it illegal'. Others who should also have been in a position to know, thought differently. A public servant stated, 'There are such cases but they are not at all common', while a reporter also believed abortion to be 'not at all common'.

Sterilisation

Finally, the question of sterilisation was broached. It was feared initially that most respondents would not understand what was being discussed, but preliminary testing, as well as the main survey, showed that, if the question was supplemented with a little discussion, this was not so. Doctors have performed sterilising operations on a very limited scale in Ghana and other Commonwealth countries in tropical Africa. Their patients have usually been expatriates or members of the urban elite. A senior public servant said that the operation used to be quite common in

Ghana but was not so by the time of the survey. A midwife of twenty-five years' experience said that some women 'do like this method'.

Many more respondents than had been anticipated felt Ghanaians, and perhaps more particularly themselves when they had sufficient children, would accept sterilisation. Thus, nearly a third of the female respondents and over a third of the males were found to approve the method. A woman who had borne eleven children in twenty-two years said she 'hadn't thought to discuss it, but if a doctor would do me, even if it cost a lot of money, I want it'.

However, the replies to a subsequent question about whether the operation should be done to the wives or the husbands cast grave doubt on the meaningfulness of the 'yes' responses listed in Table 9:11. For instance, although nearly a third of female respondents believed that Ghanaians would accept sterilising operations, only a sixth felt that such

TABLE 9:11 Responses to the question, 'In a few countries parents who think that they have enough children can get an operation done (i.e. sterilisation) so that they cannot have any more children. Do you think Ghanaians would ever like this method?'

Response	Female survey (n = 331)		Male survey (n = 296)	
	No.	Per cent	No.	Per cent
Yes	102	31	104	35
Qualified yes	5	2	0	0
Some would	17	5	9	3
No	171	52	164	55
Qualified no	4	1	0	0
Not certain, don't know	1	0	5	2
No response	31	9	14	5
Total	331	100	296	100

operations are preferably performed upon women. And, more strikingly, while over a third of the males believed sterilisation would find favour, only one-twentieth thought that it was preferably done upon men. This is not merely a case of physical apprehension, it is also a measure of the struggle between a desire to limit family size and an unwillingness to lose one's personal fecundity.

Certainly the weight of opinion was on the side of sterilising, if anyone, the wives. To a large extent this was the case because this operation had been the one usually performed by doctors. A woman teacher, married to an accountant, corrected the interviewer, 'The operation cannot be performed on men'. A public servant's wife explained, 'Here, so far it is done on the woman', and a journalist believed, 'It is normal to expect it to be done to the mother'. Many also believed this to be the safest course. A party official said, 'Sterilisation for mothers, because they will not suffer any defects'. A trader, 33 years old and with four children, married to a driver seven years older than herself, explained, 'Because it is the mother who produces the baby. Something bad may happen to my

TABLE 9:12 Responses to the question, 'Would they prefer it (sterilisation) done to the wives or the husbands?'

Response	Female survey (n = 331)			Male survey (n = 296)		
	No.	Per cent	Per cent of those believing Ghanaians in favour of sterilisation	No.	Per cent	Per cent of those believing Ghanaians in favour of sterilisation
Respondents except those in Table 9:11 replying 'yes' or 'qualified yes' or 'some would'	207	62	—	183	62	—
'Yes' or 'qualified yes' or 'some would' in Table 9:11:						
Same sex as respondent	52	16	42	15	5	13
Opposite sex to respondent	55	17	44	88	30	78
Either sex	17	5	14	10	3	9
Total	331	100	100	296	100	100

husband's organs'. A public servant's wife felt, 'It depends on the background of the wife and husband. If the parents of the wife do not agree to her undergoing such an operation then the man should surely do so'.

It is harder to define the members of the Ghanaian elite who would be likely to favour sterilisation than it is to do the same thing with regard to contraception. Age, occupation, birthplace, parent's occupations, religion, marriage structure, household structure, or condition of pregnancy were not associated in the surveys, but education is still of some importance, although statistically significant (at 5 per cent) only in the female survey, while sterilisation was favoured by 36 per cent of respondents with education beyond middle school compared with only 26 per cent of those with lesser schooling. Associations were found only with the most non-traditional of family behaviour. For instance, parents who take their children on outings are more likely to favour sterilisation, although statistical significance (at 5 per cent) was achieved in the female survey only, where the margin was 38 per cent of those undertaking outings in favour compared with 24 per cent of those not involved in such outings.

However, the position is different with regard to behaviour or views in the field of pregnancy and its prevention. In the male survey there was an association (at 1 per cent) with the view that family size was not largely a matter of fate. And associations (at 1 per cent) occur with attempts to prevent pregnancy, the discussion of contraception, the purchase of contraceptives, their use, approval of family planning clinics, and willingness to use them. For instance 40 per cent and 49 per cent of females and males respectively who would use family planning clinics believe that Ghanaians would like sterilisation, while only 16 per cent and 8 per cent respectively of those who would not use clinics hold this view. Clearly personal needs strongly influence social assessments.

Those respondents who believed that Ghanaians would not like sterilising operations were asked why they thought this was so. The replies listed in Table 9:13 show that fears of the operation's irreversibility and danger are much stronger than are protests based on religious or moral convictions. Indeed the latter are less frequently mentioned than is the desire for more children on either traditional, personal grounds or for the national good. Many believed too that prestige would suffer with sterility, distinguishing in most cases quite clearly between that condition and impotence. However, fairly frequently the opposite could not apparently be so clearly defined, and almost certainly many respondents quoting the danger of the operation were referring to the risk they believed there to be of impotence or reduced potency.

This question was important in that many respondents felt that it was so extreme that they should take the opportunity to restate the whole African position with regard to child-bearing. In this sense some of the replies added perspective to the whole investigation.

Part of the protest against sterilisation is the fact that in practice it can be regarded, at least to date, as irreversible. This may not be important in a stable, monogamous marriage where both partners survive to old age, but where divorce and remarriage are common, or where the death of a spouse in middle life is far from improbable, or where death may even suddenly reduce the number of children in the family, there may well be

TABLE 9:13   Responses to the question, 'Why do you think this (that Ghanaians would not like sterilisation)?'

Response	Female survey (n = 331)			Male survey (n = 296)		
	No.	Per cent	Per cent of those believing Ghanaians not in favour of sterilisation	No.	Per cent	Per cent of those believing Ghanaians not in favour of sterilisation
Respondents except those in Table 9:11 replying 'no' or 'qualified no'	156	47	—	132	45	—
'No' or 'qualified no' in Table 9:11:						
Irrevocable, other methods available	41	12	23	26	9	16
Fear of operation, dangerous (danger unspecified)	39	12	22	27	9	16
Desire children	21	6	12	26	9	16
Ghana needs children	7	2	4	28	9	17
Immoral, not right, unnatural	18	6	10	26	9	16
Against God's law, forbidden by religion	8	2	5	3	1	2
Loss of prestige through such an operation	15	5	9	19	6	12
Fear of impotence or reduced sexual ability	4	1	2	2	1	1
No response	22	7	13	7	2	4
Total	331	100	100	296	100	100

grave difficulties. A woman or man who cannot be offered in marriage as a potential parent may not be regarded as marriageable. Parents who cannot replace dead children may themselves be replaced in marriage. These mortality conditions may already have passed at least for the urban elite, but their attitudes are affected by the traditions, views, and condition of the whole society, and in any case this question was framed so as to have general application.

A draftsman in the government service, by religious persuasion a Jehovah's Witness, opposed sterilisation, 'Because this has some permanence about it which frightens people. What if they later want to have more children? The risk involved should not be ignored. This practice goes against Christian divine principles'. A civil servant also discussed the problem of permanence: 'There is too much finality about such an operation. What if one feels like having more children?' A lawyer's wife protested, 'If the older children die, the couple would not be able to have any more children'. With these age-old problems of the society in mind, a 22-year-old wife of a clerk, mother of two children one of whom had died, judged the suggestion as 'horrible to the African'.

Coupled with the question of irrevocability was commonly the observation that there were other methods of preventing pregnancy. An ex-teacher, wife of a businessman, argued that, 'Effective contraceptives are better than dangerous operations'. And an army officer's wife protested, 'It will be objectionable with all the other methods available'. The choice of a method of limiting births may depend on age and family size. A teacher, wife of a public servant and mother of ten living children, believed, 'The older woman prefers sterilisation to abortions; young girls will use clinics but not sterilisation'.

Many respondents feared such operations, and were sceptical of reports of their simplicity. The wife of a carpenter and mother of his nine living children believed, 'Most people, like myself, are afraid'. A supervisory draftsman, father of eleven living children, was opposed to sterilisation, 'Because it is not traditional and has its dangers'. Some respondents claimed that the fear of sterilisation was merely part of a more widespread apprehension of all operations. A young woman teacher said, 'No, as Ghanaians, we fear and try to avoid all kinds of operations, including sterilisation, which is not very important'. The mother of eight children, who had hitherto attempted to control family size by the rhythm method, but who would readily use any better method suggested to her, observed, 'Generally, Ghanaians fear operations of this nature'. While a woman teacher, considering whether Ghanaians were ever likely to favour sterilisation, remarked, 'I just feel they wouldn't'.

Many respondents put again the general case for large families, sometimes distinguishing between birth control methods which permitted the spacing of pregnancies and those which terminated them. Often the respondents referred not to their own position, or that of the other members of the urban elite, but to the general populace. A woman teacher, mother of five children and wife of a sports coach, observed, 'Ghanaians boast of more children; those with more children are more respected'. A female clerk, wife of a bank officer, did not think sterilisation would find wide acceptance, 'Because, in Ghana, many tribes boast of the number of children they have and so many want to have more'. This was suggested by a businesswoman, mother of seven children by a husband twenty-eight years older than she was, who stressed, 'Africans do generally like children'.

Traditional morality and the principles of some imported religions may seem to run together. The wife of a man who had established a successful fishing business and mother of eleven children felt, 'Our consciences will worry us too much, because our culture and tradition wouldn't accept it'. Religion may, however, exert influences in opposite directions. For Catholics who have to confess their sins and thereafter mend their ways, there may be advantages in committing a single, irrevocable sin. A 38-year-old Catholic woman, mother of ten living children born during the preceding twenty years and pregnant, though pleased about it, at the time of the survey, reported, 'Catholics seem to prefer sterilisation to clinics'. A similar situation has been described in Puerto Rico.

Summary

Throughout this chapter and some of the preceding ones, two aspects of the life of the urban elite emerge very clearly. One is the increasing pressures resulting from high fertility in a situation where nearly all children survive to demand extended education, high standards of dress, opportunities for entering high status occupations, and so on. The other is resistance to innovation, and particularly such radical innovations as the use of modern contraceptives.

The two themes should be clearly distinguished. Sometimes greater unwillingness to employ facilities to prevent or postpone pregnancy arise from lesser pressures exerted by the support of children. Thus, in the previous chapter it was seen that fewer women with less than five children would use a method for preventing pregnancy than was the case with mothers of larger families. And, to take an extreme example, we have shown elsewhere that problems of family size are felt only to a small degree in rural populations engaged in subsistence agriculture and outside the range of schooling facilities.

Nearly all the urban elite do feel that very large families do give rise to basic problems in the new way of life in which they find themselves. In these circumstances, the willingness to use contraception is modified largely by the inability to accommodate to innovation and to a much lesser extent by personal circumstances and philosophies.

Thus extended schooling does not really teach greater appreciation of contraception, but it does make it easier in all kinds of ways to break with traditional practices. Nor is extended schooling the only preparation for innovation: throughout this chapter a greater willingness to experiment has been shown to exist amongst those born and brought up in the large towns and especially in the middle- and upper-class families in those towns.

There are other features which can also be shown to be associated with readiness to accept innovation in the family planning field, but they are of a different kind, in that they are more likely to represent other evidence of the degree of the break with social traditionalism than to be the cause of that break. However, change is self-reinforcing; it can certainly prepare those involved for more of it. Thus monogamous, stable marriage, with a relatively small age gap between spouses, is more likely to be associated with family planning than are the converse forms of marriage. So is an increase in the amount of joint outings between spouses or between spouses and children.

Religious views are something very different, for the strongest resistance to contraception comes from the most highly educated Catholics, although there is a sex bias here as this statement is truer for females than males. It is precisely amongst those Catholics who have most broken with the Ghanaian past, who are most Westernised, and are most likely to be living in a stable, monogamous marriage, that opposition to contraception is strongest. However, certain qualifications must be made. The most important is that Catholics approach much more closely to Protestants where action or expected action occurs than they do in the realm of ideas. Thus, although the margin between Protestants and Catholics is considerable on the question of establishing family planning clinics, it is much smaller when it comes to who might use them. In fact, almost three-fifths of the Catholic respondents in each survey would expect to make use of such facilities.

Cutting across the whole question of innovation and traditionalism is that of communication. As seen in the last chapter, the practice of contraception depends largely on the ability to discuss the subject. Such discussions are themselves innovations and depend on two types of conditions. The first is a society which accepts easily enough communication between husband and wife, especially on non-traditional matters. On the whole, Ghanaian society does this. The second is precisely that group of characteristics already listed as encouraging innovation in action: education, upbringing, and so on. Thus, innovation in the field of contraception is a two-step process, whereby these conditions, especially if they are found in both spouses, encourage communication which in turn may encourage action, but communication is nearly always imperfect. The findings in this chapter tend to show that members of the Ghanaian, urban elite accept innovation much more readily than their spouses believe. Thus, the acceptance of radically new ideas about contraception does not vary very greatly with educational or occupational status. However, the beliefs of husbands and wives about the acceptance of such ideas by their spouses, or their own ability to employ such innovations, varies markedly with the educational and occupational status of these spouses.

Finally, Table 9:14 summarises some of the more important findings of this chapter. Over two-thirds of the respondents would favour the establishment of family planning clinics, in spite of a markedly discouraging official climate of opinion on such matters at the time. Two-thirds of them would expect to use such facilities.

These statistics have to be placed against the equally attested facts, that love of children and pride in large families are deeply entrenched characteristics of African society. Conditions are changing in the economically better-off suburbs of Ghana's towns. The worry about illegal abortion, and its higher incidence in the towns, is evidence of this. The things discussed here, contraception and even abortion and sterilisation by

TABLE 9:14   Summary of certain responses to questions on population control

Response	Female survey (n = 331) Per cent*	Male survey (n = 296) Per cent*
Favouring the establishment of family planning clinics	73	68
Willing to use facilities of family planning clinics	64	67
Believing abortion to be very common	35	45
Believing Ghanaians would like sterilisation	33	35
Believing Ghanaians would like sterilisation and that it should be performed on persons of the same sex as the respondent	16	5

* Total of 'yes' and 'qualified yes' responses.

medical practitioners, are not new ideas to many members of the urban elite. Such practices already have a considerable history in Ghana's larger towns, even if they do not penetrate deeply into the lower strata of urban society or into the countryside.

10

Conclusions: The Urban Elite and Population Change

In this study an attempt has been made to find clues suggesting the onset of incipient fertility decline, at least amongst the urban elite, in Ghana. With one exception, census data available at the time of the survey could not be made to yield evidence of any major fertility movement in the country; that exception was important as an indicator of the effect that social change might have upon fertility levels. For it seems likely, although the data could possibly be somewhat differently interpreted, that urban fertility levels were up to an eighth lower than were those of the rural areas in the same part of the country. This would have amounted on average to a margin of almost one birth per completed family. A more recent release of census data, analysed in the Appendix, in general confirmed this point, and suggested that the fertility of the most elite urban quartile might be almost a fifth below that of the villagers.

The Reality of Fertility Differentials and the Explanation Offered by Marital Behaviour

Ultimately, the reality of a fertility transition amongst the urban elite will not be judged by the kind of evidence considered at length in some of the previous chapters as to whether attempts are being made to prevent or defer pregnancies or whether they are increasingly likely to be made. The substantive evidence will be that of declining family size, but knowledge of those aspects of family life and of relations within the family, of the type considered here, will still be necessary to explain the fall in birth rates. So will some knowledge of the mechanics of the fertility decline.

Some of these mechanics have already been considered at considerable length. It is pertinent to ask how effective have been various types of action in reducing family size, whether this was the primary aim of such actions or not. In this way some light may be thrown on the rural-urban and socio-economic fertility differentials, on the likelihood of other differentials coming into existence and on the possibility of a more general fertility decline.

Thus, the data gathered in the survey will be used for a brief examination of family size by age of mother and by other characteristics of experience or behaviour, in spite of an earlier warning that a sample sufficiently small to allow interviews in depth could hardly be expected to provide significant demographic results. To obtain such results large-scale governmental inquiries will probably be necessary. Some data of this type has already been gathered by the 1960 Census Post-enumeration

171

Survey. However, little more than descriptive impressions will now be essayed. Most of the examination will be confined to the female respondents, for, in a society of unstable and polygynous marriage, male fertility measures are exceedingly difficult to make meaningful. Nor, if success were achieved, would they necessarily remain meaningful, for transition appears to be occurring in the marriage structure itself towards monogamous, and perhaps stabler, marriages.

However, there is one point on which even a very small sample can leave little doubt. The deferment of female marriage to an older age does on average reduce family size. Table 10:1 shows that, with later marriage, average family size is smaller for each maternal age group, although the margins become successively narrower with progress through the reproductive period. Nevertheless, some margin remains until the end of that period. Indeed, a deferment of marriage from under 19 to over 23 years of age may reduce the size of the completed family by as much as a third.

Several points should be noted. First, respondents have been grouped according to age at marriage into only three groups, the central group covering the four years of age when the majority of urban elite wives married for the first time. The other two divisions can be regarded as atypically early and late marriages. These groupings have been made so that individual cells should contain sufficient respondents. Nevertheless, even when the table is expanded so as to list separately respondents' ages at marriage by single years, the average number of live births per respondent falls consistently, and with very few irregularities in each age group from those respondents who married youngest to those who married at the oldest ages. Amongst the respondents nearing the end of their reproductive span, the one who had married under 17 years of age had borne thirteen children, while the four who had first married when 30–34 years old had averaged two children and the one respondent marrying after 35 years had borne only a single child.

Nor does the decline in average family size with increased deferment in age of marriage measure the full reduction in the birth rate arising from such postponement. In fact the birth rate tends to decline disproportionately more because with later child-bearing the average length of the generation increases and hence the multiplication experienced in one or more generations takes a greater number of years to transpire.

It is clear that deferred female marriage might well provide most of the explanation of the rural-urban and socio-economic fertility differentials. First marriages are often delayed in the towns. Part of the explanation is the need for and availability of extended training in the towns. Full-time education must of itself produce some differential effect. Table 10:2 shows that in the towns almost a fifth of 17-year-old females and nearly a tenth of 18-year-olds are still undertaking full-time schooling, compared with much lower proportions in rural Ghana. A factor in creating this situation has been the sending of girls to secondary school in the town, but this factor is probably a minor one, and in any case the great majority of these rural-urban migrants are certain to remain town residents.

The specific effect of full-time school attendance should not be overstated. Marriages in towns can be delayed by many things, such as part-

TABLE 10:1 Average issue of female respondents, by age at the date of survey and age at first marriage

Age at first marriage years / Age at date of survey	Number of respondents*			Average number of live births per respondent			Index†		
	Under 19	19–22	23 and over	Under 19	19–22	23 and over	Under 19	19–22	23 and over
20–24	10	34	3	2·3	0·9	0·7	100	39	30
25–29	8	51	39	4·1	2·4	1·0	100	59	24
30–34	8	37	36	5·8	4·0	3·0	100	69	52
35–39	4	24	26	7·3	5·2	3·9	100	71	53
40 –44	9	24	8	7·0	6·3	4·4	100	90	63
Total respondents	39	170	112						
Percentage distribution of respondents	12%	53%	35%						

* Of 331 female respondents, 5 have been omitted as under 20 at the date of the survey and 5 because of insufficient information.
† Issue of respondents married under 19 years = 100.

TABLE 10:2   Percentage of females attending school, by age and rural-urban
residence, 1960

| | *Age (years)* | | |
Residence	*17*	*18*	*19*
Urban	19	9	5
Rural:			
All rural population	9	4	2
Residents of centres with under 200 inhabitants	3	2	0·4

Source: 1960 Population Census of Ghana, Advance Report.

time training, the pursuit of higher salaries, the enjoyment of independence,
and by the absence of the pressure to marry from family and circumstances, so often felt in rural areas. Indeed, if the delay is caused mainly
by extended training, there should be a much greater disparity between
fertility levels in the upper- and lower-class sections of the towns than
has so far been evidenced by census and survey.

An examination of male respondents showed that their fertility also
falls with advance in age at marriage; and, doubtless partly because of a
correlation between the ages of spouses, even the fertility of the wife or
wives declines with increase of age at first marriage of their husbands.
Thus the average number of children borne by all women to men whose
oldest wife is 30–34 years is for men who married first at over 30, 25–29,
and 23–24 years, 64 per cent, 69 per cent and 77 per cent respectively
of that of men who married under 23 years of age.

There is no similar relation between fertility and attempts to prevent
pregnancy, even when an examination of these attempts is confined to
those purchasing contraceptive materials (or materials believed to have
contraceptive properties) from chemists or doctors. This bears out earlier
evidence that such contraception was usually surprisingly unsuccessful,
presumably largely because of the unsatisfactory nature of the contraceptives used. Table 10:3 compares the fertility of those female respondents who claimed to have attempted the prevention of pregnancy, those
who claimed success for such attempts, and those claiming the use of
contraceptives purchased from chemists or doctors with in each case the
remainder of the respondents.

Strictly, the only comment which should be made about the table is
that it does not show any certain relation between fertility and attempts
made to reduce it, but, with the aid of other supplementary observations,
various surmises can be hazarded.

Interviewers frequently reported that attempts to practise contraception
were discussed generally either during the interview or more often at its
close. The impression most often conveyed was that attempts to prevent
pregnancy were regarded as emergency measures rather than as actions
which should be expected in a well-regulated marriage. Hence the adoption
of contraception was often explained in terms of large family size or
repeated pregnancies within a short period. The first of these two reasons

TABLE 10:3   Issue of female respondents by age and by attempts to prevent pregnancy

Respondents*	Age (in years)				
	20–24	25–29	30–34	35–39	40–44
(i) Claiming attempts to prevent pregnancy:					
Number of respondents	10	29	32	20	13
Percentage of respondents†	20	32	40	38	30
Average issue	1·4	2·3	3·7	4·4	7·4
Index of average issue‡	127	105	95	92	128
Remainder					
Number of respondents	39	61	48	33	30
Average issue	1·1	2·2	3·9	4·8	5·8
(ii) Claiming successful attempts to prevent pregnancy:					
Number of respondents	8	19	26	11	5
Percentage of respondents†	17	21	33	21	12
Average issue	1·4	2·1	3·7	4·4	7·0
Index of average issue‡	117	91	97	94	125
Remainder					
Number of respondents	39	70	53	42	37
Average issue	1·2	2·3	3·8	4·7	5·6
(iii) Claiming use of contraceptives§:					
Number of respondents	10	25	26	17	5
Percentage of respondents†	24	30	34	33	13
Average issue	1·4	2·4	3·6	4·3	7·0
Index of average issue‡	108	114	95	90	109
Remainder					
Number of respondents	32	59	51	35	35
Average issue	1·3	2·1	3·8	4·8	6·4

* All respondents except 11 in (i), 16 in (ii), and 31 in (iii) who did not provide sufficient information and 5 under 20 years of age.
† I.e. percentage making this claim of all respondents in the section and age group providing all information.
‡ In each section and age group the issue of the remainder equals 100.
§ I.e. claiming to have bought materials from chemists or doctors to prevent pregnancy.

seems to be borne out by the increased attempt to prevent pregnancy with increase of age to the mid-thirties. The subsequent decline, especially after 40 years of age, may well be related to falling fecundity; it may also mean that we are examining an older group less affected by the temptation to innovate increasingly felt by the young during recent years. Only in the age groups exhibiting the maximum effort to prevent pregnancy are those making such efforts less fertile than other respondents. The failure of these attempts in other age groups, and indeed the frequently higher fertility found amongst those trying to prevent pregnancy, may not be quite the absurdity it first appears. Firstly, it is quite possible that those who practise birth control tend to be the most fecund and have on average succeeded in reducing their fertility. If this is so, they will have achieved some reduction in elite and urban fertility without having produced a fertility differential between family planners and others in the process. Secondly, even those purchasing contraceptive materials were not obtaining particularly satisfactory purchases. Intra-uterine devices were unknown in the country at the time and the use of oral contraceptives was apparently very rare. Considerable use was made of foaming tablets and contraceptive jellies, as well it would seem of patent mixtures which probably had no contraceptive properties at all. Governmental disapproval of contraception certainly retarded the spread of accurate information and discouraged shops and doctors from improving the quality of their supplies. The male questionnaires, although once again presenting greater problems in analysis, undoubtedly displayed a pattern which was in all points of substance identical with those of the females. Attempts at pregnancy prevention failed to produce a significant, or even clear, fertility differential.

However, if the small 40–44-year-old group in Table 10:3 is ignored as atypical, and if the other age groups are regarded as being similar to a cohort, where high initial fertility is likely to lead to attempts to control subsequent pregnancy, with a modicum of success, then the position in the 35–39 years group indicates that the completed fertility of those attempting to prevent pregnancy might be 8 per cent lower than among those making no attempts.

No other clear differentials in female fertility by behaviour patterns were found. Fertility was not lower amongst wives in polygynous marriages. This finding does not necessarily conflict with widespread findings in Africa that the average fertility of wives in such marriages is usually depressed, because we were dealing in the great majority of cases with the wife with whom the husband usually resided. Nor was there clear evidence that successive, unstable marriages had significantly lowered female fertility. Part of the reason may be linked to the earlier finding that such women are less likely to be practising contraception, and part to the fact that women in unstable marriage had first married significantly earlier than had the other females. However, as would be anticipated, it was found that male fertility rose markedly with the practice of polygyny.

Thus, in the course of the whole study two clear pieces of evidence on fertility differentials have been found. In the earlier examination of the background characteristics of respondents a significant relation with education was discovered; respondents in each survey with education beyond the middle school level were a fifth less fertile than those with lesser schooling once the age of the two groups was standardised. In the examination of marital behaviour patterns delayed marriage has been shown to exert a depressant effect upon fertility throughout the reproductive span.

The two findings are related. Table 10:4 shows that extended education in Ghana tends to delay marriage. However, there is no exact relation; all delayed marriage cannot be explained mechanically merely by the inroads into adulthood of time being spent in full-time education. Nor, probably, is delayed marriage the only mechanism whereby the fertility of the more educated is lowered. Certainly, the more educated are twice as likely to be employing contraception and some of them may do so more efficiently.

TABLE 10:4 Age at first marriage by highest level of education reached and by sex

Sex	Highest level of education	No. of respondents*	Percentage distribution of respondents by age at first marriage†		
			Under 19 years	19–22 years	23 years and over
Female	Primary school‡	64	30	53	17
	Middle school	137	14	60	26
	Beyond middle school	117	3	47	50

			Percentage distribution of respondents by age at first marriage†			
			Under 23 years	23–24 years	25–29 years	30 years and over
Male	Primary school‡	40	15	25	52	8
	Middle school	102	15	21	46	18
	Beyond middle school	153	12	26	51	11

* Excludes 13 females and 1 male respondent providing insufficient information.
† Different age ranges have been used for each sex in accordance with the distribution of ages at first marriage.
‡ Includes those with no education and a few not stating educational levels.

Only the female ages at first marriage show a statistically significant association (at 1 per cent) with educational levels attained, doubtless partly because female marriage ages are in general much lower than are those of males. So distinctive is the female pattern that marriage delay amongst them can probably explain about two-thirds of the observed fertility differential found amongst them by education. There is no equivalent direct link amongst males, but there may well be an indirect one through their wives, for there is a tendency for more educated males to marry more educated females, who on average marry later and bear fewer children than do other females.

Finally, it might be noted that, if more extensive demographic-type surveys do establish definite associations between marriage types or marital behaviour and fertility, yet another link between education and fertility will probably have been demonstrated, for associations between education and marriage can be established amongst the elite. Amongst female respondents, only 5 per cent of those with secondary or university education were found in polygynous marriages compared with 15 per cent of those with lesser education and only 3 per cent of the former had been married more than once compared with 11 per cent of the latter (both statistically significant at 1 per cent). Similar margins were found amongst the males. Only 4 per cent of those with secondary or university education were found to be polygynously married, as in fact was a similar proportion with middle school education, but below this educational level the proportion of polygynists climbed to 11 per cent (significant at 1 per cent); unstable marriage did not decline markedly until the university educated group was reached, where the incidence of previous marriages and divorces fell to 17 per cent compared with 29 per cent amongst the rest (significant at 5 per cent).

The Role of Various Influences upon the Elite

In this study various aspects of demographic, family, and attitudinal change have been examined and related to aspects of the respondents' experience or behaviour. It is equally valid to examine these various influences and to inquire about their effect on the whole range of demographic and family change.

There are certain influences which have necessarily been considered less important in a study of this kind than they would have been in an examination of the whole population. Location and age are probably the most important of these.

There are undoubtedly important differences in outlook and behaviour between the farmers of the hinterlands of Accra, Kumasi, Sekondi-Takoradi, and Cape Coast; probably too the bulk of the urban population differs, although perhaps less markedly, but the striking thing about the elite populations is the similarity between them. Ethnically they are often heterogeneous within each centre, for men in administrative and professional positions will often be posted to a centre from afar. In experience, an initial saturation in Westernised education and subsequent responsibility, more often than not in government service, the elite have drunk from the same cup, and the drink has certainly diluted the effects of different antecedent traditions. Occasionally we have noted that residence in Kumasi, the centre of the Ashanti cultural tradition, may render respondents somewhat less likely to denounce polygyny or to take their children on family outings, but the margins are small, and it is their smallness or non-existence that is the most important point.

Age is a characteristic which must be handled with great care. In the population as a whole only the young adults have had more than a small chance of attending school and consequently they are more given to welcoming innovation and are more capable of coping with responsible jobs in the modern sector of the society. The urban elite are by their very nature composed almost entirely of persons who have successfully coped with innovation—indeed, who are in many cases directing innovation. Thus, it is not surprising that the older members of the elite are just as prone as the younger members to disapprove polygyny and unstable marriage, to approve the establishment of family planning clinics, or to take the whole family out for entertainment.

Therefore, although the elite are not sharply divided by ages the existence of any age divisions is of considerable interest in that evidence might thus be provided of likely changes in attitudes or practices. Thus it is significant that almost twice the proportion of young males as of older males believed the existing rate of population increase was too high and a similar ratio held with regard to the view that too many children harmed the chances of maximum economic development. Similarly the young of both sexes were somewhat more inclined to favour the Westernised family way of life, as presented to them, and were slightly more likely to have discussed pregnancy prevention.

The study failed to show a continuing decrease in the age gap between spouses in the elite, but almost certainly that gap is smaller amongst the elite, and probably in all urban society, than in traditional society. In both surveys, where the age gap was smaller a larger proportion of married couples went out together and a greater proportion held discussions on the desired number of children. Evidence was found, particularly in the female survey, that where the gap was smallest, parents were more likely to go out with their children, favour the picture of the Western family and discuss pregnancy prevention.

However, compared with some other characteristics of the respondents, the differences found between the younger and older or between spouses of closer and more distant ages are small. Birthplace exerts a stronger influence. Second generation urbanites are much more likely than those coming from rural areas to know of a method for preventing pregnancy, to have discussed such methods with their spouses, and to have employed them. They are also more prone to use contraceptives for the purpose and to favour the extension of opportunities for securing family planning services.

Second generation membership of the middle and upper classes has a similar, if less marked, effect to second generation residence in the large towns. To an extent, of course, these two factors are almost certainly linked. Where the respondents' fathers held urban, upper-class jobs, the respondents themselves are more likely to favour the establishment of family planning clinics, to have discussed pregnancy prevention, and, amongst male respondents at least, to be using contraceptives.

Amongst the elite a discussion of the role of religion must necessarily be confined to Christianity, and any comparisons must be between Protestantism and Catholicism. The gulf between the two groups was not wide, being at its greatest in the case of females. Catholics tended to favour slightly more children, although, it should be noted, they were less likely to have discussed the matter with their spouses up to the time of the survey. They were less likely to have discussed either pregnancy prevention in general or the specific use of contraception, and fewer Catholic females knew anything about such things. Fewer Catholic than Protestant couples had tried to prevent pregnancies or were currently practising contraception; indeed, fewer wanted knowledge about how to do so spread by family planning clinics, but the differences were marginal, and amongst both religious groups there was a far more significant margin between what people were doing and what they would like to do. Only a third of Protestants were actually practising contraception, while almost three-fifths of Catholics would like to be assisted by family planning clinics to do so. Indeed, the religious margin was much more marked in the field of general ideas than in that of anticipated personal behaviour.

However, the most marked divisions wrought amongst the elite were those created by education. The effect of schooling and of more extended education far exceeds those springing from background or from any other form of experience. Even amongst the elite, who have largely been created by modern education and who have mostly received a considerable amount of schooling, different periods of education have produced markedly different results. Obviously the divisions in the country as a whole, especially between those who have received a substantial amount of schooling and those who have been raised without schooling in a largely illiterate area, must be very great indeed.

The major impact of more extended education amongst the elite has not been in the acceptance of changes in family structure from traditional patterns. Such changes are far too widely accepted amongst educated, urban Ghanaians for prolonged education to be a necessary factor in their acceptance by any member of the elite. However, it is true that unstable marriage and polygyny are less likely to be either practised or advocated by the highly educated and that later marriage is, amongst females at least, associated with extent of education. It is also true that the more highly educated are more likely to go out with each other or their children.

Where education does make its presence felt is in its effect on innovation in either attitudes or practices with regard to the control of family size. There are probably two causes. The first is that more extended education does make the acceptance of innovation easier. The second is that those who owe their job and income to extended education are likely to feel stronger obligations to secure the same advantages for their children and to realise the difficulty of doing so if the obligation spreads to too many children.

In both surveys there was a very significant difference (at 1 per cent) between respondents with education beyond middle school and those with lesser education in their views or behaviour with regard to various birth control matters. The former group were much more likely to have held discussions on the maximum preferred size of their family, to know of some way of preventing pregnancy, to use such a method, to have discussed contraception, and to employ it. They are also more likely to believe that it is possible to restrict successfully family size to some desired limit.

When desired action is considered, however, the margin between the more and less educated is much smaller, though it does not entirely disappear. The more educated are somewhat more inclined to advocate smaller families, to disbelieve the role of fate in deciding family size, to feel that they would employ a contraceptive method recommended by a doctor, to favour the establishment of family planning clinics, to consider they would use clinics once established, and to believe that Ghanaians would accept sterilisation as a method for limiting family size.

Occupation produces a pattern of views and behaviour very similar to that recorded for education. This may be because occupational position is largely determined by education, but in the case of both education and occupation it may be something a good deal more complex. More ready acceptance of innovation may be partly the product of extended education and partly the product of the greater sophistication engendered in the more responsible occupational positions secured by such education. In this case change in attitudinal and behaviour patterns would be associated both with high educational levels and high occupational positions, as is indeed the case.

There are a few noteworthy deviations or modifications of the response pattern according to occupation. Pregnancy prevention is particularly likely to be discussed where the wife has a high status job, perhaps partly because it is important that she should avoid pregnancy so as to retain her relatively large income-earning capacity. Respondents of both sexes were more inclined to feel that, the higher the occupational status of the spouse, the more likely was agreement to use family planning clinic facilities.

Of equal importance was the type of marriage or marriage experience. The partners in a monogamous, first marriage were far more likely to enjoy a mutual intimacy that made the discussion and practice of family planning possible than were wives or husbands in polygynous marriages or marriages where either spouse had been previously married. This may partly reflect educational levels, for the more educated are more likely to be participating in monogamous, first marriages, but education alone cannot explain all the difference in attitudinal and behaviour patterns. It may also reflect the difference between those less and more orientated to traditional society, for the latter are presumably more likely to participate in polygynous and unstable marriages. Certainly the partners in monogamous, first marriages are much more likely to have discussed desired family size and pregnancy prevention, to be employing contraception, to advocate family planning clinics, and to be ready to follow advice on contraception given by doctors or clinics.

Rather surprisingly, family size exerted much less pressure on ideas or practices. The most marked association with family size, whether measured by the number of births or the number of survivors, was that with the discussion of the desired number of children. Perhaps curiously the discussions were less likely to have been held by the parents of large families with severe resultant financial and other problems than by those with small families. There may here be some evidence of success in limiting family size once a limit has been clearly visualised, but the position is complicated by the likelihood that the more educated both had smaller families and were more likely to have discussed family size. However, the former proposition receives some support from the finding that in both surveys those with smaller families were somewhat more likely to be using contraceptives. A finding of very considerable interest and significance for the future was that the larger the number of children borne by a woman, especially after four had been passed, the more likely was she to assert that she would follow any advice given by a doctor on how to prevent further pregnancies.

Equally surprisingly the response pattern of women who were pregnant at the time of the survey differed hardly at all from the responses of those who were not pregnant. A slightly higher proportion of pregnant women said that they would follow the advice of a doctor on how to avoid pregnancy, but no other clear differences in attitude or practice were discernible at all. Certainly the onset of pregnancy does not seem to produce in most respondents any emotional shock leading to gloom and a desperate desire for advice on birth control. Nor does it lead to euphoria and a raising of the number of desired children.

The way of living of the family is important. Where the nuclear family lives alone, without boarding any other relative or outsider, both husband and wife are more likely to be using contraception and to favour the establishment of family planning clinics. Furthermore, one kind of family innovation is related to another. Where husband and wife go out together, or where they sometimes also take the children, the use of contraception is more likely, as is the advocacy of family planning clinics and the willingness to use them.

However, in breaking with tradition it is not merely actions but also ideas and the discussions from which ideas evolve that are important. It is those who demonstrate traditional viewpoints by maintaining that family size is largely a matter of fate who are least likely to attempt contraception, recommend the establishment of family planning clinics, or believe that Ghanaians would accept sterilisation. Conversely, it is those who have broken with tradition by discussing contraception who are most likely to employ it, to favour the setting up of family planning clinics and to believe that sterilisation would be acceptable.

The high degree of association between various ways of breaking traditional patterns goes much beyond decisions about personal behaviour. There is a link between what is regarded as good for oneself and what is approved for the whole society. Persons are more likely to be apprehensive about the economic effects of rapid population growth in the country if they have discussed family size, considered the possible use of contraceptives, or practised contraception. Furthermore, they are much more likely to believe in the establishment of family planning clinics if they have done any of these things. This correlation of beliefs extends to family matters beyond the control of family size. For instance, respondents who believed that stable, monogamous marriage was the only satisfactory married state were more likely to believe that family planning clinics should be established.

However, the advocacy of family planning clinics by those already obtaining contraceptive materials from doctors or chemists is not merely a case of the correlation of private and public views. There is little doubt that most of this group would expect to obtain a more satisfactory contraceptive service from a clinic. Certainly most of them would expect to switch their source of contraceptive supplies from the chemists and doctors to the clinics. In each survey 95 per cent of those currently using contraceptives would expect to get them from family planning clinics if established.

General Summary

Without repeating the conclusions set out in the summaries at the ends of the chapters, it is possible to assemble a general picture from those summaries of the elite family and of the implications which change within it might have for the country's population growth.

The economically better-off urban families do not have a tradition of their own stretching back for centuries and widening in the course of its evolution. On the contrary the history of such families does not really begin until at the earliest the late nineteenth century. It is only within the last few years, largely since independence in 1957, that their numbers have increased greatly to a point where their ways of life and attitudes affect each other. The great majority of these families are found in the four towns studied here, Accra, Kumasi, Sekondi-Takoradi and Accra-Tema.

The urban elite are to a very great extent the product of the educational system which has developed during the present century in Ghana. They were forced to create new traditions because the old traditions were essentially those of village life and offered no guidance for many of the problems of town life, especially relatively affluent town life. Necessarily many of the new traditions have drawn heavily on Western traditions, partly because they were to a large extent concerned with urban life, and partly because the substance of the new mission and state schooling was saturated with them.

The above statement describes correctly enough the full extent of the transition from old Ghana to the new Ghana of the middle- and upper-class suburbs. Yet in its simplification it misses out an essential point about the transition without which much of the pattern of responses revealed by the present study cannot be fully understood. European cultural influences arrived first in strength not in the form of contemporary, secular, Western education but through the missions. Mission churches and schools spread their influence rapidly during the second half of the nineteenth and first half of the twentieth centuries. Their teachings found a very receptive audience. In most of Ghana, and certainly in the south, they found no entrenched world religion, such as Islam, hostile to proselytism. Much of the New Testament, and much more of the Old Testament, described ways of life and problems which were curiously familiar to the villager. By the mid-twentieth century a new blended culture was paramount in most of southern Ghana, even in the small and remote villages. Christian attitudes to life, to the family, and to marriage had penetrated deeply. These were not wholly Western ideas. Even the major Protestant and Catholic churches had, with long residence, and with a growing number of indigenous ministers or other church functionaries, experienced something of a sea-change. In addition more 'African' splinter Protestant sects—the so-called Ethiopian churches—were appearing, but the real blend of Africa and Western Christianity was not so much in the churches as in the individuals. A symbolic example of this is the high proportion of Ghanaians who marry according to both Christian and traditional rites, the latter having, in so far as the two can be separated, more significance for the couple concerned in terms of the link with traditional culture than with traditional religion. The same kind of fused cultural attitudes has affected much of the population of southern Ghana, and certainly influences views on family matters. Many of the responses quoted in the study, often claiming to represent the way Ghanaians or Africans have always felt, in reality hark back not to the undiluted traditional way of life but to this mission-produced twilight of it.

Most of the elite, and many other Ghanaians, have in addition been subject to more specifically Western-type Christianity in their schools and to modern, European secularism in the towns, in their jobs, in the state schools, and from the mass media. It is the strength of these influences which tends to separate them from the mission-traditional culture of the countryside and often of their parents or grandparents.

A small elite is not necessarily the most proper subject for study, but this is not the case with the examination of social change in Africa, as an increasing intellectual concern with the tropical African elite demonstrates. For, whilst the cultural pattern of tropical Africa is a blend of indigenous and imported elements, it is the imported elements which have produced by far the greater part of the change. Furthermore, they first affect the elite of the towns, which, as governmental and business centres and as importers and diffusion points for the externally produced mass media, are far more in contact with the outside, non-African world. Urban elites have been the harbingers of social change in many, perhaps most, societies, and they play a particularly conspicuous role in this regard in tropical Africa. The recent history of most of tropical Africa, certainly of Ghana, has shown that the new patterns of living adopted by the wealthier residents of the towns are likely to diffuse down to the urban poor and out to the villagers. Two factors assist this. One is the geographical and social mobility of the population. The town population, even the elite, travel back repeatedly to visit and advise their relatives and other residents still living in their ancestral villages. Furthermore, the schools, rather than any class-based system of preference, have thrown men into highly placed, responsible jobs while they still have many relatives amongst the rural and urban poor. Their promotion in the socio-economic scale has not cut them off from their relations. Indeed their relations often try to bring themselves more forcibly to notice. Often they succeed in placing a child, perhaps a nephew, within the successful man's household, thus ensuring the flow of social change beyond the latter's nuclear family. The other factor is a ready acceptance of social innovation. Ghanaian culture does not try fiercely to preserve its age-old values from incursion. Most Ghanaians who have experienced any form of social transition from the pure, traditional system—and nearly everyone in southern Ghana has—accept new ways of living with astonishing ease and enthusiasm.

Our study has shown, then, that the urban elite are largely a product of modern education. Over half the males had secured some degree of secondary education or its equivalent and on the basis of these qualifications had usually secured a professional or administrative post in the governmental service. Even amongst the wives, more than a third had been educated beyond middle school and had frequently reached elite-type occupations without the prior aid of a 'successful' marriage. Indeed a large proportion continued in employment, assisted by the fact that relatives often helped with the domestic work in their homes. To a considerable degree, and perhaps a surprising one in view of the small size of Ghanaian towns of a generation ago, the elite were self-recruited, for a wholly disproportionate fraction were second-generation urbanites, coming particularly from the town middle and upper classes. There is evidence here that Ghana may not be able to maintain its recent high rate of social mobility.

Amongst the elite, most women married for the first time between 20–24 years of age and most men between 25–29 years, and, although the majority probably had first experienced sexual relations at younger ages, very few births before first marriage were recorded. By the standards of many developed countries these are not early marriages. Two-thirds of the respondents investigated were enjoying first, monogamous marriages. The older couples were likely to be completing their family with on average, if they were more educated, five children, and, if less educated, six.

Half or more feel that economic development would probably be assisted if Ghanaians bore fewer children, but not all are sufficiently impressed by the economic argument to proceed to the conclusion that it would be preferable if there were fewer children. Between a fifth and a sixth believed the 1963–4 rate of population growth to be a bad thing, in spite of a very definite official viewpoint to the contrary, and another tenth refused to agree that it was a good thing.

Within the elite families there has certainly been movement from older patterns in both ideas and practices, each evidence of social change and the two necessarily interrelated. Certainly there has been a marked movement even within the last few years towards stable, monogamous marriage. Two-thirds of the respondents stated their awareness that their own family life differed from that traditionally lived in Ghana, and some of the remainder seemed to be more concerned with defensively emphasising Westernised aspects of the traditional pattern than arguing that they had succeeded in maintaining an indigenous, non-imported way of life or that they had not been socially affected by economic success. In fact two-fifths saw nothing at all wrong with a rather extreme description of Western, middle-class, family life—a way of life which on the whole has only proved possible in societies where family size is rather rigorously limited. Most of those who appreciated that family change was occurring identified much of that change as making the family more child-centred, especially in the sense of being concerned about the children's education. The turning in of the nuclear family's interest upon itself has been assisted by the fact that half the elite families now reside in the form of parents and their children only, without any other relatives or non-relatives.

Most parents are aware of questions of family size, over two-thirds having discussed such matters with their spouses. In fact between a quarter and a third want no more children, the proportion rising very much higher in the case of wives who have already borne four or more children. Two-thirds believe that some people can successfully control family size. However, a similar fraction claim to have perceived that there is at present a larger proportion of children in both society and individual families because of rising chances of survival with falling mortality.

However, it is equally clear that the increased expenditure upon children, which nearly all families report, is not primarily a product of the rise in the number of surviving children. It is more closely related to the expense of training children for high status, urban occupations. This means long years of schooling followed perhaps by university or teachers' college training. Yet the relation between the training of children and occupational placement is not merely mechanistic. Part of the acquiescence by fathers in further training undoubtedly springs from the greater importance of the views of wives and of children themselves in families which are ever more likely to be housed in the form of nuclear families only and which are strengthening the emotional bonds between spouses and between parents and dependent children at the expense of bonds with other relatives. With increased education the position of the children in the family and their ability to communicate with their parents becomes ever stronger. Thus it is the educated children who are often in a position to accelerate change in the family structure, even in terms of the relationship between their parents. Certainly they can exert pressure to be allocated a greater share of the family expenditure and to extend their own schooling.

It is therefore the transition to an urban, middle- or upper-class way of life that disproportionately increases the strain exerted by the large family. Some strain has accompanied modernisation even in rural areas, but the intense strain is felt amongst the economically better-off families of the towns. The analysis in the Appendix suggests that this strain may extend far beyond the urban elite, and, in the larger towns at least, may be felt by half the population. The writer has also shown elsewhere that this expenditure upon the education of children can be partly regarded as a form of investment. Hitherto, it has been the type of investment which might in time be returned in full. Even now, almost five-sixths of university students expect to spend, from their future earnings, considerable sums on their parents and three-quarters expect to be in the same position with regard to their siblings. But, in this investigation, some evidence, mostly in the form of descriptive testimony, was found that the certainty of a return of some of the expenditure and in any case the proportion likely to be returned was probably least amongst the children who had been raised in the urban elite.

In spite of these increasing strains, frequent or unexpected pregnancy is not yet regarded as a major disaster in most elite families. At the time of the survey the proportion of pregnant female respondents or of males with pregnant wives was such as to suggest that no rapid fertility decline was underway. Of the pregnant women, 93 per cent and of the husbands of pregnant women 86 per cent, stated themselves to be pleased by the occurrence of pregnancy. However, the most significant evidence of transition from very high fertility ideals may be that only about a third of wives or husbands in marriages where pregnancy did not currently exist wished the position was otherwise.

The continuing attempt to prevent pregnancy is, in fact, on a considerable scale. A third of the respondents claimed to have attempted the prevention of pregnancy and a quarter that they were currently using contraceptive materials, or materials believed to be suited to that purpose, purchased from doctors or chemists. Contraception was more likely to be employed by the second-generation urbanites, by the second-generation members of the modern middle and upper classes, by those in monogamous, first marriages, and by Protestants and more particularly those with Protestant wives. These attempts to prevent or postpone pregnancy were made almost entirely to prevent families from becoming over-large or to space out pregnancies. The desire to employ contraception to avoid child-bearing altogether is practically unknown. There was very little evidence of success in attempts to prevent or postpone pregnancy, although some success might be disguised by a greater likelihood of such methods being used by the more fecund and the more fertile. Nevertheless, no definite association between family size and the use of contraception could be shown. Furthermore, only 5 per cent of female respondents and 7 per cent of males explained even one gap of three years or more between successive pregnancies as the consequence of deliberate action to achieve this result. Admittedly, contraception was being practised in Ghana in conditions of unusual difficulty.

The readiness to prevent pregnancy is much more common than the successful efforts to do so. Four-fifths of respondents felt that they could discuss such matters with their spouses and two-fifths claimed that they had already done so. Over two-thirds would be willing to follow the instructions of a doctor or a family planning clinic on how to practise contraception, providing that the means were simple, but those who would persist with troublesome and complex methods were few more than those already using contraceptives. The lesser educated and Catholics are both less likely than others to know about contraception, to have discussed it, or to be employing it, but almost as many of both groups would use methods to prevent pregnancy if they knew of them.

Over two-thirds of all respondents favour the establishment of family planning clinics and almost three-fifths would expect to use them. There is a marked religious differential on the first point but not on the second. The explanation is that, with very few exceptions, only those Catholics who wished for personal reasons to use clinics favoured a public policy of establishing them. In contrast, considerable numbers of Protestants, who, for various reasons such as nearness to the end of the wife's reproductive span or small size of family, would not wish to use clinics nevertheless favoured their establishment.

A Few Cardinal Observations

A few observations, mentioned here and there throughout the study, seem of such general interest that we might conclude by reiterating them.

The first is that while Ghana is obviously a very different society from, for instance, England of the mid-nineteenth century, many rather similar signs of incipient fertility decline are present. Socio-economic and urban-rural residence fertility differentials, though as yet small, have come into existence. Changes in ways of life are making large families more burdensome, especially for the middle and upper classes of the towns. There is evidence that a significant proportion of these groups is attempting to prevent or postpone pregnancy.

Private and public acceptance of population control are interrelated. Persons who are compelled to consider limiting their own family size are much more likely to approve national efforts to curb rapid population growth. The whole process is probably circular, or perhaps helical, in that national approval of family limitation probably inspires more limitation and more private approval of public action in that field. It may well be a widespread phenomenon of crucial importance in fertility decline in many developing countries.

There is considerable evidence, amongst the elite at least, that a smaller incidence of family planning amongst the less educated, the rural-born and the first generation members of the elite is not indicative of a desire for relatively large families but of greater general problems in coping with social and technological innovation and with—another case of innovation itself—communication about innovation. Most of the individual respondents in these groups show almost as much desire to prevent pregnancy as do their counterparts in the complementary groups, but are likely to do so only if contraceptive methods are simple enough and presented to them in an easy enough fashion to reduce to a minimal level the problem of coping with innovation and if public acceptance is sufficiently widespread or sufficiently publicised to reduce their problems of communicating with their spouses and doctors.

Some of these problems exist in the case of other sub-groups. Catholics, because of viewpoints adopted by their church, are likely to have greater problems communicating with their spouses, but would be almost as interested in preventing pregnancy. Communication between spouses is easiest in monogamous, first marriages where the age gap between spouses is relatively small. Thus spouses in other types of marriage were less likely to have discussed contraception and less likely to be employing it, even though polygynously married wives would be as ready as monogamously married wives to prevent pregnancy.

Difficulties of communication are not the only barriers to family limitation in polygynous or unstable marriages or marriages where residence was not essentially in the form of the nuclear family. Social change has been in the direction of reducing the proportion that such marriages make up of all marriages amongst the urban elite, almost certainly amongst all urban population, and probably, to a lesser extent, amongst the whole population. Thus all persons who have experienced successive marriages and divorces or separations, as well as the husbands at least in polygynous marriages, are more likely to be social traditionalists and less likely to favour innovations especially as they affect marriage. This position is reinforced by the fact that such marriages, for fairly obvious reasons, are likely to be less child-centred and perhaps less burdened by concern for the extended education of children.

Finally, it should be noted that problems of communication almost certainly cause both husbands and wives to underestimate their spouses' ability to innovate, either in the field of action or that of communication. Repeatedly respondents of both sexes reported that they would be able to communicate on family planning or practise it only when the association between these replies and the education or occupation of their spouses demanded much higher levels in these regards of the spouses than of the respondents themselves. Catholic spouses were more likely to believe each other unwilling to accept contraception than they were themselves. Thus, in a country, and in particular a section of its society, which has experienced rapid social change, individuals seems to give others less credit for ability to adjust to that change than they give themselves.

Socio-Economic and Fertility Differentials

Fertility Differentials—the Earlier Evidence

Data from censuses prior to that of 1960 were insufficient for any analysis of fertility differentials except for a rough estimate of that between regions. This will certainly not be the case when the full 1960 Census and Post-enumeration Survey is analysed and published. At the time of the survey described in this book the only census findings available were those contained in three *1960 Population Census of Ghana* publications: Vol. I, Vol. II, and the *Advance Report*.

The volumes did not provide data on the subdivisions of the towns and so could not be used to distinguish the economically better-off residential districts or to test for socio-economic differentials in fertility in urban areas, but Vol. II did allow the construction of crude fertility measures, child-woman ratios (the number of children under five years of age per thousand women between their fifteenth and forty-fifth birthdays), which could be used to compare the fertility of regions or of towns with the regions in which they were located. The *Advance Report of Volumes III and IV* provided further data allowing such indexes to be computed separately for aggregate urban and aggregate rural population,* and supplied age data by 5-year groups for the regions and 1-year groups for the whole country and its urban and rural divisions which permitted age-standardisation of the potentially reproductive female population during fertility comparisons.

Age-standardised child-woman comparisons did show regional fertility deviations from the national mean as much as 15 per cent below in the Northern and Upper regions and the Accra Capital District to 14 and 16 per cent above in Ashanti and Brong-Ahafo regions respectively.† Child-woman ratios (not standardised for age because of insufficient data for the towns), as set out in Table A:1, exhibited urban values 8 per cent below the national level and 10 per cent below the rural one. Accra-Tema had ratios 12 and 14 per cent respectively below those of the total and the rural population. All the major towns of Southern Ghana exhibited ratios well below those found for the whole population of their regions, but this was not the case in the Upper and Northern regions. The four towns examined in this study all recorded ratios about one-eighth below that found in the whole region of which each formed a part.

Strictly speaking these comparisons are only indirectly of fertility (i.e. the level of births) for they are really measures of surviving children and do not take mortality into account. Nor are they standardised for the age distribution of the females in the 15–44 years of age range. However, they were regarded

---

* 'Urban' population is composed of those persons enumerated in centres with 5,000 or more inhabitants; the rest of the population is 'rural'.
† In this Appendix the Upper and Northern regions and the Western and Central regions will each be treated as the single unit they were at the time of the 1960 Census, as the census data have appeared in this form.

TABLE A:1   Ghana, child-woman ratios, 1960 (children, 0–4, per thousand females, 15–44)*

Population	Sub-population	Child-woman ratio	Percentage ratio sub-population forms of that of whole population
Ghana		885	
	Urban population	816	92
	Accra-Tema	777	88
Rural population		908	
	Urban population	816	90
	Accra-Tema	777	86
Eastern Region†			
and Accra Capital District		888	
	Accra-Tema	777	87
Ashanti Region		993	
	Kumasi	846	85
Western and			
Central regions		899	
	Sekondi-Takoradi	790	88
	Cape Coast	791	88

* The female range, 15–44, is employed because the data in Census Vol. II does not permit the use of the 15–49 age range used in a later part of the analysis.
† The Accra Capital District is officially part of the Eastern Region but is so often treated separately that it is advisable to specify when it is included.

Source: Derived from *1960 Population Census of Ghana,* Vol. II and *Advance Report.*

during the final planning of the research project as clear evidence of an urban-rural fertility differential. In the first place, infant and child mortality is almost certainly lower in the towns than in the countryside and any cognisance of its existence would widen the urban-rural fertility differential. Secondly, the towns contain a disproportionate number of females in the most fertile age groups, and an examination of female age structure and fertility would suggest that the real urban-rural fertility differential is even greater than that suggested by the child-woman ratios. On the other hand Ghanaians frequently leave their children with grandparents and other relatives. In some cases young women come periodically or even for long periods to town without their children ; in other cases town families send children back to their village of origin so as to prevent them becoming entirely cut off from their ancestral roots. No population survey work carried out by the writer, either in the towns or villages of emigration, suggested that these occurrences were common enough to explain the major part of the differential shown in Table A:1. Furthermore, analyses described below show that the differential is greatest when comparison is being made with upper-class urban areas, precisely those areas where, as is shown in the present study, mothers are most likely to have all their children with them.

Socio-economic Differentials within the Towns

Some method of scaling the subdivisions of Accra-Tema, Kumasi, Sekondi-Takoradi and Cape Coast according to socio-economic characteristics was necessary for two reasons. Firstly, some measurement external to the survey itself was necessary to justify the selection of elite residential areas. Secondly, some determination was needed as to whether socio-economic differentials in fertility did exist within the urban areas. If they did, the significance of various fertility associations described in this study and the efficacy of some of the methods for reducing fertility would be shown in a new light. It seemed likely, once the urban-rural fertility differential was shown to exist, that socio-economic differentials would be found. If urban fertility was substantially lower than rural fertility, it was unlikely that the same reduction had taken place amongst rich and poor, or amongst immigrants from the villages and the town-born. Where the towns were so new, it was unlikely that homogeneity existed in the attainment of a new, lower level of fertility.

Such an analysis became possible when, subsequent to the completion of the survey program, three more *1960 Population Census of Ghana* publications appeared, Vol. III, *Demographic Characteristics,* Vol. IV, *Economic Charac-teristics of Local Authorities, Regions and Total Country,* and *Special Report 'A': Statistics of Towns with 1,000 Population or more.* The last was of particular importance, for

Each of the three cities were subdivided into *Statistical Areas*: Sekondi-Takoradi—10, Accra—17 and Kumasi—15. These areas were created by agglomerating geographically contiguous E.A.s [Enumeration Areas] with apparent homogeneous physical and social characteristics. This grouping of E.A.s was based mainly on a field survey of the urban functions of the various zones in the city area (e.g. industrial, commercial and administrative, services, residential etc. zones). In some cases also other sources of information such as rentable values of buildings were used. The traditional division of the town into various zones was also taken into consideration . . . . They were given names taken from what the Census Office considered as typical for the area. Most of these names are known features of the area and several S.A.s bear the traditional name of the area though the boundaries of the two may differ (*Special Report 'A',* ix).

No direct information on socio-economic status was available, for definitions of such status vary widely; nor was there anything on income; but there were data on occupation and education, the latter, as we have seen, being closely correlated with urban occupation in Ghana. Socio-economic status was believed, for some of the reasons set out in this study, to be measured by the following available criteria: (i) the sending of children to school (measured by the percentage of 7-year-olds at school); (ii) the main-taining of adolescents at school (measured by the percentage of 15-year-olds at school); (iii) the past schooling of parents (measured by the percentage of 35–39-year-olds who had ever been to school); (iv) higher educational qualifications in the form of secondary schooling or teacher-training (measured by the proportion—number per thousand population—whose highest educa-tional qualification was this type of education);* (v) higher educational qualifications in the form of university education (measured by the pro-portion—number per 10,000 population—who had ever attended university); (vi) higher occupational status (measured by the percentage of the employed occupied in professional, administrative, executive, managerial and clerical positions).

From these measurements a social status index was constructed for each statistical area in the three cities and for the whole of Cape Coast. The number

---

* There is a case for also including commercial and technical education in this measurement, but inquiry indicated that the most reliable component of an index could probably be formed from secondary education and teacher-training (which to a considerable degree parallels secondary education) alone.

of separate components in the index helped to compensate for irregularities in individual ones. For instance, the two measures of higher educational qualifications ((iv) and (v)) were needed to buttress the occupational measure (vi) for the professional, administrative and clerical classifications include not only modern, elite occupations but also such persons as midwives, herbalists, jujumen, fortune tellers, fetish priests, dancers, chiefs, letter-writers and others more closely tied to traditional or transitional society. The general measure of schooling (iii) makes the index more reliable when comparing elite with non-elite suburbs. The measures of children's schooling ((i) and (ii)) are good measures of the kind of responsibilities for training discussed at length in the present study, but should not be given too much weight in the index because they are affected by whether an area contains a boarding school or not, a not insignificant point when examining the elite.

Four points should be noted about the index. Firstly, the weighting set out in Table A:2 is constructed so that in the majority of statistical areas the score after weighting for occupational classification (vi) approximately equals the sum of the weighted scores of all the educational measures ((i)—(v)), and in the latter the weighted schooling scores ((i)—(iii)) approximately equal the weighted scores of higher qualifications ((iv) and (v)). For the highest and lowest socio-economic areas, these relations no longer hold, and, although the index remains a satisfactory method for scaling relative socio-economic position too much meaning should not be placed on the relative size of scores. In the first ten and last ten statistical areas the special higher qualifications add disproportionately too much and too little weight respectively to the index. Secondly, the index is specifically constructed to measure the importance of the urban elite in various suburbs, and its occupational component measures the employment which is important for those groups. Thus, the index is not very meaningful when applied to rural populations, although, for comparative purposes, such use has been mentioned passingly below. Thirdly, some evidence for the satisfactory nature of the components of the index is provided by the fact that in general each moves as the index itself moves.

The index cannot be compared with income figures for the statistical areas because of lack of income data and because the measure of socio-economic status in the modern sector of society cannot be completely correlated with income. The one set of figures of this type are Szereszewski's (1966, p. 92) for Gross Value Added Per Capita, by Regions, 1960, which correlates closely in rank order with computed status indexes for the regions, the exception being a downward displacement of Brong-Ahafo partly because of its relatively low level of urbanisation.

No suburb is completely elite, partly because the richest suburbs contain considerable numbers of servants, poor relatives of the wealthy or others offering services. Conversely, poor suburbs such as James Town or Ussher Town which are traditionally the urban centres for a specific people, in these cases the Gas, may house some well-off members of the same group. These are the reasons for some of the apparent anomalies in the table and the reason why only some of the households in even the highest status statistical areas come within the survey universe.

In general the proportion of 7-year-olds at school falls from about three-quarters in the highest status areas to below half in the lowest. It should be noted that school attendance was for this age group officially compulsory and that schools are reasonably plentiful in urban areas. Similarly, the proportion of 15-year-olds at school declined, somewhat more irregularly, from well over half to about a quarter. Both sets of figures, and especially the latter, confirm that the education of children is a very heavy burden in urban Ghana. This is particularly so for the higher status half of town populations, for the evidence shows that the second quartile keep almost as many children at school as does the first, although there is enough evidence from their occupations and education to indicate that the adult populations average substantially lower incomes.

It had been posited before the survey that families who found it very difficult to keep adolescents at school would be most likely to terminate their daughters' education. The calculation of a sex ratio for 15-year-olds still at school shows this to be substantially correct, for, with decline in status, the ratio of boys to girls receiving full-time schooling rose from under one-and-a-half times to five times or more. Nevertheless, the relationship with status proved to be too inconsistent to warrant including the measure within the status index.

A more constant relation is found with the education received by the adult population. An examination was made of the 35–39-year-old group, most of whom are parents without as yet being grandparents. With declining status the proportion who had received any schooling fell from about three-fifths to one-fifth or less. The drop in the proportion of residents with high educational qualifications, the very hall-mark of the urban elite, is even steeper with the decline in socio-economic status. The highest status suburb houses proportionately fifty times as many persons with secondary education or teacher-training as does the lowest and hundreds of times as many university-educated persons as several of the lowest status areas. In fact the first quartile of suburbs contains three-quarters of the university educated and half those with secondary schooling.

With decline in status the proportion of all employed persons found in 'white-collar' occupations falls from over a quarter to a twentieth or less. So constant is the fall, and so rare the real anomalies, that this component of the employment is particularly reliable. This is not merely the product of the large part it forms of the total index, for there is a very high correlation between the employment component and the balance of the index. Two-fifths of those professionally, managerially, and clerically employed are found in the first quartile of statistical areas.

One particularly striking point is the high status of Accra, the national capital at a time when the bureaucracy was expanding remarkably rapidly. With only half the total population of the four towns, it contained almost two-thirds of the secondary educated and over two-thirds of the university educated. In contrast is the traditional capital of the Ashanti, Kumasi. It had never been the seat of government, unlike Cape Coast and Accra, nor a port, unlike the other three, nor a creation to meet the needs of the modern economy, unlike Takoradi or Tema. Probably it offered more cultural resistance to the arrival of Western schooling than did the other three major centres. In every component of the status index it ranked the lowest.

The nature of the social status index, especially as it relates to the quartiles which will henceforth be increasingly used, is analysed in Table A:3, where marked discrepancies between the scaling of index components and the total index are noted. It can be seen that the index is closely related to the scale of adult occupations obtained by calculating the percentage of 'white-collar jobs' and to that computed from the education of the 35–39-year-olds. The proportion of university educated is more capricious, in that it is affected by only a small fraction of the population of even the most elite suburbs, but it is important for the purposes of this study. The child schooling components are obviously less closely related to the index, although marked variation occurs only in one-fifth of the measures of the education of 7-year-olds. However, their inclusion in the index is important, for the earnest endeavour to

TABLE A:2   Status indexes for statistical areas of Accra-Tema, Kumasi, and Sekondi-Takoradi and for Cape Coast, 1960.

(1)	(2)	(3)	(4)	(5)	(6)	(7)	(8)	(9)	(10)	(11)
Aggregate population percentile position from top	Statistical area*	Population	Percentage at school of 7-year-olds	Percentage at school of 15-year-olds	Sex ratio of 15-year-olds at school†	Percentage of 35-39-year-old with any schooling	Persons with secondary schooling or teacher-training per 1,000 population	Persons with university education per 10,000 population	Percentage of employed working in professional occupations‡	Status index§
0·5	Ridge Area (K)	3,719	54	29	129	57	103	409	28	2,124
3·8	Cantonments Area (A)	25,984	74	57	154	63	90	340	28	1,932
5·1	Kokomlemle (A)	10,106	76	48	124	69	82	207	34	1,604
6·3	Harbour Area (S)	9,424	73	68	272	54	80	143	19	1,168
6·9	Technology Area (K)	5,245	53	37	130	40	26	175	16	989
11·7	Adabraka (A)	37,836	71	49	143	53	63	70	26	988
13·4	Kaneshie (A)	13,054	74	56	161	55	48	67	27	962
15·3	Nungua and Eastern Outskirts (A)	15,186	62	70	199	33	20	175	13	958
17·7	Korle Gonno (A)	18,748	77	62	117	46	34	42	28	861
20·5	Osu (A)	22,063	85	70	110	52	37	35	25	823
22·9	Mamprobi (A)	18,885	75	65	167	53	43	37	23	801
24·4	Odum/Lake Rd (K)	11,159	60	45	128	38	49	47	19	735
26·0	Sekondi Zongo (S)	13,044	76	55	110	45	35	34	21	719
27·6	Sekondi Bay Area (S)	12,307	71	59	108	43	31	42	18	680
29·5	Tema (A)	14,937	61	34	148	48	35	60	14	652
32·6	Market Circle Area (S)	24,289	65	52	147	41	25	14	21	611
39·3	Cape Coast	41,230	63	66	142	35	24	39	15	593
37·8	Abossey Okai (A)	11,842	73	61	160	40	23	15	19	592
41·2	Suntresu (K)	15,055	78	47	100	42	26	7	20	586
44·5	Labadi (A)	25,939	71	61	149	42	27	14	17	569
45·5	New Takoradi (S)	7,224	39	37	167	31	19	47	15	545
46·8	Effiakuma (S)	10,167	57	59	112	36	24	9	18	539
51·6	James Town (A)	38,104	73	53	118	42	27	10	16	535
52·9	Kwadaso (K)	10,386	57	59	489	30	15	35	14	520
54·6	Southern Outskirts (K)	13,236	59	50	753	17	25	31	12	486

Status index*	Place	Population								
	(K)		57	47	124	30	21	12	13	482
59·7	Northern and Western Outskirts (A)	15,559	57	47	213	31	25	28	10	454
64·9	Ussher Town (A)	40,804	73	52	125	35	27	9	11	444
68·7	New Town (A)	30,034	55	43	158	34	19	14	13	439
69·8	Essikadu (S)	9,162	60	52	216	33	17	11	13	437
73·1	Ashanti New Town (K)	25,590	63	49	132	26	18	17	12	435
75·2	New Town Extension (K)	15,992	51	33	206	22	12	18	12	388
77·0	Nkotompo-Ekuase-Adiembra (S)	14,011	57	49	238	23	9	8	12	372
79·5	Amakom (K)	19,742	54	36	260	26	15	17	10	372
81·0	Ketan-Fijai Area (S)	11,935	47	44	333	18	6	11	8	288
82·7	Sabon Zongo (A)	13,460	52	34	267	23	8	4	8	273
85·9	Zongo (K)	25,466	62	34	200	26	7	4	7	267
89·9	Nima (A)	30,969	47	28	284	22	8	6	6	235
90·9	Suame (K)	8,298	56	36	367	18	6	6	5	226
93·5	Teshie (A)	19,823	48	52	149	19	5	1	5	217
94·8	Tafo (K)	10,909	41	35	257	20	4	0	6	204
96·5	Northern Outskirts (K)	13,385	55	40	621	12	4	2	4	189
98·0	Sekondi-Takoradi Outskirts (S)	11,750	34	23	471	12	3	1	5	161
100·0	Aboabo (K)	15,567	42	27	545	20	2	0	3	143
	Accra-Tema	403,333	68	53	146	42	34	56	17	705
	Kumasi	218,172	59	41	204	27	17	25	11	429
	Sekondi-Takoradi	123,313	59	51	166	34	24	28	16	556
	Cape Coast	41,230	63	66	142	35	24	40	15	596
	Total four towns	786,048	63	50	160	36	27	42	15	596
	First quartile four towns‖	191,409	73	57	146	52	55	124	25	1,119
	Second quartile four towns‖	214,138	68	57	132	32	27	25	17	585
	Third quartile four towns‖	185,186	62	47	173	31	21	17	12	401
	Fourth quartile four towns‖	195,315	51	36	263	21	7	5	7	256

* (A) = Accra-Tema, (K) = Kumasi, and (S) = Sekondi-Takoradi.

† Not included in status index.

‡ Includes administrative, executive, managerial, and clerical.

§ Status index = columns (4) + (5) + (7) + 3 × (8) + 3 × (9) + 16 × (10).

‖ These groupings of statistical areas are as near quartiles as the use of statistical areas as units will allow. They are shown in the table as areas separated by broken lines.

TABLE A:3   Marked discrepancies between the ranking order of status index
components and of the total status index. Number of statistical
areas exhibiting values for components above or below the
average values for the next higher or next lower quartile value
respectively*

	First	Quartile† Second	Third	Fourth	Total discrepancy	Percentage of all placements
Schooling of 7-year-olds	—3	+2 −3	+1	0	9	20
Schooling of 15-year-olds	—2	+4 −3	+2	+1	12	27
Post-schooling of 35–39- year-olds	0	0	+4 −1	0	5	11
Persons with secondary education as teachers training	—2	—1	0	0	3	7
Persons with university education	0	—5	+3	0	8	18
Proportion employed in professional, managerial, or clerical positions	—2	0	+1	0	3	7
Total quartile	—9	+6 −12	+11 —1	+1	40	15

* Average quartile values are the average values for the component exhibited by
statistical areas falling within quartiles determined by the total status index.
† Values above the average for the next lowest quartile shown '+' and those below
the next highest quartile shown '—'.

educate children is an indication of one kind of social status especially as it
relates to non-traditional society, and it is this inclusion which has changed
the rank position, as determined by occupation, of several statistical areas
where occupation alone seems to provide insufficient guide to socio-economic
status.

The Selection of Survey Areas

The survey areas were selected and surveyed before the census data on the
statistical areas became available. Nevertheless, the areas of choice were largely
those indicated by the status index. Furthermore, the same kind of problems
were realised that are perhaps thrown into somewhat greater relief by the
computation of the status index.

Firstly, as suggested above, the elite are not distributed in the same
proportions as is the total population, and this must be taken into account

TABLE A:4   Distribution of total population and socio-economically high status population in the four towns, 1960

	Total population	First quartile*	First third*	First and second quartiles*
Population	786,048	191,409	255,986	405,547
Accra-Tema				
Number of persons	403,333	161,862	176,799	252,684
Percentage of persons	51·3	84·6	69·1	62·3
Kumasi				
Number of persons	218,172	20,123	20,123	35,178
Percentage of persons	27·8	10·5	7·8	8·7
Sekondi-Takoradi				
Number of persons	123,313	9,424	59,064	76,455
Percentage of persons	15·7	4·9	23·1	18·8
Cape Coast				
Number of persons	41,230	—	—	41,230
Percentage of persons	5·2	—	—	10·2

* These are the approximate divisions made possible by the statistical areas and form 24·4 per cent, 34·1 per cent, and 51·6 per cent respectively of the total population. Percentages show the distribution of population in each column.
Source: Derived from 1960 Census data.

when designing the sample. Table A:4 shows that, whilst only half the total population lives in Accra, five-sixths of the first quartile population does and not far short of two-thirds of the population of the combined first and second quartiles. Thus substantially more survey work was done in both Accra and Sekondi-Takoradi than their populations alone would seem to warrant.

Secondly, the heterogeneity of the families within residential areas means that there is no simple division between using all the first quartile population as survey universe and rejecting the rest. What it meant in the survey was that a higher proportion of residences within the highest status areas was chosen than in those areas that succeeded them. But some sub-areas within the first third and a few within statistical divisions as low as the bottom of the second quartile had to be included. Furthermore, Cape Coast had to be subdivided because in fact it contained areas of each quartile type.

Thirdly, these observations should not be taken as discrediting the selection of statistical areas, for, as the census quotation previously noted, these areas are not necessarily to be more than approximately identified with the suburbs after which they are named. In the survey, however, it was necessarily the suburbs as such which are referred to by these names.

The Fertility Levels of Statistical Areas

The simplest measure of fertility derived from the census data is that of child-woman ratios, or the ratio of the number of young children to the number of females in the age groups from which the children's mothers were probably drawn. These measures are set out in Table A:5.

Such ratios have two disadvantages. Firstly, they measure not all children born to all mothers but only the ratio of the survivors of each group. This problem will be examined later. Secondly, bias is introduced by variations

TABLE A:5   Child-woman ratios and standardised fertility indexes for statistical areas of Accra-Tema, Kumasi, and Sekondi-Takoradi and for Cape Coast ranked according to status index, 1960

Cumulative population percentile position	Statistical area*	Town	Child-woman ratio†	Standardised fertility index‡
0·5	Ridge Area	Kumasi	791	74
3·8	Cantonments Area	Accra	735	68
5·1	Kokomlemle	Accra	647	61
6·3	Harbour Area	Sekondi-Takoradi	782	73
6·9	Technology Area	Kumasi	954	91
11·7	Adabraka	Accra	668	64
13·4	Kaneshie	Accra	788	75
15·3	Nungua and Eastern Outskirts	Accra	799	77
17·7	Korle Gonno	Accra	734	69
20·5	Osu	Accra	764	73
22·9	Mamprobi	Accra	921	87
24·4	Odum/Lake Rd	Kumasi	648	61
26·0	Sekondi Zongo	Sekondi-Takoradi	778	75
27·6	Sekondi Bay Area	Sekondi-Takoradi	772	74
29·5	Tema	Accra	690	65
32·6	Market Circle Area	Sekondi-Takoradi	760	70
39·3	—	Cape Coast	797	77
37·8	Abossey Okai	Accra	840	79
41·2	Suntresu	Kumasi	840	79
44·5	Labadi	Accra	877	83
45·5	New Takoradi	Sekondi-Takoradi	916	85
46·8	Effiakuma	Sekondi-Takoradi	801	75
51·6	James Town	Accra	771	74
52·9	Kwadaso	Kumasi	879	83
54·6	Southern Outskirts	Kumasi	992	92
57·7	Fante New Town/Asafo	Kumasi	790	77
59·7	Northern and Western Outskirts	Accra	858	80
64·9	Ussher Town	Accra	767	74
68·7	New Town	Accra	780	74
69·8	Essikadu	Sekondi-Takoradi	818	78
73·1	Ashanti New Town	Kumasi	833	82
75·2	New Town Extension	Kumasi	854	80
77·0	Nkotompo-Ekuase-Adiembra	Sekondi-Takoradi	772	73
79·5	Amakom	Kumasi	854	79
81·0	Ketan-Fijai Area	Sekondi-Takoradi	778	73
82·7	Sabon Zongo	Accra	863	80
85·9	Zongo	Kumasi	825	77
89·9	Nima	Accra	724	67
90·9	Suame	Kumasi	940	88
93·5	Teshie	Accra	888	84

Cumulative population percentile position	Statistical area*	Town	Child-woman ratio†	Standardised fertility index‡
94·8	Tafo	Kumasi	836	77
96·5	Northern Outskirts	Kumasi	993	94
98·0	Sekondi-Takoradi Out-skirts	Sekondi-Takoradi	813	75
100·0	Aboabo	Kumasi	814	76
	Accra-Tema		776	74
	Kumasi		846	80
	Sekondi-Takoradi		790	74
	Cape Coast		797	77
	Total Four Towns		799	76
	First quartile Four Towns		750	71
	Second quartile Four Towns		797	76
	Third quartile Four Towns		820	78
	Fourth quartile Four Towns		828	77

* Broken lines show quartiles as in Table A:2.
† Children, 0–4 years of age, per 1,000 females, 15–44.
‡ Percentage formed by children, 0–4 years, of the theoretical number of births over the five preceding years calculated by applying national age-specific birth rates to the female population, 15–49 years, during the time when the births occurred. The 0–4-year-old group has been adjusted for a loss of 3 per cent by age advancement. Age-specific birth rates employed were: 15–19, 0·141; 20–24, 0·259; 25–29, 0·306; 30–34, 0·259; 35-39, 0·213; 40–44, 0·165; 45–49, 0·117. These are not corrected for age misstatements which it is assumed were equal in fertility surveys and census. (For justification of estimate of age advancement, age-specific birth rates and for corrections for age misstatement, see J. C. Caldwell in *Some Aspects of Social Structure*, op. cit., pp. 38, 84–9, 164–5.) The 15–49 years range has been chosen because of the apparent high fertility in the 45–49 years of age group (largely due to age misstatement). The child-woman ratios have continued to employ the 15–44 age range for comparability with Table A:1.

in the distribution of female population by age. This is an important point when comparing two suburbs, one of which, being an immigrant suburb, might contain a particularly high proportion of young, adult, female, rural-urban migrants in their most fertile years.

Such bias can be removed by suitably standardising the female ages so that each community's index has the same representation of women in each age group. This can be done by choosing a convenient standard population. Alternatively, it can be done indirectly as in Table A:5 by applying national age-specific birth rates to the women of reproductive age in each area and then expressing the actual number of enumerated 0–4-year-olds as a percentage of the theoretical number of births during the preceding five years. This percentage we have described as the *standardised fertility index*. The index would equal 100 if the women of a particular area actually exhibited the same level of fertility as did all the women of the country, if no children had died, and if all living children of mothers resident in the area currently lived in the same area while no children had entered it without their mothers. The approach has the advantage of overcoming the problem of a differential distribution of females by age and does express enumerated children as a proportion of the estimated national birth level. The standardised fertility index falls in numerical value between a tenth and an eleventh of the child-woman ratio.

There is no constant relation between socio-economic status and fertility, but there is a general association which is clear even without consulting the quartile summaries. The fertility indexes tend to record lower values as position on the socio-economic scale rises. In the first quartile only two statistical areas record child-woman ratios above 800 or standardised fertility indexes above 80, while in the fourth quartile nine areas exceed the former level and five the latter. It is precisely in this kind of comparison that the standardised fertility index is valuable because the child-woman ratios tend to overstate the fertility levels of fourth quartile suburbs which are somewhat more affected by immigration and often contain a relatively high number of younger women in their most fertile years. Applying the same kind of test used in Table A:3, it is found that over half the areas in each quartile exhibit both child-woman ratios and standardised fertility indexes which are above the average of those in the next higher quartile and below the average of those in the next lower quartile.

The measures certainly vary from town to town, being highest in Kumasi in the heartland of the Ashanti high-fertility tradition and lowest in Accra-Tema and Sekondi-Takoradi. The effect of these variations on the quartile figures will be examined later.

When the analysis is confined to quartiles it can be seen that child-woman ratios continue to rise as socio-economic status falls, while the standardised fertility index also does so except between the third and fourth quartiles. However, the most marked differential is that between the first quartile and the rest. The first quartile is over 7 per cent lower than the fourth quartile by either measure.

The Effect of Mortality

However, even a constant level in these measures from quartile to quartile would be almost certain proof of a considerable socio-economic differential in live births, for these measures are indicators of survival and this certainly varies considerably with socio-economic status.

The health conditions, especially in their impact upon young children, obviously vary very greatly from first quartile to fourth quartile suburbs. In Accra, for instance, the Cantonments and Nima come to within a mile of each other, but, in the former, houses are large and spacious, children are well fed, and parents have the money, social position, and sophistication to secure medical attention whenever required. Many Ghanaian families live in the same way as British and other expatriates who apparently record mortality figures no lower than do the middle classes of their own homelands. In contrast, however, in the latter, children live in conditions that are usually more congested and squalid than in the villages from which the rural-urban migrants came, but in terms of health this may be offset by the nearness of hospitals.

Thus, it seems improbable that the expectation of life at birth in the first quartile suburbs is below 50 years and in the fourth quartile much above 40 years. In Table A:6 a conservative assumption has been made that the variation is from about 52½ years in the former to about 42½ years in the latter.

TABLE A:6 Estimates of relative fertility levels obtained by making corrections for mortality to standardised fertility indexes, the four quartiles, 1960

| | *Quartile* | | | |
	First	*Second*	*Third*	*Fourth*
Standardised fertility index	71·1	75·6	78·2	77·3
Assumed joint expectation of life at birth (years)	52½	50	45	42½
Mortality correction factor*	1·140	1·158	1·194	1·214
Mortality corrected standardised fertility index	81·1	87·5	93·4	93·8
Percentage mortality corrected index forms of fourth quartile mortality corrected index	86	93	100	100

* *United Nations Model Life Tables* have been used to calculate a mortality correction factor by dividing the chance of 15–49-year-old female survival for half the period divided by the chance of survival from birth to the 0–4 age group. No adjustment has been made for the sex ratio at birth as this is believed to be near parity, although no certain evidence exists.

The real difference may well be much greater but even this relatively small margin is sufficient to establish that a marked fertility differential apparently exists.

The exact figures depend not only on the size of the mortality gulf between the quartiles but on the prevailing levels of mortality in the country as a whole. In these analyses it is assumed that in the five years preceding 1960 the expectation of life at birth in the whole country was about 42½ years, in rural Ghana about 40 years, in urban Ghana about 45 years and in the four towns 47½ years. These estimates are close to those suggested by the writer elsewhere. (Caldwell, 1967a, pp. 89–92). The precision of the estimates and the exact nature of the urban-rural mortality differential do little to affect the resulting conclusions about fertility differentials. The more important points are the validity of the estimates of socio-economic mortality differentials within the towns themselves and the mortality schedules used to distribute mortality by age. For the latter purpose *United Nations Model Life Tables* have been used, as these were the only tables available when the analysis was begun but other sets, perhaps more suitable, are now available.*

If the relative sizes of the 0–4 and the adult female groups can be taken to reflect survival accurately, the mortality corrections suggest that the birth levels in the first quartile are a seventh or more below those of the fourth quartile. With a greater mortality differential, but one still within the bounds of possibility, a continuing fertility rise from quartile to quartile can be produced and the first can fall to a fifth or more below the fourth.

If mortality assumptions are also made about the other segments of Ghana's population we obtain the rather interesting picture presented in Table A:7.

* The Coale and Demeny tables (Coale and Demeny, 1966) are now also available, of which the 'North' set is believed to be more suited to tropical African mortality conditions.

The basic pattern is clear enough from the child-woman ratios. Fertility, in so far as it can be measured by the children enumerated in any area, is lower in the urban areas than in the rural areas. The pattern becomes clearer with the mortality corrections to the standardised fertility index.

Lower urban fertility has apparently reduced the overall national figure by about 4 per cent. Fertility is about an eighth lower in urban areas than in rural areas. It is lower again in the four main towns. The reason for this is the fertility differentials by socio-economic division within the main towns. For the two lower socio-economic divisions exhibit levels similar to those found in the smaller urban areas. The lowest rates are found in the first quartile suburbs which exhibit levels at least a fifth below those of rural Ghana.

Influences on the Differentials

The measures discussed so far only establish true fertility differentials if the children enumerated in any area can be approximately equated with the surviving children. Furthermore, the use of quartiles is justified only if they reflect true socio-economic fertility differentials; it is, for instance, possible that the apparent differences arise from the quartiles being formed from different proportions of the populations of the four towns, for, as seen in Table A:5, the child-woman ratios of the towns do vary quite markedly.

Taking the latter point, which is the simplest, first, doubts can be settled by analysing separately those parts of each quartile found in each town. This has been done in Tables A:8 and A:9.

These tables establish that socio-economic fertility differentials do exist in each town, but, except in Kumasi, they are smaller than the analysis of the four towns in aggregate had suggested. The differentials in the aggregate have been magnified by the disproportionately large share taken up in the fourth quartile by residents of Kumasi, the centre with the highest fertility levels of the four.

Several conclusions can be drawn. Differentials do exist and are most marked in the two largest towns. In spite of generally higher fertility levels in Kumasi, the first quartile population of that town are no more fertile than the first quartile population of Accra. A conservative estimate of the mortality differentials indicates that birth levels, as estimated from enumerated surviving children in each area, are, in the first quartile of Accra and Kumasi at least, a tenth and a sixth respectively below those of the fourth quartiles. In each of the three largest towns fertility appears to be definitely depressed in both the first and second quartiles, more markedly so in the former.

A more difficult problem is that of deciding whether mothers and children have been enumerated generally in the same areas. Rural-urban migrants often leave children behind in their home villages for periods or subsequently send them home. Even amongst the elite of the present survey, of whom only half were rural-urban migrants, almost a fifth of children were living apart from their mothers at the time of the survey. Such a fraction is large compared with the kind of differentials we have been investigating, but it should be remembered that many of these children were away at school or even in employment, occurrences not associated with the 0–4-year-olds used in this analysis. Furthermore, urban families often take in child relatives from the countryside for domestic help or to assist them to attend a suitable school. Sometimes wives have living with them children by their husbands' former marriage. Most interviewers were given to understand that the sending and receiving of children was least in the case of the very young, who were mostly found with their mothers.

No direct analysis is possible, but if tendency to send children away is closely related to extra-urban origins, a measure can be obtained by relating

TABLE A:7 Estimates of relative fertility levels obtained by making corrections for mortality to standardised fertility indexes, various segments of Ghana's population, 1960

Population segment	Child-woman ratio	Standardised fertility index	Assumed joint expectation of life at birth (years)	Mortality correction factor	Mortality corrected standardised fertility index	Percentages mortality corrected index forms of rural Ghana mortality corrected index
Rural Ghana*	908	84·1	40	1·235	103·9	100
All Ghana	885	82·4	42½	1·214	100·0	96
Urban Ghana outside Four Towns	839	78·4	45	1·194	93·6	90
All urban Ghana*	816	76·8	45	1·194	91·7	88
Four Towns:						
All quartiles	799	75·7	47¼	1·175	88·9	86
Fourth quartile	828	77·3	42½	1·214	93·8	90
Third quartile	820	78·2	45	1·194	93·4	90
Second quartile	797	75·6	50	1·158	87·5	84
First quartile	750	71·1	52½	1·140	81·1	78

* Urban population is population in centres with 5,000 or more inhabitants, while the remainder is rural population.

TABLE A:8 Fertility measures for each quartile analysed separately by towns, 1960

Quartile	Measure	Accra-Tema	Kumasi	Sekondi-Takoradi	Cape Coast
First	Population	161,862	20,123	9,424	—
	S.F.I.*	71·1	70·5	72·8	—
	% S.F.I. forms of fourth quartile S.F.I.	95	87	99	—
	M.C.S.F.I.†	81·1	80·4	83·0	—
	% M.C.S.F.I. forms of fourth quartile M.C.S.F.I.	89	82	93	—
Second	Population	90,822	15,055	67,031	41,230
	S.F.I.	75·4	79·5	74·1	76·7
	% S.F.I. forms of fourth quartile S.F.I.	101	98	101	—
	M.C.S.F.I.	87·3	92·1	85·8	88·8
	% M.C.S.F.I. forms of fourth quartile M.C.S.F.I.	96	94	96	—
Third	Population	76,397	89,627	9,162	—
	S.F.I.	74·9	81·4	78·4	—
	% S.F.I. forms of fourth quartile S.F.I.	100	101	107	—
	M.C.S.F.I.	89·4	97·2	93·6	—
	% M.C.S.F.I. forms of fourth quartile M.C.S.F.I.	98	99	105	—
Fourth	Population	64,252	93,367	37,696	—
	S.F.I.	74·9	80·8	73·3	—
	% S.F.I. forms of fourth quartile S.F.I.	100	100	100	—
	M.C.S.F.I.	90·9	98·1	89·0	—
	% M.C.S.F.I. forms of fourth quartile M.C.S.F.I.	100	100	100	—

* Standardised fertility index.
† Mortality corrected standardised fertility index.

TABLE A:9 Summary comparison of percentage measures in each quartile form of fourth quartile measure

Measure	Quartile	Four Towns	Accra-Tema	Kumasi	Sekondi-Takoradi
Standardised fertility index	First	92	95	87	99
	Second	98	101	98	101
	Third	101	100	101	107
	Fourth	100	100	100	100
Mortality corrected standardised fertility index	First	86	89	82	93
	Second	93	96	94	96
	Third	100	98	99	105
	Fourth	100	100	100	100

the standardised fertility index to the proportion of population born in each statistical area. In Table A:10 the statistical areas have been divided into quartiles according to the proportion of enumerated population claiming local birth at the 1960 Census and standardised fertility indexes have been calculated for each quartile.

The interpretation of Table A:10 does present some difficulties. Not all persons born outside the locality are rural-urban migrants; indeed, because of the small size of localities in the peripheral areas of the towns some of them may have been born a comparatively short distance from where they were enumerated. Furthermore, the percentage of adults born in the locality will usually be much lower than the figure for total population because many of their children will have been born recently in the area. Nevertheless, the measure probably does serve as a reasonable index of continuing links beyond the town of residence.

There can be no doubt that there is an association between birth outside the locality and a reduction in such measures as the standardised fertility index and the child-woman ratio. Almost certainly the main explanation is that those groups who have come to the town more recently are more likely to have children with relatives elsewhere. This association can be seen more clearly still if the statistical areas are graded according to fertility and the fertility quartiles are compared with place of birth. Table A:11 shows that where the child-woman ratio is above 840 over half the population are locally born, while where it is below 765 only a third are.

This relation between enumerated children and migration is as striking as that between the former and socio-economic class. Furthermore, subsequent analysis failed to find any other census data which showed similar associations. Thus it is clear that any analysis of the connection between child-woman ratios and socio-economic class will have to hold the migration factor constant, while analyses seeking to relate the proportion of enumerated children to the degree to which a community is a settled, urban one will have to hold socio-economic class constant. This has been attempted in Table A:12 where the statistical areas have been subdivided two ways, into quartiles by socio-economic class as in Table A:2, and into quartiles by proportion of population born in the locality as in Table A:10. A theoretical case could be argued for

TABLE A:10 Standardised fertility indexes and mortality corrected standardised fertility indexes for population of statistical areas classified by birthplace, the four towns, 1960

Birthplace quartile*	Percentage born in locality where enumerated†	Standardised fertility index	Percentage S.F.I. forms of first quartile S.F.I.	Mortality corrected S.F.I.‡
First	85·1–58·4	78·6	100	92·4
Second	56·9–42·6	78·5	100	92·2
Third	41·0–28·8	73·3	93	86·1
Fourth	27·7–11·7	71·9	91	84·5

* The following are the statistical areas in each quartile with the percentage of locally born:

Quartile	Statistical Area	Percentage locally born	Quartile	Statistical Area	Percentage locally born
First	Teshie	85·1	Third	Fante New Town	41·0
	Mamprobi	68·4		Aboabo	40·3
	Cape Coast	64·8		Essikadu	37·2
	Osu	63·7		Northern and Western	
	Labadi	62·5		Outskirts—Accra	37·0
	Ussher Town	61·8		Adabraka	36·9
	Northern Outskirts—			Sekondi Zongo	35·5
	Kumasi	58·8		Suntresu	32·2
	Korle Gonno	58·4		Tafo	31·7
				Nkotompo-Ekuase-	
Second	James Town	56·9		Adiembra	30·3
	Abossey Okai	50·9		New Town Extension-	
	Kaneshie	50·8		Kumasi	30·2
	Southern Outskirts—			Kokomlemle	29·4
	Kumasi	50·1		Technology	29·0
	Sekondi-Takoradi			Odum/Lake Rd	28·8
	Outskirts	49·4			
	Zongo-Kumasi	48·3	Fourth	Amakom	27·7
	Suame	46·8		Kwadaso	27·5
	Sekondi Bay	44·8		New Town—Accra	27·5
	New Takoradi	44·6		Ketan-Fijai	26·9
	Ashanti New Town	44·1		Nima	25·3
	Nungua and Eastern			Market Circle	23·8
	Outskirts—Accra	43·3		Tema	23·6
	Sabon Zongo	42·6		Cantonments	22·7
				Effiiakuma	14·4
				Ridge Area—Kumasi	13·3
				Harbour Area	11·7

The four quartiles contain 25·6 per cent, 24·9 per cent, 25·2 per cent, and 24·3 per cent respectively of the aggregate population of the four towns.
† Locality, as defined in the 1960 Census, meant a separate 'nucleated and physically distinct settlement'. Accra-Tema consisted of 46 localities, but 81 per cent of the population lived in Accra Locality; Kumasi of 52 localities with 83 per cent in Kumasi Locality; Sekondi-Takoradi of 57 localities with 33 per cent in Takoradi Locality, and 28 per cent in Sekondi Locality; and Cape Coast of 33 localities with 72 per cent in Cape Coast Locality.
‡ Assuming for all quartiles the expectation of life at birth of 47·5 years estimated for the four towns.

TABLE A:11 Percentage of population born in locality by fertility quartiles, 1960

Fertility quartile*	Child woman ratio†	Standardised fertility index†	Percentage born in locality of enumeration
First	993–840	94–79	50·1
Second	840–791	79–75	46·5
Third	790–767	75–73	43·7
Fourth	764–647	73–61	34·1

* The quartiles contain 25·4, 23·2, 26·3, and 25·1 per cent of the population respectively.
† Approximate equivalents only.

TABLE A:12 Standardised fertility indexes and mortality corrected standardised fertility indexes for statistical areas, subdivided into socio-economic quartiles and birthplace quartiles, 1960

Quartiles by percentage born in locality

		(i) First	(ii) Second	(iii) Third	(iv) Fourth
I First		I (i) Korle Gonno (A) Osu (A) Mamprobi (A)	I (ii) Kaneshie (A) Nungua (A)	I (iii) Kokomlemle (A) Technology (K) Adabraka (A) Odum/Lake Rd (K)	I (iv) Ridge Area (K) Cantonments (A) Harbour Area (S)
		Population 7·6% S.F.I. 76·1 M.C.S.F.I. 86·8	Population 3·6% S.F.I. 76·1 M.C.S.F.I. 86·8	Population 8·2% S.F.I. 64·9 M.C.S.F.I. 74·0	Population 5·0% S.F.I. 69·6 M.C.S.F.I. 79·3
II Second		II (i) Cape Coast (ii) Labadi (A)	II (ii) Sekondi Bay (S) Abossey Okai (A) New Takoradi (S) James Town (A)	II (iii) Sekondi Zongo (S) Suntresu (K)	II (iv) Tema (A) Market Circle (S) Effiakuma (S)
		Population 8·5% S.F.I. 79·0 M.C.S.F.I. 91·5	Population 8·9% S.F.I. 75·6 M.C.S.F.I. 87·5	Population 3·5% S.F.I. 77·5 M.C.S.F.I. 89·5	Population 6·3% S.F.I. 70·1 M.C.S.F.I. 81·2
III Third		III (i) Ussher Town (A)	III (ii) Southern Outskirts (K) Ashanti New Town (K)	III (iii) Fante New Town (K) Northern and Western Outskirts (A) Essikadu (S) New Town Extensions (K)	III (iv) Kwadaso (K) New Town (A)
		Population 5·2% S.F.I. 73·8 M.C.S.F.I. 88·1	Population 5·0% S.F.I. 84·7 M.C.S.F.I. 101·1	Population 8·3% S.F.I. 78·7 M.C.S.F.I. 94·0	Population 5·1% S.F.I. 75·8 M.C.S.F.I. 90·5
IV Fourth		IV (i) Teshie (A) Northern Outskirts (K)	IV (ii) Sabon Zongo (A) Zongo (K) Suame (K) Sekondi-Takoradi Outskirts (S)	IV (iii) Nkotompo - Ekuase - Adiembra (S) Tafo (K) Aboabo (K)	IV (iv) Amakom (K) Ketan-Fijai (S) Nima (A)
		Population 4·3% S.F.I. 88·3 M.C.S.F.I. 107·2	Population 7·5% S.F.I. 79·1 M.C.S.F.I. 96·0	Population· 5·1% S.F.I. 75·0 M.C.S.F.I. 91·1	Population 8·0% S.F.I. 72·0 M.C.S.F.I. 87·4

Quartiles by socio-economic status — I First, II Second, III Third, IV Fourth

Note: Population = percentage of population of the four towns found in the cell; S.F.I. = standardised fertility index; M.C.S.F.I. = mortality corrected standardised fertility index employing the corrections set out in Table A:6; A = Accra-Tema, K = Kumasi, S = Sekondi-Takoradi.

subdividing again by major towns; for instance, the standardised fertility index for cell III (i) would almost certainly have been higher if the single entry had been an Ashanti suburb of Kumasi and not a Ga suburb of Accra. However, the data would have been spread too thinly.

The table is subject to fluctuations, most of which can be plausibly explained by the inclusion in the cell of different proportions of the four towns, but the overall trends are clear. Holding socio-economic class constant, the indexes tend to fall as the proportion of locally born declines. In only three out of twelve comparisons between adjacent quartiles by locality of birth in the same socio-economic quartile is the fertility index higher in the quartile where fewer are locally born. This is set out more clearly in Table A:13.

TABLE A:13   Percentage formed by standardised fertility index* in each place of birth quartile of index in first quartile, calculated separately

Quartiles by socio-economic status	Quartiles by percentage born in locality			
	First	Second	Third	Fourth
First	100	100	85	91
Second	100	96	98	89
Third†	100	115 (95)	107 (88)	103 (85)
Fourth	100	90	85	82

* For this comparison S.F.I.s and M.C.S.F.I.s yield the same result.
† Accepting the argument presented above that the first cell of this line is unrepresentative and depressed, the succeeding cells have been rescaled (in parentheses) so that the fourth cell records a value intermediate between the cells above and below it. It is these rescaled values which are employed in Table A:15.

There is some evidence from the table that higher socio-economic status families are less likely to be separated from their children than are lower socio-economic status families. Thus, while the first status quartile drops with the full fall in the proportion of locally born across the table by 9 per cent, the fourth status quartile falls by twice as much. Furthermore, the whole table shows a similar pattern if we make allowance for the low fertility index in cell III(i) of Table A:12.

More importantly, from the viewpoint of the present analysis, the fertility indexes tend to rise with falling socio-economic status providing birthplace is held constant. The comparison is less clear than that just examined, for the standardised fertility index fails to rise with falling status in five of the twelve possible comparisons and the mortality corrected standardised fertility index in four of the comparisons. Table A:14, where this is examined, produces difficulties not experienced in Table A:13, for in the latter the comparisons were within status quartiles and did not depend upon estimates of the mortality differentials between quartiles.

Part (b) of Table A:14 suggests that the birth level in the first quartile is between a tenth and a fifth below that of the fourth quartile.

European* households are a conspicuous feature of many first quartile suburbs. In 1960 three-quarters of all European females in the four towns

* I.e. European, American, Australian, etc.

TABLE A:14 Percentages formed by (a) the standardised fertility index and (b) the mortality corrected standardised fertility index in each socio-economic status quartile of the index in the fourth quartile, calculated separately by locality of birth quartiles

Quartiles by socio-economic status	Quartiles by percentage born in locality			
	First	*Second*	*Third*	*Fourth*
	(a) Standardised fertility index			
First	86	96	87	97
Second	89	96	103	97
Third	84	107	105	105
Fourth	100	100	100	100
	(b) Mortality corrected standardised fertility index			
First	81	90	81	91
Second	85	91	98	93
Third	82	105	103	104
Fourth	100	100	100	100

were to be found in such suburbs. Therefore, it might be felt that their presence helped to explain the lower level of fertility in this quartile. But in the creation of the differentials shown in Table A:14 their effect must have been practically insignificant. Even in the first quartile suburbs European females made up less than 3 per cent of all females. Furthermore, the child-woman ratio of this group was, at 566 per thousand, surprisingly high in terms of their countries of origin. It was more than three-quarters of that of all first quartile population and over seven-tenths of that of the aggregate population of the four towns.

The whole analysis presents one interesting possibility. This is that the birth level of the fourth quartile population is not far below that of the rural population. In the cell of Table A:12 where socio-economic status is lowest and local birth highest, cell IV (i), the M.C.S.F.I. is above 100; but birth levels in much of the rural south of the country are undoubtedly above the national average. In fact the standardised fertility index for Teshie and Kumasi's Northern Outskirts is identical with that of the Eastern Region (including the Accra Capital District) and Ashanti respectively, and, if we assume, reasonably enough, no mortality differential, the birth levels would also be similar. It may, however, be objected that both Teshie and Kumasi's Northern Outskirts are in many ways rural centres which have been partially submerged by the growth of Accra and Kumasi respectively and are not in this sense truly urban. An examination of cell IV (ii) shows that in two of the four suburbs in it the standard fertility index is no lower than the index for the whole region than might be reasonably explained by some absent children. For instance, Sabon Zongo in the heart of Accra exhibits an index only 4 per cent below that of the whole Eastern Region, but the other two suburbs appear to supply evidence for some rural-urban fertility differential even at this level. An enumeration of adjoining cells appears to supply more evidence for the reality of such a differential.

The Components of Apparent Urban-Rural Fertility Differentials

In Table A:15 an attempt has been made to summarise the findings by presenting them in the form of a fertility balance sheet. In section (a) the differentials between the four towns and the regions encompassing them are presented, and then more correctly the comparison with those people of the regions living outside the four towns. It might have been more proper to have confined the comparison to that between the towns and the rural population only, but in southern Ghana the smaller towns have for two generations been almost as much a feature of the countryside as the villages.

The table shows that differentials in female age distribution are not great enough to prevent the child-woman ratio being an effective index. The only

TABLE A:15   Fertility differentials existing between the four towns and the remainder of the surrounding regions,* 1960

(a) Apparent extent of differentials

	Whole regions Per cent	*Regions without four towns Per cent*
Relative level of child-woman ratio	—13	—16
Relative level of standardised fertility index	—13	—16
Probable effect of urban-rural mortality differential†	— 3	— 3
Relative level of apparent birth levels	—16	—19

(b) Suggested explanation of differential between towns and remainder of regions

	Extent‡ Per cent	*Total effect on rural fertility level Per cent*
(i) Urban-rural fertility differential not explained by (ii) and (iii)	—5	— 5
(ii) Socio-economic fertility differential within towns§	—6	—11
(iii) Absence of living children from towns‖	—9	—19

* I.e. Eastern Region (including Accra Capital District), Ashanti Region, and Western Region.
† Assuming an expectation of life at birth of 47·5 years in the towns and 42·5 years in the remainder of the regions.
‡ These extents are relative to the levels without them and not to the original rural level; hence, although they add to 20 per cent, their cumulative effect is only 19 per cent.
§ See Tables A:6, A:12, A:14.
‖ See Tables A:10, A:12, A:13. These tables show an overall reduction in fertility indexes of 7 per cent if it is assumed that no children are absent from birthplace quartile (i), and if the rescaling shown in parentheses in Table A:13 is employed, but, as even in this quartile a third of the population were not born in the locality, 9 per cent appears to be a better estimate of the likely total effect.

correction needed is one to allow for the somewhat better mortality conditions probably found in the towns.

In section (b) it is shown that the socio-economic fertility differentials and the apparent differentials in the absence of children discussed in this Appendix are not in themselves sufficient to explain the differences between the numbers of children enumerated in the towns and the remainder of the regions. It is probable that the birth level in the towns is about one-ninth below that of the rest of the regions and that only a little over half of the explanation lies in socio-economic fertility differentials within the towns themselves.

This does not mean that the fertility differentials in every section of the urban community are around the average. Thus, although internal socio-economic differentials probably contribute to a drop of only 5 per cent in fertility amongst the whole population of the four towns, the fall on this account is probably 14 per cent in the top socio-economic quartile. Similarly, the absence of living children may explain as much as 12 per cent of the apparent fertility drop in the birthplace quartile in which the least number of persons had been born in the locality of enumeration.

Finally, it should be noted that the explanation for the 'unexplained' urban-rural fertility differential may be of a very similar nature to that which explains socio-economic fertility differentials within the towns. The way of life of townspeople may be subject to pressures which makes the marriage and child-bearing pattern of the villages inappropriate. The pressures may merely be greater in the first socio-economic status quartile.

Explanations for the Fertility Differentials

Fertility differentials can be explained in only a limited number of ways: a later age at female first marriage, periods thereafter not in a conjugal condition, and reduced marital fertility either without apparent cause, or because of conscious effort to avoid pregnancy, or arising from some aspect of the marital condition such as polygyny.

By far the most important explanation for the differentials noted in this Appendix is undoubtedly the delay in female marriage. Surveys indicated that females in Ghana's towns probably marry at least $1\frac{1}{2}$ to 2 years later than do girls in the villages (Caldwell, 1967a, pp. 68-9). Such a delay would, in terms of the 1960 distribution of females and of age-specific birth rates, reduce fertility by 8 to 11 per cent, more than the full amount of the 'not explained' differential. This would imply that abortion or contraception played no greater role in urban than in rural areas. It is possible that the role of delayed marriage is somewhat overstated here, because urban-rural difference in age at first marriage may not be as great in the advanced southern part of the country as in the whole nation.

It is possible now to construct a table of hypothetical average ages at female marriage on the assumption that all real fertility differentials can be fully explained by delay in such marriage. New work on the 1960 Post-enumeration Survey has shown that 84 per cent of females, 15–24 years of age, in the whole country and 66 per cent in the Accra Capital District have been married at least once (Tetteh, 1967). Because of substantially fewer females enumerated as 15–19 years than 20–24 years, probably largely because of age misstatement, this implies average ages of marriage of $16\frac{3}{4}$ and $18\frac{3}{4}$ years respectively in the two areas. Rural age at marriage would be somewhat below the national figure, but it is reduced by very low marriage ages in the north. Farther south it is probably at least 17 years, which is the figure Tetteh found in his studies on the border of the Brong-Ahafo and Northern Region (Tetteh, 1967, p. 202). In Table A:16 this is assumed to be the average age of female

TABLE A:16   Estimated average ages of females at first marriage in rural
areas and the socio-economic status quartiles of the four towns
on the assumption that all fertility differentials can be explained
by delayed female marriage

	Rural southern Ghana	Socio-economic status quartiles			
		Fourth	Third	Second	First
Assumed average age of female marriage (years)	17	—	—	—	—
Percentage fertility below rural Ghana*	—	5	6	12	18
Estimated average age of female marriage (years)†	(17)	17·9	18·1	19·2	20·3

* From Tables A:8 and A:14.

† Estimating from age-specific birth rates and enumerated female population a delay of one year in marriage should produce a fall in births of about 5½ per cent assuming equal annual fertility from average age at marriage until 25 years.

marriage in the rural areas from which most of the immigrant families in Accra are drawn. The estimated reductions in the birth rate, as estimated from the number of 0–4-year-olds, is calculated from the national age-specific birth rates employed earlier and the population structure as enumerated at the 1960 Census in the four towns.

Table A:16 receives support from several sources. For instance, Table 10:1 demonstrates that later marriage does reduce fertility in Ghanaian towns and is not cancelled out by higher marital birth rates subsequent to marriage amongst those delaying marriage. The present study showed an average age at marriage amongst female respondents of 21·6 years, which in view of their smaller numbers and the greater degree of selectivity involved than in choosing the first quartile females, corresponds well with an average marriage age of 20·3 years amongst the latter group, especially if we assume some success amongst this group in the attempt to prevent pregnancy. Moreover, it is in general agreement with the Post-enumeration Survey figure given by Tetteh (1967) for the Accra Capital District. The figures he gives for proportions married suggest an average female age at marriage of about 18¾ years. If the assumption of a 17-year marriage age for rural population applies to the Accra Capital District outside Accra-Tema, which makes up a fifth of the population of the whole district, and, if account is taken of the distribution of population by quartiles in Accra-Tema as shown in Table A:8, Table A:16 suggests a marriage age of just over 19 years.

The explanation for the socio-economic differential within the towns, and hence of its contribution to the urban-rural differential, may not be quite as simple as this discussion suggests. It is likely that a minor cause for the socio-economic fertility differential is greater success by those in the upper quartiles in the prevention of unwanted pregnancies. The evidence of such success quoted in Chapter 10 was not impressive even amongst the urban elite. Only in the 30–34 and 35–39-year-old ranges were fertility levels lower amongst those attempting to prevent pregnancy and even then only 5 and 8 per cent respectively lower. There was some evidence that the picture may have been obscured by greater pressures upon the more fertile to attempt the prevention of pregnancy.

Summary

An urban-rural fertility differential does exist in Ghana and could presage a fall in the national birth rate. The true differential is certainly less than half that implied by the enumeration of children in the towns. Nevertheless, birth rates in the four major towns are probably about one-ninth lower than in the rest of the surrounding regions. Half the explanation lies in internal socio-economic differentials, and half lies in very similar differences between the towns as a whole and the countryside. In fact one might better imagine a continuum of socio-economic change from the rural areas to the highest socio-economic division of the towns accompanied by a continuing reduction in fertility levels. The chief mechanism in achieving this reduction is undoubtedly increasingly delayed female marriage; nevertheless, a minor influence, especially in the higher socio-economic groups, may be the attempt to prevent pregnancy within marriage. Both delayed female marriage and the attempt to prevent pregnancy are, as seen earlier, positively associated with extended education. They are also associated with second generation town-living and membership of the upper and middle classes. Presumably, with continuing economic development both will increase.

Bibliography

A OFFICIAL REFERENCES

The population censuses of the area of modern Ghana are shown as:

1921 Census	1948 Census
1931 Census	1960 Census

In each case the year refers to the year of enumeration.

The various volumes of the *1960 Population Census of Ghana* are as follows:

Vol. I, *The Gazetteer: Alphabetical List of Localities*, Accra, 1962.

Vol. II, *Statistics of Localities and Enumeration Areas*, Accra, 1962.

Advance Report of Volumes III and IV, Accra, 1962.

Vol. III, *Demographic Characteristics*, Accra, 1964.

Vol. IV, *Economic Characteristics of Local Authorities, Regions and Total Country*, Accra, 1964.

Special Report 'A', Statistics of Towns with 10,000 Population or More, Accra, 1964.

Special Report 'E', Tribes in Ghana, by B. Gil, A. F. Aryee, and D. K. Ghansa, Accra, 1964.

Vol. V, *General Report*, by G. Gil and K. T. de Graft-Johnson, Accra, 1964.

Atlas of Population Characteristics, Accra, 1964.

The current development plan at the time of the survey was the *Seven-Year Development Plan for National Reconstruction and Development, Financial Years 1963/64–1969/70*, Accra, 1963, and is shown as *Seven-Year Development Plan*.

B OTHER REFERENCES

Acquah, A. I. 1949. 'Marriage and Family Life Among the Educated Africans in the Urban Areas of the Gold Coast', M.A. thesis, University of London.

Acquah, Ioné, 1958. *Accra Survey*, London.

Apter, David E. 1955. *The Gold Coast in Transition*, Princeton (revised and expanded as *Ghana in Transition*, New York, 1963).

Baker, Tanya and Bird, Mary, 1959. 'Urbanisation and the Position of Women', *Sociological Review*, New Series, Vol. VII, pp. 99–122.

Banks, J. A. 1954. *Prosperity and Parenthood: a Study of Family Planning among the Victorian Middle Classes*, London.

Banton, Michael, 1957. *West African City: a Study of Tribal Life in Freetown*, Oxford.

Berelson, Bernard, 1966. 'KAP Studies on Fertility', in Berelson *et al.* (eds.), *Family Planning and Population Programs: a Review of World Developments*, Chicago, pp. 655–68.

Birmingham, Walter, Neustadt, I., and Omaboe, E. N. 1967. *A Study of Contemporary Ghana*, Vols. I and II, London.

Borrie, W. D. 1948. *Population Trends and Policies: a Study in Australian and World Demography*, Sydney.

Brown, William O. (ed.), 1955. *Contemporary Africa: Trends and Issues*, Vol. 298 of *Annals of the American Academy of Political and Social Science*.

Busia, K. A. 1950. *Report on a Social Survey of Sekondi-Takoradi*, London.

—— 1954. 'Some Aspects of the Relation of Social Conditions to Human Fertility in the Gold Coast', in Frank Lorimer, *Culture and Human Fertility*, Paris, pp. 341–50.

—— 1956a. 'The Present Situation and Aspirations of Elites in the Gold Coast', in UNESCO, *International Social Science Bulletin*, Vol. VIII, No. 3.

—— 1956b. 'Social Survey of Sekondi-Takoradi', in UNESCO, *Social Implications of Industrialization and Urbanization in Africa South of the Sahara*, Paris, pp. 74–86.

—— 1961. 'The Conflict of Cultures', in Peter R. Gould (ed.), *Africa: Continent of Change*, Belmont, California, pp. 177–83.

Caldwell, J. C. 1962. 'The Population of Malaya', Ph.D. thesis, Australian National University.

—— 1963a. 'Fertility Decline and Female Chances of Marriage in Malaya', *Population Studies*, Vol. XXVII, No. 1, pp. 20–32.

—— 1963b. 'The Demographic Background', in T. H. Silcock and E. K. Fisk (eds.), *The Political Economy of Independent Malaya: a Case-Study in Development*, Canberra, pp. 59–92.

—— 1965. 'Extended Family Obligations and Education: a Study of an Aspect of Demographic Transition amongst Ghanaian University Students', *Population Studies*, Vol. XIX, No. 2, pp. 183–99.

—— 1966a. 'The Erosion of the Family: a Study of the Fate of the Family in Ghana', ibid., Vol. XX, No. 1, pp. 5–26.

—— 1966b. 'Africa', in Berelson *et al.* (eds.), *Family Planning and Population Programs*, Chicago, pp. 163–81.

—— 1966c. 'Family Formation and Limitation in Ghana: a Study of the Residents of Economically Superior Urban Areas', ibid., pp. 595–613.

—— 1967a. Population Sections of ,Walter Birmingham, I. Neustadt, and E. N. Omaboe (eds.), *A Study of Contemporary Ghana*, Vol. II, *Some Aspects of Social Structure*, London.

—— 1967b. 'Fertility Attitudes in Three Economically Contrasting Rural Regions of Ghana', *Economic Development and Cultural Change*, Vol. XV, pp. 217–38.

——1967c. 'Introduction: the Demographic Situation', in John C. Caldwell and Chukuka Okonjo (eds.), *The Population of Tropical Africa*, Vol. I, *Demography*, London.

—— 1967d. Fertility Differentials as Evidence of Incipient Fertility Decline in a Developing Country ; the Case of Ghana. *Population Studies*, Vol. XXI, No. 1.

—— 1967e. 'Population Policy: a Survey of Commonwealth Africa', paper presented to the First African Population Conference, Ibadan, 1966, to be published in J. C. Caldwell and C. Okonjo (eds.), *The Population of Tropical Africa*, Vol. II, *Population Policy and Study*, London.

Coale, Ansley J. 1966. 'Estimates of Fertility and Mortality in Tropical Africa', *Population Index*, Vol. XXXII, No. 2, pp. 173–81.

—— and Demeny, Paul, 1966. *Regional Model Life Tables and Stable Populations*, Princeton.

Coleman, James S. 1960. 'The Politics of Sub-Saharan Africa', in Gabriel A. Almond and James S. Coleman (eds.), *The Politics of the Developing Areas*, Princeton.

Crabtree, A. I., 1950. 'Marriage and Family Life Amongst the Educated Africans of the Gold Coast', M.Sc. thesis, University of London.

Davis, Kingsley, 1945. 'The World Demographic Transition', *Annals of the American Academy of Political and Social Science,* Vol. CCXXXVII, pp. 1–11.

Dorjan, V. R. 1958. 'Fertility, Polygyny and their Interrelations in Temne Society', *American Anthropologist,* Vol. 60, No. 5.

—— 1959, 'The Factor of Polygyny in African Demography', in William R. Bascom and Melville J. Herskovits (eds.), *Continuity and Change in African Cultures,* pp. 87–112.

E.C.A. 1965. Economic Commission for Africa, 'Recent Demographic Levels and Trends in Africa', *Economic Bulletin for Africa, 1965.*

Falade, Solange, 1963. 'Women of Dakar and the Surrounding Urban Areas', in Denise Paulme (ed.), *Women of Tropical Africa,* London, pp. 217–29.

Forde, Daryll, 1956. 'Introductory Survey', in UNESCO, *Social Implications of Industrialization and Urbanization in Africa South of the Sahara,* Paris, pp. 11–50.

Fortes, Meyer, 1954. 'A Demographic Field Study in Ashanti', in Frank Lorimer, *Culture and Human Fertility,* Paris, pp. 253–339.

——, Steel, R. W. and Ady, P. 1956. 'The Ashanti Survey', in UNESCO, *Social Implications of Industrialization and Urbanization in Africa South of the Sahara,* Paris, pp. 91–6.

Frazier, E. Franklin, 1956. 'Education and the African Elite', *Transactions of the Third World Congress of Sociology, 1956,* Vol. V, *Changes in Education,* Part 2, 'Education and Social Mobility in Economically Underdeveloped Countries', London, pp. 90–6.

Freedman, Ronald, Whelpton, Pascal K., and Campbell, Arthur A. 1959. *Family Planning, Sterility and Population Growth,* New York.

Friedlander, D. 1966. 'Measuring Fertility in Ghana', paper presented to the First African Population Conference, Ibadan, January.

Gaisie, S. K. 1966. 'Some Aspects of Fertility Studies in Ghana', ibid.

Gamble, David P. 1963. 'The Temne Family in a Modern Town (Lunsar) in Sierra Leone', *Africa,* Vol. XXXIII, No. 3, pp. 209–26.

Glass, D. V. and Grebenik, E. 1954. *The Trend and Pattern of Fertility in Great Britain: a Report on the Family Census of 1946, Part I: Report, Papers of the Royal Commission on Population,* Vol. VI, H.M.S.O.

Goode, William J. 1964. *The Family,* Glenwood Cliffs, N.J.

de Graft-Johnson, K. E. 1966. 'The Evolution of Elites in Ghana', in P. C. Lloyd (ed.), *The New Elites of Tropical Africa,* Oxford, pp. 104–17.

Hunter, Guy, 1962. *The New Societies of Tropical Africa,* Oxford.

Hurd, G. E. 1967. 'Education in Ghana', in Walter Birmingham, I. Neustadt, and E. N. Omaboe (eds.), *A Study of Contemporary Ghana,* Vol. II, *Some Aspects of Social Structure,* London.

Innes, J. W. 1938. *Class Fertility Trends in England and Wales, 1876–1934,* Princeton.

Jahoda, Gustav, 1954. 'The Social Background of a West African Student Population: I', *British Journal of Sociology,* Vol. V, pp. 355–69.

—— 1955. 'The Social Background of a West African Student Population: II', ibid., Vol. VI, pp. 71–9.

—— 1958. 'Boys' Images of Marriage Partners and Girls' Self-images in Ghana', *Sociologus,* New Series, Vol. VIII, No. 2, pp. 155–69.

—— 1959. 'Love, Marriage and Social Change: Letters to the Advice Column of a West African Newspaper', *Africa,* Vol. XXIX, pp. 177–90.

—— 1961. 'Aspects of Westernization: a Study of Adult-Class Students in Ghana: I', *British Journal of Sociology,* Vol. XII, pp. 375–86.

Killick, Tony, 1966. 'Policy and Planning', in Walter Birmingham, I. Neustadt, and E. N. Omaboe (eds.), *A Study of Contemporary Ghana*, Vol. I, *The Economy of Ghana*, London, pp. 365–438.

Kimble, George H. 1960. *Tropical Africa*, 2 vols., New York.

Leith-Ross, S. 1956a. 'Nigeria', in International Institute of Differing Civilizations, *Development of a Middle Class in Tropical and Sub-tropical Countries*, Brussels, pp. 174–83.

—— 1956b. 'The Rise of a New Elite amongst the Women of Nigeria', in UNESCO, *International Social Science Bulletin*, Vol. VIII, No. 3, pp. 481–8.

—— 1956c. International Institute of Differing Civilizations, *Development of a Middle Class in Tropical and Sub-Tropical Countries*, Brussels, 1956.

Leslie, J. A. K. 1963. *A Survey of Dar es Salaam*, Oxford.

Little, Kenneth, 1955. 'The African Elite in British West Africa', in Andrew W. Lind (ed.), *Race Relations in World Perspective*, Honolulu, pp. 263–88.

—— 1959. 'Some Urban Patterns of Marriage and Domesticity in West Africa', *Sociological Review*, New Series, Vol. VII, pp. 65–97.

—— 1964. 'West African Urbanization as a Social Process', in William John Hanna (ed.), *Independent Black Africa: the Politics of Freedom*, Chicago, pp. 137–49.

—— 1966. 'Attitudes Towards Marriage and the Family among Educated Young Sierra Leoneans', in P. C. Lloyd (ed.), *The New Elites of Tropical Africa*, Oxford, pp. 139–62.

Lloyd, P. C. 1966. Introduction, ibid., pp. 1–65.

Lorimer, Frank, 1954. *Culture and Human Fertility*, Paris.

—— 1961. *Demographic Information on Tropical Africa*, Boston.

——, Brass, William, and van de Walle, Etienne, 1965. 'Demography', in Robert A. Lystad (ed.), *The African World: A Survey of Social Research*, London.

—— and Karp, Mark, 1960. *Population in Africa: Report of a Seminar held at Boston University*, Boston.

Lystad, Robert A. 1965. *The African World: a Survey of Social Research*, London.

McCall, Daniel F. 1961. 'The Dynamics of Urbanization in Africa', in Peter R. Gould (ed.), *Africa: Continent of Change*, Belmont, California, pp. 183–95.

Marris, Peter, 1961. *Family and Social Change in an African City: a Study of Rehousing in Lagos*, London.

Notestein, Frank W. 1945. 'Population—the Long View', in Theodore W. Schultz (ed.), *Food for the World*, Chicago, pp. 36–57.

Ohadike, P. O. 1966. 'A Demographic Note on Marriage, Family and Family Growth in Lagos, Nigeria', paper presented to the First African Population Conference, Ibadan, January.

Okigbo, Pius, 1961. 'Social Consequences of Economic Development in West Africa', in Peter R. Gould (ed.), *Africa: Continent of Change*, Belmont, California, pp. 211–21.

Omari, T. Peter, 1960. 'Changing Attitudes of Students in West African Society Towards Marriage and Family Relationships', *British Journal of Sociology*, Vol. XI, pp. 197–210.

Paulme, Denise (ed.), 1963. *Women of Tropical Africa*, London.

Peil, Margaret, 1965. 'Ghanaian Students: the Broadening Base', *British Journal of Sociology*, Vol. XVI, pp. 19–28.

Pool, D. I. 1966. 'The Ghana Fertility Survey', paper presented to the First African Population Conference, Ibadan, January.

Smythe, H. H. 1958. 'Nigeria's Marginal Men', *Phylon Quarterly,* Vol. XIX, No. 3, pp. 268–76.
—— and Smythe, Mabel M. 1960. *The New Nigerian Elite,* Stanford.
Som, R. K. 1966. 'Some Demographic Indicators for Africa', paper presented to the First African Population Conference, Ibadan, January.
Sydenstricker, Edgar and Notestein, Frank, 1930. 'Differential Fertility According to Social Class', *Journal of the American Statistical Association,* Vol. XXV, No. 169, pp. 9–32.
Szereszewski, Robert, 1966. 'The Macroscopic Structure', in Walter Birmingham, I. Neustadt, and E. N. Omaboe (eds.), *A Study of Contemporary Ghana,* Vol. I, *The Economy of Ghana,* London, pp. 37–117.
Tetteh, P. Austin, 1966. 'Emergent Family Patterns and Household Structure', ibid., Vol. II, *Some Aspects of Social Structure,* London.
Thompson, Warren S. 1929. 'Population', *American Journal of Sociology,* Vol. XXXIV, No. 6.
UNESCO, 1956. *International Social Science Bulletin,* Vol. VIII, No. 3.
United Nations, 1956. United Nations, Department of Economic and Social Affairs, *Population Studies No. 25: Manuals on Methods of Estimating Population, Manual III: Methods for Population Projections by Sex and Age.* New York.

Index

219